the red review

A Liverpool FC Almanac

An in-depth statistical and analytical assessment of Liverpool's players, formations and tactics during the Rafael Benítez era

Oliver Anderson • Paul Tomkins

SPECIAL LIMITED FIRST EDITION COPY

"Nobody has managed to capture the spirit of the Rafa-lution at Liverpool like Paul Tomkins - that rare example of a fan who can write about his subject with intelligence as well as passion"

Football365

Harcourt
Publishing

www.paultomkins.com
harcourt_books@btinternet.com

The Red Review: A Liverpool FC Almanac
ISBN 0954958055

Published By Harcourt Publishing

© Oliver Anderson and Paul Tomkins 2006
All rights reserved.
The moral right of the author has been asserted.

Printed in Great Britain by the Anchor Print Group Ltd.

First edition published 2006

contents

the **red review**

Acknowledgements

The statistics published herein are nearly all unique to *The Red Review*. However, many are calculated from information gathered from a huge variety of published sources, in order to form new types of calculation and analysis. Very occasionally third-party statistics are published in their original form, and acknowledgements are duly accredited in the text.

A big thanks to Andy at www.liverweb.org.uk, whose considerable statistical collections were invaluable when checking and double-checking the raw data. Its slogan says it all:

Liverweb – the one stop shop for all your Liverpool FC Needs

Other information — such as line-ups, shots on target, corners, etc — was taken from a number of sources, including www.liverpoolfc.tv, the Guardian, Match magazine and www.soccernet.com. Where discrepancies in the figures between these sources existed, an average figure was taken.

Thanks From Oliver

Special thanks to Dad for all his help, for being there to talk about all things Red and helping with many aspects of the book, and thanks to Mum for being there to talk about all things non Red. Thanks to Tom for all his ideas and discussions, and for his 'insider' Spanish knowledge. Thanks to Emily for all her help on the journalistic side, and for all her contacts. Thanks also to Emma for her love and guidance, and Mitch for being patient while the cricket teachings were postponed.

Next, a huge thank-you to Paul Tomkins, who has been fantastic throughout the project. Thanks for adding your own thoughts throughout the book, and thanks for all your help, guidance and tolerance of a first-time writer hell-bent on including too many dodgy one-liners.

Thanks to Garreth Cummins, Dan Symonds and Stephen Davies for advice and input. Finally, thanks to those websites which have offered to run excerpts. Thanks to everyone else who helped out, and who believed in the book.

Feedback

You are now the proud owner of a 'limited' first-edition book. If you have any comments, positive or negative (although preferably constructive), please email us at harcourt_books@btinternet.com. This also applies to any queries with the findings or the methodology, and any errors that can be corrected ahead of the second edition.

Foreword

Lies, damned lies and statistics — a famous aphorism, sometimes attributed to 19th-Century novelist Mark Twain. Did he have a point? Possibly so, although it's easy to lazily follow Twain's lead and try to discredit statistics without bothering to investigate what they actually convey. Of course, it should also be noted at this stage that *The Adventures of Huckleberry Finn*, while a seminal work of American literature, shows no apparent understanding of the relative merits of the 4-5-1 and 4-4-2 systems. So Twain cannot necessarily be trusted.

The greatest problem with statistics is not the information they provide, but the way in which this information is often presented. The statistics themselves don't aim to lie, nor to mislead. If accurately calculated, they are factual figures. However, any statistics used to present only one side of an argument are clearly not to be trusted. Used selectively, stats can skew perceptions.

That is not the aim of *The Red Review*, not least because of the order in which the information was collected by Oliver Anderson. Whatever happened over the course of the 2005/06 season was noted and entered into a database, and whatever the information revealed is what forms the basis of the analysis; it was not designed with the premeditated notion of casting certain players in a positive light, nor proving that other players simply aren't very good. Their performances speak for themselves, in a statistical sense, and for good measure, comparisons can be made with the previous season, Benítez's first, so evidence of progress and regression can be easily traced.

The analysis that accompanies the findings never ignores the impressions we formed through watching the players — statistics should never be used to judge a player without having seen him in action (although in recent years I've seen a few people claiming that the latest Peruvian sensation should be purchased on account of his fantastic Championship Manager ratings). The results herein supplement what we've seen with our own eyes, and what others can see either at the game or on television. But it doesn't stop there.

As well as a whole host of detailed figures that confirm our suspicions, there are also plenty of surprises; important factors and trends not always easily perceptible when viewing a match, or taking each game as it comes without the aid of the larger picture. Why was Steve Finnan, a defender, the third-highest assist maker during the season, ahead of a whole raft of more creative, attacking players? Why did the Reds score so few goals when Xabi Alonso was in the side? Sometimes detailing a hidden trend can lead to enlightenment, although very occasionally it leads to investigation undertaken with no little head scratching. But that's football; while essentially a simple game in its purest form — pass, move, tackle, score — there are layers and layers of complexity involved. We all form impressions, but are those impressions backed up by the figures? If so, why? And if not, why not?

Was Fernando Morientes a failure because he didn't score enough goals, or was he a success because the team won an incredible percentage of its Premiership matches when he was in the side? He was the team's worst striker when it came to minutes-per-goal, but the best when it came to calculating the average points taken from each league encounter. Did Peter Crouch have a poor first season because 13 goals 'wasn't good enough for Liverpool', as plenty of people suggested, or were his 18 assists more than ample recompense? How did Djibril Cissé's goals-per-minute compare with other Premiership strikers, including new signing Craig Bellamy? And was Cissé more productive on the right or up front? Can the fact that John Arne Riise's presence in the back four resulted in less goals being conceded qualify his season as a definite success, even though some still doubt his defensive ability? Or did his poor goals output when playing left-back lead to the need for more goals from that position? How did Fabio Aurelio's figures from Spain compare?

Football is a team game, and we cannot look at a player outside the context of the side as a whole; while their individual stats are presented, their effect in the team is also examined. Which players and formations suited Liverpool best? Players do not exist in isolation; they need other players to blend with, who suit their styles and who, in return, will benefit from their presence. It's the same in all areas of life. After all, certain clothes suit certain people and look terrible on others. The Donna Versace dress worn by Liz Hurley in the mid-90s may now be regarded as an iconic fashion item, but it wouldn't have acquired quite the same status had it been worn by Rosanne Barr.

None of the tables and statistics presented in this book are designed to be taken as definitive *proof* of anything. Each is merely a strong hint at a player's (or indeed the team's) strengths and weaknesses, as no single statistic in isolation can tell you the whole story. However, when the myriad forms of evidence are assessed in unison they go to form a detailed picture.

We are presenting a circumstantial case. When prosecuting a criminal, lawyers may point out that the killer wore size nine shoes, based on a footprint left at the scene. The lawyer might add that eye-witnesses claimed the killer was of South American descent, and overweight. Evidence at the scene may have suggested the killer was left-handed and short — about 5ft 5" — in keeping with the man on the stand. (Any similarity to Diego Maradona is, of course, purely coincidental.) A hair found at the scene may be consistent with those of the accused, but not contain the crucial hair-tip follicle that would enable scientists to make that billion-to-one DNA match. Criminal profilers may suggest that the perpetrator was in his mid-30s and have a hatred of women based on a domineering mother, again fitting the man on trial. None of these 'facts' in isolation would finger any culprit. But combined they present a strong circumstantial case: enough to convict or acquit. The more detail and depth gone into, the clearer the picture should become. And that is definitely the case here.

Looking only at the below average amount of goals Liverpool score when Xabi Alonso plays, for example, could lead you to conclude he's not an effective player; and yet this from someone with such bounteous creative skills. But the analysis needs to be taken in conjunction with the amount the team concedes (which is also less than the average) and the points the team wins; as well taking into account the quality of opposition — was Alonso saved to play only in the more difficult games? And how many goals did he himself score and create?

Let's get one thing straight from the start. As with Alonso, it doesn't take a series of statistics to tell anyone that Steven Gerrard is a top-class footballer. But what is his best position? Just how effective is he on the right compared with the middle? Who is his best partner in a central position? Just how often does he contribute to a Liverpool goal, either by scoring or assisting? Do Liverpool score more or less when he is in the side? Do they concede a greater or lesser amount when he is playing? Do they win more or less frequently when his name is in the teamsheet? How many mistakes did he make that led directly to Liverpool conceding goals? In which competition did he perform best?

These are the kind of questions asked and answered within this book — for Gerrard, for Alonso, and for all the other members of the Reds' squad. But it doesn't stop there. What striking partnership was the most effective? What back four was the strongest? How did the central midfielders perform in tandem? Do the figures suggest zonal marking actually works, or is it Benítez's grand folly? How did Liverpool's key players compare with those of their rivals?

But don't just take our word for what we believe the figures suggest; after all, it's just our interpretations, even if we trust we've seen things for how they really were. With the full detailed results tables published for every category, you can look at the raw data and come to your own conclusions.

Paul Tomkins
August 2006

Chapter One
Statistics – What Are They Good For?

Gérard Houllier's frantic protestations about how many corners the Reds won did his reputation no good at all. For that matter, they didn't help the reputation of football statistics, either.

Of course, the amount of corners a team wins *should* count for something in football analysis; not in terms of points, but it's yet one more measure of how territorially successful a team was in a game. When a manager is having to explain away a 0-0 draw he may call on such things as evidence of his side's hard luck, but in that context it often seems desperate, especially if it doesn't fit with what the fans have just witnessed. Winning 15 corners but not having a single shot on or off target doesn't represent a good day at the office.

But that does not make such statistics immaterial. Corners are a good way to score goals, and if you are winning 20 corners every match you have to be doing something right in open play; however, if you're not scoring from any of them, then that's equally indicative of an area of failure. In the Club World Championship final against São Paulo in December 2005, Liverpool had all the possession, and thoroughly deserved a victory. However, the Brazilians won the game 1-0. Afterwards Benítez said: "We had 21 shots and 17 corners, hit the bar twice and scored three [disallowed] goals. We couldn't have done any more to win." In those circumstances, it seems acceptable to point out such facts.

It's fair to say that the majority of football statistics still centre around counting simple figures such as corners or fouls, although the most popular continue to revolve around the amount of goals scored by an individual. Often these are the only stats seen on pre- or post-game shows, in newspapers or on internet sites. They are usually either in a box to the side of the text or scrolling along the bottom of the screen but rarely incorporated in the commentary or article, and are often left unexplained. For example, in a pre-match report you may see a graph of when a team scores alongside data as to when its opponents score. But there is very rarely a description of what is being shown or what the information in the graph might tell us. Is there a team flaw? What are the reasons behind a regular late conceding of goals? The data often just sits there like a picture for the story below. In this book you will not see a statistic given just for the sake of it. The numbers and tables will all be analysed and discussed in detail — not simply left unexplained.

While 'goals scored' remains the most popular stat for an individual, with goalscoring charts published almost everywhere, in truth it tells us little about how a player is really performing. A Premiership striker — Striker A — could step-up and convert nine penalties in a season but may not have won any of them. He could score 15 goals in the season but not set up another team-mate all year, constantly choosing to shoot irrespective of whether others are better placed. This is an example of how the player could receive praise for a 15-goal season but his team-mates, and more importantly his team, would actually have suffered due to his selfishness. So without supporting figures on Striker A's team play and the team's overall performance when he is in the line-up the 15 goal tally would look impressive. In addition to that Striker A could have played in 30 games, whilst Striker B scored eight in 12 games. Looking at the goalscoring leaders for the Premiership in most years Striker A would be in the top 10 but Striker B would not figure, even though he was more prolific in his time on the field. Therein lies another problem with looking at goals in isolation. This short example reveals that through adding information or other statistics a greater understanding of a player's performance can be acquired. Equally, there's also the need to take into account the necessary willingness to have a shot at goal. It's no point being the most accurate striker in the league, converting 100% of your efforts, if you only shoot once a chance becomes truly 'unmissable' – perhaps by waiting until the keeper collapses with a pulmonary embolism. Sometimes you have to gamble.

One such stat that can add insight into a player's overall team performance and value is the assist. But not the assist as many of you might be familiar with from Opta but what is arguably a better, more team-oriented assist statistic, with a slightly different emphasis. The original system, developed in 1996 by Opta (in conjunction with former England coach Don Howe), came about after they obtained the licence to compile and analyse statistics on each and every Premiership game. Due to Sky television owning the rights to broadcast Premiership games a natural partnership was born, and Opta stats found their way into game broadcasts and Premiership statistics on the internet. The stats have improved the production and analysis of football, but more often than not media sources fall back on the same old stats. It is very rare for a goalkeeper's save percentage to fly across the screen or a striker's penalty conversion rate as he steps up to take a spot kick. But both would add to the game and the knowledge and enjoyment of viewers. Are things like this omitted due to a perceived lack of understanding on the part of the audience? Probably so, but by breaking the mould and displaying this information, with a simple explanation by the commentator, even the most casual fan would become used to it and appreciate its meaning in the context of the game.

Another of the problems with Opta statistics is that although they are available on the Sky Sports website, they are very hard to find or access. A lot of what Opta produces is not for publication unless purchased by a team or media outlet to analyse and report. This means that the bulk of their statistical information never reaches the masses and has never become commonplace in analysing and assessing the game.

The one important statistic they did bring to the game was the 'assist', or what we'll call the 'standard assist', which is given to an outfield player directly responsible for a goal by a direct cross, pass or shot. The stat appears to be given out sparingly and without any real explanation as to why it is being awarded. The assist statistic should be a great indicator of how unselfish a player is; how frequently a player sets up goals, to be used as an indicator as to how valuable a player is in terms of overall attacking performance.

The standard assist is perfect for telling who made the final pass, but that does not necessarily make it the *killer* pass; that could easily be the pass preceding the final ball, whilst the final ball could be a basic one-yard lay-off. What about an inch-perfect cross expertly headed down to the goalscorer? Don't both contributions — the cross and the knock-down — deserve equal recognition? By widening the criteria to the final two passes it gives more insight into the 'business end' of the move. Of course, you could widen it yet further, but then it starts to lose impact and relevance. As with the standard assist, the assist method used in this book does not take into account the quality or difficulty of the pass or cross, but it measures the impact of more than just one player in the creation of a goal, to give more insight into a team's cutting-edge personnel, and to name the players 'directly involved' in any goal.

Of course, not every goal scored has two passes prior to the scorer receiving the ball; sometimes possession is lost and regained with only one player setting up the goal. These are one-assisted goals. Other times the scorer himself wins possession, to score an unassisted goal (see Thierry Henry's second goal against Liverpool at Highbury for the perfect unassisted goal, due to Steven Gerrard's 'blind' backpass; similarly, Luis Garcia's winner against Chelsea in the FA Cup semi-final came from a wayward William Gallas header).

Changes in possession continually end and start the recording process of who picks up an assist on any goal scored. This statistic can be far more accurate at judging a player's performance than the more 'standard' assist used by Opta. Let's take the demolition of Birmingham in the FA Cup as an example. Steven Gerrard had a hugely productive game but had nothing to show for it in terms of goals. Looking at the Opta stats on this game, Gerrard was credited with two assists, a very high total for that statistic, but with the 'two touch' assist rule he can be credited with a further three. Describing them can show how Gerrard was directly involved in five of the seven goals. The first on the night was from a beautifully floated free-kick cross from the captain, helped on by Sissoko into the path of Hyypia to head home. The second was from a direct Gerrard cross to Crouch (a 'standard' assist was accredited here). The third came when Gerrard was able to slide and save the ball from going out of play whilst simultaneously passing it through to Luis Garcia, who subsequently fed Crouch for his second. The fourth was the captain's squared pass for Morientes to finish (again a 'standard' assist here), and finally his control and flick into the path of Riise for his wonder strike.

As you can see, without Gerrard's key contributions in all five goals they would not have been scored. Even looking at the less obvious contributions for the first and third goals, there would have been no Sissoko flick for the first, no Garcia pass for the third; Gerrard's part in the goals is very prominent. As mentioned earlier, sometimes the ball before the final ball is the one that breaks the defence — as was the case with the third goal of the night, scored by Crouch and fed by Garcia. The ball by Gerrard releasing Garcia and Crouch upfield was in many ways more important than the final feed from Garcia. With Riise's goal and Liverpool's fifth of the night you can see the current problem with the 'standard' assist. Gerrard gave a direct pass for Riise to smash home but received no 'standard' assist on the play. Why not? Without Gerrard's cushioned layoff Riise would not have received the ball, which was prime for striking, in the first place.

The goal and the assist are there to record the productive side of a team's game, but what about its defensive abilities? At present, the clean sheet is the most prevalent statistic, and is often accredited to the goalkeeper first and foremost, to the defence as a secondary measure, and occasionally to the team as a whole. Clean sheets are easy to measure; it just takes a zero on the scoresheet. But what about goals conceded, and the fault therein?

The statistic recorded for errors is herein labelled the 'Mistake'. Errors are part of football. Everyone is fallible, and part of the great wonder of the game (and indeed all sports) is the human error involved from the players, the managers, and even the officials. If you look hard enough you can always find a mistake in why a goal was scored. Someone is always at fault, somewhere down the line, if you trace a move back far enough; it could stem from a player giving the ball away five minutes earlier. But that player could justifiably argue that his colleagues didn't properly deal with the problem in the interim. There has to be a realistic level set about what constitutes a mistake that costs the team a goal. Unless being over-critical, sometimes no one can be faulted.

This statistic is very subjective, and could easily become a biased measure. For this reason, categories of types of mistake were drawn up for both outfield players and goalkeepers, to remove as much of this bias as possible and record the errors in a more systematic or classified way. The groupings for outfield players are as follows: a missed tackle, bad marking, an unnecessary or bad foul, positional mistake (failure to hold the line/slow to close down), a missed clearance and slowness to react to a loose ball or danger (serious delay). The categories for a goalkeeper are: a dropped cross, a missed cross (one within reach), a missed clearance, a positional mistake, an unnecessary or bad foul, and a poor attempt at a save.

If a defender or goalkeeper's actions fall into one of the categories mentioned above, a mistake will be counted against that player. Similar to the assist, conceding a goal can be due to a series of mistakes, but there are cases of players making a single mistake that leads directly to a conceded goal. An example would be Luton's third goal in the FA Cup 3rd-round when Sami Hyypia failed to clear and was dispossessed, ending in Luton being awarded a penalty. The penalty was conceded by Scott Carson and in normal circumstances he would also have been awarded a mistake; however, on video evidence it was clear that Carson did not bring the player down. The sole mistake that led to the Luton penalty and subsequent goal was therefore Hyypia's loose control. Another slightly less obvious example of a mistake would be Stephen Warnock's against Chelsea, at Stamford Bridge in the Premiership, for the second goal of the game. On the ball played over the top by Chelsea, Warnock was slow in stepping out with the other defenders, playing Hernan Crespo onside to give Chelsea a two-goal lead.

An example of a two mistake goal was observed against Benfica at Anfield in March. For the first goal of the game Djimi Traoré was caught horribly out of position (first mistake) and unfortunately compounded the error by slipping over. Jamie Carragher moved over to the left of centre to cover for Traoré but was unable to clear the ball after two attempts (second mistake). The ball was worked to Simao who cut inside the back-peddling Liverpool defence and curled his shot into the top corner of the net.

This statistic is flawed in some ways over a short period of time, but over the course of a season it does indicate a trend, i.e. which players are more susceptible to committing errors (and remember these are critical errors resulting in the opposition scoring because of the mistake) and cost the team in results. As with all the stats within this book they should not be looked at individually but in conjunction with other statistics to build up an overall appraisal of the player's performance. A player may have a high individual error rate but when he is in the line-up, the team might have an extremely low goals-against count.

The two statistics we have discussed here — assists and mistakes — along with the goal and many others in common usage in football, are basically 'counting' or 'tally' statistics. That is they are counted or tallied up during a game and often totalled for all games played, e.g. 15 goals, 25 assists, three mistakes etc. It may seem obvious, but the more games or minutes played the higher the player's counting statistics are generally going to be. Giving the total count alone, therefore, is not by itself adequate to judge the performance of a player or team. For example, using the example of Striker A and Striker B from the beginning of this chapter, what if Striker A collected 15 goals in 30 games whilst Striker B collected eight goals in only 12 games?

A better way to look at these totals to determine player performance would be to rate them over some kind of time period, such as 'per-game'. Striker A would then come out at 0.50 goals-per-game and Striker B at 0.67 goals-per-game. So in this assessment Striker B would be considerably better than Striker A, scoring at a much more prolific rate. This type of rate stat for goals has become more common but is still not used enough establish the best goalscorer. That is still how many total goals a player has scored over the whole season.

Such rate stats become more relevant as the game becomes more squad-oriented, and strikers face heavier rotation. Is it better to have two first-rate strikers scoring 25 a season, as was common in years gone by, or four sharing the playing time equally and scoring 15 apiece? You can do the maths. The balance for any manager is allowing strikers enough regular playing time in order to find their confidence and rhythm, but also keeping them on their toes with competition, and not over-playing them so that grow susceptible to injury or fatigue.

It's fair to say that assessing strikers in 2006 is far more complicated than it was 20 years ago. Football is played over 90 minutes (with a small amount of injury time, and sometimes extra-time), with a maximum of three substitutions allowed per team. Using goals-per-game gives no indication as to whether a player has played 90 minutes, 40 minutes or two minutes in a game; it just assumes the player has played the full 90 minutes, which is hard on the figures of a striker introduced in the 89th minute simply to run down the clock. Rating the goals over 90 minutes would give an even better indication of the player's true performance. Again using the Striker A and B example, what if Striker A had played only 60 minutes in all 30 games and been replaced on the hour as part of his manager's substitution patterns, whilst Striker B played the full 90 in all his games? The rate stat would change dramatically again. Striker A would have collected his 15 goals in 1800 minutes, or 0.75 goals-per-90-minutes and Striker B collected his eight goals in 1080 minutes, or 0.67 goals-per-90 minutes.

So after breaking the games down into minutes instead of games played, Striker A becomes the more prolific force once again. Rating a stat like goals or assists per-game, therefore, is flawed in that it credits one whole game played for any number of minutes spent on the pitch. This kind of rating will punish substitutes and reward players who end up playing in extra-time games. In this book you will find the more traditional counting statistics, but you will also find rate statistics as well. In most cases they will be rated over 90 minutes to remove any playing time discrepancies, but where relevant a 'per-game' rate will also be used.

Even with the recording of different statistics and different slants on older measurements, football is a more complex game than just goals, assists and mistakes. The interaction of players in a team leads to possession, scoring chances and goals. Figures do not, and could not, take into account step-overs, players creating space for each other, covering for a colleague, decoy runs and many more aspects that are extremely difficult to quantify. In addition, the goals, assists, mistakes, shots, and passes become individual statistics when football is very much team game. That is why in addition to the individual statistics recorded for players, a method was needed to at least attempt to quantify the effect each player has in the team's overall performance.

To do this, the scoreline and eventual result of each game in which a player featured was recorded, to calculate the team's goals-for average, goals-against average, points-for average (three for a win in all games, including cup competitions) and clean sheet percentage for each individual player. This represents, therefore, a line of statistics detailing how incorporating any player into the line-up affects the balance, shape and more importantly, performance of the team. You will see these stats discussed and analysed in the Players' and Formations' sections in more detail.

Chapter Two
Explaining the New Statistics

A variety of techniques, unique to this book, have been used to gather and assess information on the first two seasons of Rafael Benítez's reign as Liverpool manager. Most of what you read will be different from other publications, but still not too difficult to comprehend. This brief section will introduce some of the methods used in player and team evaluation.

To analyse Liverpool's improvements from last season to this, and highlight any shifting trends in play, we have looked at the team's overall record — how many wins, draws and defeats, as well as looking at the points won, points-per-game and clean sheets kept. On some occasions we analyse the clean sheets further by calculating them as a percentage of the number of games played. The main bulk of the team analyses, however, centre around the team statistics tables, an example of which is given below in Table 1.

Table 1. An example of the team statistics tables.

Season	GFA	GAA	SOG	OSOG	Fouls	OFouls	Corners	Ocorners	Offside	Ooffside	TOP	OTOP	Saves	OSaves
04/05	1.42	1.04	6.0	4.2	12.4	14.4	5.5	4.4	2.7	3.6	52.0	48.0	3.7	5.2
05/06	1.45	0.70	6.9	3.2	12.9	14.2	6.2	3.8	2.5	4.3	54.2	45.8	3.7	6.2

The majority of the team statistic tables make a comparison between last year, the 2004/05 season, and this year, 2005/06. The data contained within the table is actually quite simple and displays stats that will no doubt be familiar to you. Information is presented as averages for the season, time period or specific category being looked at. Only occasionally are the specific team stats for an individual game displayed. The first column gives the headings for the data being compared. As stated earlier, it will mostly be between last season and this, but it could be individual games or perhaps the stats from different competitions. The next 14 columns actually contain only seven different statistics but the data is presented for both Liverpool and the average of their combined opponents. The statistics given are as follows:

Goals-for average (GFA) the average goals scored by Liverpool per-game

Goals-against average (GAA) the average goals conceded by Liverpool per-game

Shots-on-goal (SOG) the average number of shots-on-goal by Liverpool per-game

Opponents' shots-on-goal (OSOG) the average number of shots-on-goal by Liverpool's opponents per-game

Fouls (Fouls) the average number of fouls committed by Liverpool per-game

Opponents' Fouls (OFouls) the average number of fouls committed by Liverpool's opponents per-game

Corners won (Corners) the average number of corners won by Liverpool per-game

Opponents' corners won (OCorners) the average number of corners conceded by Liverpool per-game

Offsides (Offside) the average number of times Liverpool were called offside per-game

Opponents' offsides (Ooffside) the average number of times Liverpool caught their opponents offside

Time of possession (TOP) the average time of possession for Liverpool per-game given as a percentage

Opponents' time of possession (OTOP) the average time of possession for Liverpool's opponents per-game given as a percentage

Saves made (Saves) the average number of saves made by Liverpool keepers per-game

Opponents' saves made (OSaves) the average number of saves made by Liverpool's opponents' keepers per-game

Players who featured in the Liverpool first team this season or last have their own player table, an example of which can be seen in Table 2, detailing the player statistics for the 2004/05 and 2005/06 seasons.

The first line for each table contains the player's name, squad number, playing age at the beginning of the campaign, his height, and primary playing position or positions. The next line contains three headers for the columns of data that follow: 'Season' for information such as year and competition, 'Individual' for individual player stats, and 'Team' for the team stats for that player. Under the 'Season' heading the statistics are broken down into the different competitions. For 2005/06 the overall statistics are separated into four categories, giving the Premier League, Cup and European player statistics, as well as the combined totals. The numbers for the 2004/05 season are displayed in the total and Premier League breakdowns.

Table 2. An example of an outfield player statistical table

John Arne Riise No.6						Age: 24	Height: 6'1"		Left-Back/Left-Midfield			
Season	Individual									Team		
YEAR COMP	GS	MINS	GOALS	ASSISTS	POINTS	GOALS (90)	ASSISTS (90)	POINTS (90)	MLG	MLG % (90)	CS	CS %	GFA	GAA	PTS
2005-06 Total	42	3906	4	13	17	0.09	0.30	0.39	3	6.91	26	59.4	1.68	0.58	2.26
2005-06 Prem	24	2263	1	4	5	0.04	0.16	0.20	1	3.98	17	68.1	1.35	0.48	2.25
2005-06 Euro	9	972	0	3	3	0.00	0.28	0.28	0	0.00	5.7	52.4	1.48	0.46	2.07
2005-06 Cups	6	671	3	6	9	0.40	0.80	1.21	2	26.83	3	40.2	3.08	1.07	2.55
2004-05 Total	52	4656	8	12	20	0.15	0.23	0.39	2	3.87	15	29	1.41	0.89	1.69
2004-05 Prem	34	2985	6	9	15	0.18	0.27	0.45	2	6.03	5.9	18	1.42	1.03	1.60

The first four columns detail the actual 'count' statistics compiled by the player during the season — so in Riise's case his Premiership counts were 24 games started (GS), 2263 minutes (MINS), one goal (GOALS) and four assists (ASSISTS). The fifth column, POINTS, is another 'count' statistic, and is a measure of the overall attacking production of the player; it is a simple addition of the player's goals and assists, combined to give a useful indication of his overall attacking effectiveness. Who is more effective in an attacking sense, the player with five goals and five assists or the player with two goals and eight assists? It could be argued that they are both equally so, as they have both contributed to ten goals being scored. In this example, in all competitions John Arne Riise scored eight goals last year and had 12 assists, for a total of 20 attacking points.

The next three columns are rate statistics for the goals, assists and points statistics. These are headed GOALS (90), ASSISTS (90) and POINTS (90). These three columns are the main attacking 'count' statistics averaged over 90 minutes. As explained in the previous chapter, averaging the statistics over 90 minutes cuts out the bias due to certain players playing a greater number of games, and thus having a better chance of compiling more counting statistics. The three columns are essentially how many goals, assists and points the player will get for every 90 minutes of football. Looking at Riise's figures above you can see that last year he averaged 0.15 goals per-90-minutes and 0.23 assists per-90-minutes, for an average of 0.39 attacking points-per-90.

The last two columns in the 'Individual' section are a count of the mistakes leading to goals (MLG) collected by the player in each season and competition, and the mistakes leading to goals as a percentage (MLG %(90)) adjusted to be the percentage per-90 minutes of football. Identical in its concept to rating the attacking statistics the mistakes-leading-to-goals percentage has been adjusted to take into account the player's on-field time, and remove all bias of certain players playing more and compiling greater mistake numbers during the course of a season. Unlike with the attacking rate stats, however, the lower the mistake percentage the better the player performed; it is simply a measure of the percentage of games (90 minutes of pitch time) in which the player made a mistake. So with this example we can see that Riise made only one costly error in the league; his figure of 3.98% meant that in 96.2% of his games he was without blame for any goal conceded.

Under the 'Team' heading are the individual player's team statistics for the season, for every competition played in. Due to football being a team-oriented game these statistics were devised to look at how an individual player affects the performance of the whole team in terms of clean sheets (CS), clean sheet percentage (CS%), goals-for average (GFA), goals-against average (GAA) and points won per-game (PTS). All the statistics collected in this section are calculated to capture the player's true contribution to the Liverpool cause, and are again rated over 90 minutes. For example, in 2004/05 the team statistics for whenever John Arne Riise appeared in the Liverpool team were 1.41 goals-for, 0.89 goals-against and 1.69 points-per-game. He contributed to 14.8 clean sheets in his minutes on the field, which worked out to be a clean sheet percentage of 29%. These statistics can give a different insight into a player's value, and suggest things that individual player statistics cannot reveal about the dynamics of professional football.

The table we have just explained would not be suitable to assess a goalkeeper so we have developed a similar table to analyse their contributions, an example of which is given in Table 3.

Table 3. An example of a goalkeeper's statistical table

Scott Carson No.20											Age: 19 Height: 6'3"				Goalkeeper	
Season	Individual											Team				
YEAR	COMP	GS	MINS	ASSISTS	POINTS	ASSIST (90)	POINTS (90)	GA	SAVES	SAVE%	MLG	MLG % (90	CS	CS %	GFA	GAA	PTS
2005-06 Total	4	360	0	0	0	0	6	13	68.4	0	0	1	25	2.00	1.50	1.50
2005-06 Euro	2	180	0	0	0	0	1	7	87.5	0	0	1	50	1.00	0.50	1.50
2005-06 Cups	2	180	0	0	0	0	5	6	54.5	0	0	0	0	3.00	2.50	1.50
2005-06 Total	9	810	With Sheff Weds					5	44	89.8	-	-	5	55.5	1.33	0.56	2.00
2004-05 Total	5	450	0	0	0	0	4	20	83.3	1	20.00	1	20	1.00	0.80	1.80
2004-05 Prem	4	360	0	0	0	0	3	15	83.3	0	0	1	25	0.75	0.75	1.50

The table is set out in much the same way as those for the outfield players, with the first row detailing the player's personal statistics, then the table separated into the same three headings. The 'Season' and 'Team' sections remain the same, but there are some changes to the 'Individual' player stats section. Most of the individual stats seen for outfield players remain (games started, minutes played, assists, points, assists-per-90, points-per-90, mistakes and mistakes-per-90). However, goals have been removed — although it would be a novel and welcome addition to the team if one could score — and some goalkeeper-specific figures added. The three columns added are goals-against (GA), detailing the goals conceded by the goalkeeper in question; saves (SAVES), giving the saves made by the goalkeeper; and save percentage (SAVES%), which gives the percentage of all goal chances (shots-on-goal, headers on goal, crosses, smothers, etc) the goalkeeper has saved.

While this chapter has explained the bulk of the statistics used in this book there are some others used, mainly in the Player and Team Statistics sections, but these will all be explained in detail as and when they are discussed.

Chapter Three
Team Statistics

Football evolves. Every few years a new system gets developed, and for a while it can trump all other variations; like a mutating virus that evades all forms of antibiotics. Then, after a while, other teams begin to work out its weaknesses, and further change is required. New strains appear.

It could be said that Rafa Benítez and Jose Mourinho represent the new school of football thinking. (The statistics suggest it's *not* Bryan Robson and Steve Bruce.) Ten years younger than Arsene Wenger, and twenty younger than Sir Alex Ferguson, these two top managers arrived from Iberia in the summer of 2004 with new ideas, and quickly blew away the old guard in many respects. Chelsea took two consecutive league titles with 90+ point hauls, while within two seasons Benítez had overturned a massive Arsenal advantage in terms of league points and equalled Ferguson's sole success in the Champions League. Like all good managers, Wenger and Ferguson are capable of adapting to the new circumstances; however, unlike in previous years, they no longer have it all their own way. And when it comes to the biggest trophies — the European

Cup and the Premiership — they have found themselves on the outside, looking in enviously at Benítez and Mourinho, who've shared three in that short time, as well as a couple of the 'lesser' ones.

The styles adopted by Liverpool and Chelsea in the past two years have differed, but proved similar in their main objectives of defending and attacking as a team. Chelsea employed Claude Makelele to protect the back four and start attacks, usually with simple passes; Liverpool had Xabi Alonso and Momo Sissoko to perform a similar role, although Alonso starts moves with greater flair. Chelsea had Didier Drogba holding the ball up and playing in runners from the midfield, whilst Liverpool signed Peter Crouch to perform a similar role, each weighing in with 10-15 goals. Chelsea's major goal threat was a midfielder, Frank Lampard, who was top scorer two seasons running, while Steven Gerrard did the same at Liverpool. Both teams employed a flat back four, and talented young keepers.

Chelsea's major advantage was clearly in wide areas, but this could well change in 2006/07, with Damien Duff having left Stamford Bridge, and with Benítez introducing the pacy, skilful pair of Mark Gonzalez and Jermaine Pennant. Mourinho added another goalscoring midfielder, Michael Ballack, and finally went for a predator up front in Andriy Shevchenko — something not previously needed. Liverpool added their own poacher, with Dirk Kuyt. Chelsea seem to be heading for a narrower formation, either 4-3-3 or 4-2-2-2, while Liverpool now have players prepared to stay wide and get chalk on their boots, in a 4-5-1 or a 4-4-2. So both teams continue to evolve.

Under Gérard Houllier Liverpool's tactics were often fairly simple: defend deep, protecting the back four with the midfield at close quarters, and counter-attack with the pace of Michael Owen and Emile Heskey. Possession football was sacrificed in order to draw the opposition out, so they could be hit on the break as quickly as possible. Under Benítez, however, things are radically different. Liverpool now play with the back four defending higher up the pitch. His method involves his side attacking and defending as a team, and not having separate units who can only see each other with the aid of binoculars. It involves keeping the ball, and spreading play with the long passes of Gerrard and, in particular, Xabi Alonso. The back four are usually protected by a two man sentry in the midfield. Then there are two wider players who tend to have more freedom than the widemen received under the previous regime. Up front there are two players, although only one may be an out-and-out striker, with the second either a forward dropping into the hole, or a midfielder pushing on.

The system is very effective, giving enough protection to the back four but also allowing for free-flowing football. The key is hitting upon the right balance. Now that Benítez has more of his own players in place it is possible to see the true flexibility in the system. The Reds can now play three very different ways. The first is possession-based, with midfielders technically superior to those seen at the club in the earlier part of the decade, and certainly so when it comes to passing, while the team's shape — more compact — helps with a short-pass possession game. The second is a longer game, where Peter Crouch can be hit with long diagonal balls, either to flick-on or to hold up for an attacking midfielder. The third, which will be more prevalent next season (2006/07) is a fast counter-attacking game, with a number of quick-heeled additions made ahead of Benítez's third year in charge. All of these styles are related to attacking; the enduring defensive philosophy remains to defend fairly high up the pitch and, as a team, to press the opposition and force them into mistakes.

Team Form

Liverpool's overall team form, despite a slow start and the stutter in the winter months, improved dramatically in Rafa Benítez's second season. The figures posted in 2005/06 were easily up on the previous campaign, and provide compelling evidence of a team heading in the right direction, and doing so at some speed.

Table 1. The overall team record over the last two seasons

Season	Wins	Draws	Defeats	Points	Points per game	Clean Sheets	Clean Sheet %
2004/05	31	10	19	99	1.65	18	30.0%
2005/06	41	10	11	131	2.11	33	53.2%

*Points calculated as 3 points for a win and 1 point for a draw in all competitive matches this season and last

The overall win total is impressive, as well as the points won (Table 1). Liverpool were able to up their points-per-game tally by an impressive 0.46 points, from 1.65 a year ago up to just over 2.11 this season. One thing to note is the sheer number of games played by Liverpool during the last two seasons. It was not only this year's tough schedule that hampered Liverpool at times; it was the great number of high intensity games played last season, compounded by lack of a proper rest during the close season, and the earlier end to this season due to the World Cup in Germany. It was always going to be tough for Liverpool, having played exactly 60 games last season and then asked to play 62 this.

One of the clearest examples of Rafa Benítez's plan to have Liverpool defend and attack as a team is visible in the huge jump in the number of clean sheets, and the clean sheet percentage. Liverpool only registered 18 clean sheets last year, but this year the figure was 33, one short of tying the club's all-time record for a single season. The Reds registered a clean sheet in 53.2 % of all the games played this year, as opposed to only 30% in 2004/05.

Table 2. The overall team statistics in both 2004/05 and 2005/06

Season	GFA	GAA	SOG	OSOG	Fouls	OFouls	Corners	OCorners	Offside	Ooffside	TOP	OTOP	Saves	OSaves
04/05	1.37	0.93	6.0	4.2	12.4	14.4	5.5	4.4	2.7	3.6	52.0	48.0	3.7	5.2
05/06	1.68	0.71	6.6	3.2	12.5	13.5	6.0	3.7	2.6	4.4	54.6	45.4	3.9	6.0

Looking at the team statistics (Table 2), you can really see where Liverpool improved this season. The goals-for average rose by 0.31 goals-per-game in 2005/06, from a figure of 1.37 goals-per-game in 2004/05, up to 1.68 in 2005/06. A similar difference can be seen in the goals-against average, which fell from last year's figure by 0.22 goals-per-game. In 2004/05 the figure was just under one at 0.93 per-game, however this year the figure is a much meaner 0.71 per-game. The swing between the two goal rates was over half a goal-per-game more in favour of the Reds. Why is this?

From the figures you can see that Liverpool have been able to reduce their opponents' shots-on-goal by one per-game this year (4.2 opponents' shots-on-goal last year to 3.2); they have been able to concede less corners than last year (0.7 per-game less); retain more possession (up 2.6%); and finally — and a key to how they play — force more offsides from the opposition. Offsides forced has increased by almost one more per-game this season compared with last, meaning that on average almost one more potentially dangerous situation per-game was nullified. This is particularly important since under Benítez the Reds defend much higher up the pitch, and are therefore sometimes susceptible to balls over the top releasing fast forwards in on goal. It is evident that the offside trap has been well practised and well drilled into the Reds under Benítez.

As mentioned earlier, Liverpool's time of possession has increased by 2.6% this season, aided by the arrival of Peter Crouch. But an increase in possession is not significant unless something more substantial is produced with it; something the Reds did. Possession not only means more chances to create openings, but the opposition cannot score without the ball (unless it's from a spectacularly suicidal own-goal). Liverpool increased their shots-on-goal by almost one per-game, and also increased the number of corners won by a similar amount, all bringing about the increase seen in goals-for. Had Liverpool's strikeforce's finishing been more consistent, the scoring average would have been even higher by the end of the year.

Premiership Form
As mentioned in the previous section, the league form saw a huge improvement. The Premiership took a backseat to the European run last year, but this year a much stronger challenge was produced (see Table 3).

Table 3. The Premiership team record over the last two seasons

Season	Wins	Draws	Loses	Points	Points-per-game	Clean Sheets	Clean Sheet %
2004/05	17	7	14	58	1.53	7	18.4%
2005/06	25	7	6	82	2.16	22	57.9%

It is unusual to see the club's league form almost match that of the overall form. Although win percentage was slightly lower, the Premiership form did produce more points-per-game than the all-games record of the team in 05/06. The form was a stark turnaround, winning eight more games than a year ago, with a total of 25 wins this season compared with only the 17 picked up last year. The most impressive thing was that those eight wins all came from the loss column, as the team decreased its number of defeats this season from 14 last year, the 7th worst figure in the Premiership, to only six this year, the 3rd best in the league. This has primarily been achieved with an extremely tight defence — registering the greatest number of clean sheets (22), at a percentage of 57.9%, in the league. Putting that into context means the Reds kept a clean sheet in well over half their Premiership matches this year, approaching a rate of two for every three games played.

Table 4. The team statistics for Premiership games in both 2004/05 and 2005/06

Season	GFA	GAA	SOG	OSOG	Fouls	OFouls	Corners	OCorners	Offside	Ooffside	TOP	OTOP	Saves	OSaves
04/05	1.37	1.08	6.4	4.1	11.6	14.1	5.8	4.1	2.6	3.4	53.2	46.7	3.7	5.7
05/06	1.50	0.66	7.5	3.3	11.6	14.0	6.2	3.6	2.8	4.7	54.6	45.4	4.2	6.9

The team statistics for the Premiership campaign (Table 4) make interesting reading. The goals-for average has decreased from the overall total we saw in Table 2, as has the goals-against average. But the most interesting stats are that the shots-on-goal have been almost a whole shot-per-game greater in the Premiership than the overall numbers. This is further highlighted in the opponents' saves-per-game, observed as being 6.0 overall to 6.9 saves per-game in the Premiership.

Comparing the last two years, a similar pattern emerges to that witnessed in the overall team stats; the most significant change being the decrease in goals-against average without much of a change in goals-for average. The team conceded 16 fewer goals this season in Premiership play and also scored five more, for a 21-goal swing in the team's favour. A look at the Premiership stats reveals the same patterns for the strength and continuing development of the team under Benítez. In terms of moving forward and attacking as a team, measures such as shots-on-goal (from 6.4 to 7.5 per-game), the corners won (from 5.8 to 6.2 per-game), the time of possession (54.6% compared with 53.2% last year) and the opponents' saves (from 5.7 last year to 6.9 this year) have improved from last year's figures; whilst in terms of defending as a team, measures such as opponents' shots-on-goal (4.1 – 3.3 per-game), opponents' corners (4.1 – 3.6 per-game), opponents' time of possession (46.7% – 45.4%) and offsides (3.4 – 4.7 per-game) have all improved in favour of the Reds.

Premiership Home Form

One of the few pleasant surprises of 2004/05's poor overall Premiership form was the return to something resembling 'Fortress Anfield', where an inconsistent team still managed 12 wins in the 19 games. But even that has been bettered this season.

Table 5. The Premiership Home record over the last two seasons

Season	Wins	Draws	Loses	Points	Points per-game	Clean Sheets	Clean Sheet %
2004/05	12	4	3	40	2.11	6	31.6%
2005/06	15	3	1	48	2.53	14	73.7%

Last year's home form kept Liverpool in the hunt for 4th place, and without it they would have been way down the table (Table 5). This year the wins were increased and the defeats reduced, securing Liverpool the 2nd-best home form in the league, trailing only Chelsea, with the only home loss coming at the hands of London club in the 4-1 rout in early October. The Reds increased their points total here by eight, primarily due to an amazing defensive record. Excluding the four goals the Reds conceded to Chelsea, they conceded on only four other occasions throughout the whole of the 2005/06 season at Anfield; those goals being a first-half effort conceded to Fulham in the 5-1 win in March, Xabi Alonso's unfortunate late equaliser for Birmingham in the 1-1 draw on Robbie Fowler's 'second coming', and one apiece in the Merseyside derby and the last home game of the year, against Aston Villa. The Reds kept 14 clean sheets in the 19 home games this season, for a whopping clean sheet percentage of 73.7%.

Table 6. The team statistics for Premiership Home games in both 2004/05 and 2005/06

Season	GFA	GAA	SOG	OSOG	Fouls	OFouls	Corners	OCorners	Offside	Ooffside	TOP	OTOP	Saves	OSaves
04/05	1.63	0.79	7.3	3.2	10.2	14.7	6.9	3.5	2.2	2.9	55.9	44.1	3.6	7.3
05/06	1.68	0.42	9.3	2.6	10.3	14.5	8.3	3.4	2.5	4.2	57.3	42.7	4.1	9.4

An interesting thing about the team stats, given above in Table 6, is how similar the 2004/05 home form was to the all-game form of the team shown this season. The very good — if not amazing — home form of Benítez's first season became the template for all games in his second. In 2005/06 the home form improved yet further, and the dreadful away form became far more respectable, averaging out at the Anfield levels seen a year earlier.

That home form indicated that Liverpool, as a team with a new style, were heading in the right direction, with increased goal production and a miserly defence, but that the type of football they wanted to play wasn't working away from home, due to confidence issues and gaps in personnel. The most significant change is seen in the goals-against average, decreasing from an already low 0.79 goals-per-game to only 0.42 goals conceded per-game this year. Liverpool reduced the goals they conceded at home this season from 15 in 2004/05 down to only eight in 2005/06. As mentioned earlier four of those goals were conceded in one game against Chelsea, therefore meaning that in the other 18 home Premiership games Liverpool conceded only four goals. The team did this by further restricting the opponents' shots-on-goal, reducing them by a figure of 0.6 per-game, to only 2.6 in 2005/06. Liverpool managed just one more goal at home this season compared with 2004/05, netting a total of 32 goals at Anfield. It is actually hard to fathom how the Reds didn't manage to increase this total by even more. The shots-on-goal at home increased by a massive two per-game from last year, up to a figure of 9.3 per-game, whilst the corners also increased by a large amount: from 6.9 per-game last year to 8.3 this season. Time of possession was also seen to increase in the favour of Liverpool, up by a figure of 1.4%, to a very dominant 57.3%. If Liverpool had finished with their overall Premiership chance-conversion rate (which in itself was disappointing) the team would have netted 36 times at Anfield, not 32.

The problem was finishing the many chances that were created. The extra two shots-on-goal per-game led to just that single extra goal — but did result in a massive increase in saves by opposition goalkeepers.

Premiership Away Form

If the home form in the Premiership was the reason Liverpool stayed in the hunt for the final Champions League spot in 2004/05, then the improved away form (see Table 7) was the reason for the dramatic league improvement.

Table 7. The Premiership Away record over the last two seasons

Season	Wins	Draws	Loses	Points	Points-per-game	Clean Sheets	Clean Sheet %
2004/05	5	3	11	18	0.95	1	5.26%
2005/06	10	4	5	34	1.79	8	42.1%

Only three teams (Southampton, Norwich and Portsmouth) had more away defeats than Liverpool in 2004/05 and two of the three were relegated. This season the form improved to place Liverpool 3rd in the league in away points, only two points behind champions Chelsea in 2nd-place. Liverpool's points-per-game average away from home this season was higher than the team's total

Premiership points-per-game figure for the whole of 2004/05 (1.79 compared with 1.56). The clean sheet increase was not just limited to Anfield, with the Reds able to register seven more away clean sheets this season compared with last, resulting in a clean sheet percentage of 42.1% this year — compared with an embarrassing 5.26% last season.

Table 8. The team statistics for Premiership Away games in both 2004/05 and 2005/06

Season	GFA	GAA	SOG	OSOG	Fouls	OFouls	Corners	OCorners	Offside	Ooffside	TOP	OTOP	Saves	OSaves
04/05	1.11	1.37	5.5	5.1	13.0	13.5	4.7	4.8	3.0	4.0	51.3	48.7	3.7	4.2
05/06	1.32	0.89	5.6	3.9	12.8	13.5	4.1	3.8	3.2	5.2	52.6	47.4	4.4	4.6

Looking at the team stats from last year (see Table 8) the main problem was conceding too many goals away from home. Liverpool conceded 26 goals for an average of 1.37 per-game, but only scored 21 in reply (1.11 per-game).

One area that Rafa Benítez highlighted at the end of his first season was the inability of the Reds to possess the ball away from home for any kind of advantage. The reason for needing to do this away from home is to take the sting out of the crowd, create more chances, whilst also reducing those for the opposition. This was the main reason for the acquisition of Peter Crouch. The benefits of purchasing Crouch came in all forms of the game, not just away from home, but it was in away games where his presence was most keenly felt. Away from home the time in possession increased, by 1.2% over the level of a year ago. This figure might not be a significant increase at home, but away from home such a difference can be crucial.

The biggest improvement, however, was not in creating chances and scoring more goals away from home but in trying to control the game and limiting the opposition's scoring. Like every cut of the team statistics this year, the goals-against average decreased from last year's figure, dropping from 1.37 per-game down to below a single goal (0.89 per-game). This is not only due to the increased possession Liverpool have enjoyed away from home but from restricting the home team's shots-on-goal (down from 5.1 to 3.9 per-game), reducing the number of corners conceded (4.8 to 3.8 per-game) and increasing the number of offsides won (increased from 4.0 to 5.2 per-game). The increase in offsides forced is key here, and indicates that Liverpool rarely change their style of play even away from home. The style is very much to remain defending higher up the pitch, and force offsides from the home team using a trap practiced to near-perfection. It indicates that Liverpool are intent on taking the play back to the home team, and are not intent on forcing draws away from home by playing only counter-attacking football.

Form against the Premiership top five
Another much-publicised area where Liverpool needed to improve was in

their form against the top five in the Premiership. These are always seen as the juiciest fixtures, and are where titles appear to be won and lost. Last year the top five included nose-bleeding Everton, while this year Tottenham made their way into the big five, but with the look of a team who could hang around there.

Table 9. The Premiership record against the other top five teams over the last two seasons

Season	Wins	Draws	Defeats	Points	Points-per-game	Clean Sheets	Failure to Score
2004/05	2	0	6	6	0.75	0	4
2005/06	2	2	4	8	1.00	4	4

Looking at the records for this season and last (Table 9) you can see the slight improvement the Reds have made in the high profile games in the Premiership. The two point increase is significant in that it is a conversion of two defeats into two draws from the season before; while adding only two points to the Reds' haul, it subtracts four from the opposition. The games at the top of the table are invariably tight, with often only one or two goals in it. The fact that Liverpool were able to attain four clean sheets in the eight games (as opposed to zero last year) shows that the Reds are now more able to defend against the very best attacks the league offers. The problems appear to lie with the inability to score or convert chances; exactly mirroring the clean sheet record by failing to score in four games of the eight games played against other top five opposition.

Table 10. The team statistics against the other top five Premiership teams for both 2004/05 and 2005/06

Season	GFA	GAA	SOG	OSOG	Fouls	OFouls	Corners	OCorners	Offside	Ooffside	TOP	OTOP	Saves	OSaves
04/05	0.75	1.38	5.5	4.6	13.0	16.6	4.8	3.5	2.8	2.5	49.7	50.3	3.5	5.3
05/06	0.50	1.13	6.0	3.9	15.5	14.0	5.3	3.4	2.3	6.1	51.8	48.1	3.8	6.0

Looking at the team stats for these games (Table 10) the problem becomes even more apparent. It is often said that in the tightest of games your weaknesses will be exposed and your strengths solidified. Well, this really was the case here. As with many of the different cuts with these team statistics, the increased shots-on-goal, corners and possession has not led to many more goals. Similarly on the other side, decreased shots allowed on goal, increased possession, reduced corners given away and more offsides has decreased opponents' goalscoring. That is significant, however, because to do it over the course of a season playing so-called 'lesser' opposition is one thing, but to make big strides like this against the other teams in the top five is very encouraging, even if the final scoreline did not always reflect these improvements.

Further proof of how strong Liverpool are becoming is that they were able to turn a deficit in time of possession last year into a surplus this year, having almost 52% of the ball in contests against top five opposition — which countered claims made by Jose Mourinho and Alex Ferguson about Liverpool being purely a long-ball team. The massive increase of 3.6 more offsides per game shows how effectively Benítez is implementing his system, with the players becoming comfortable enough to play his style against the Premiership's best. It was just the finishing that let Liverpool down.

Table 11. The Premiership record against the other top five teams both Home and Away over the last two seasons

Season	Home/Away	Wins	Draws	Defeats	Points	Points-per-game	Clean Sheets	Failure to Score
2004/05	Home	2	0	2	6	1.50	0	2
2004/05	Away	0	0	4	0	0.00	0	2
2005/06	Home	2	1	1	7	1.75	3	1
2005/06	Away	0	1	3	1	0.25	1	3

Separating these key fixtures down into home and away games (Table 11), the form becomes much more apparent. Last year Liverpool won two and lost two at home against the other top five teams, whilst this year one of the defeats has been turned into an extra point with a draw. The same can be said of the away form, where Liverpool lost all four games last year, but managed one point this year, with a draw and three defeats. But how did they play? Were the defeats deserved?

Table 12. The team statistics against the other top five Premiership teams at home for both 2004/05 and 2005/06

Season	GFA	GAA	SOG	OSOG	Fouls	OFouls	Corners	OCorners	Offside	Ooffside	TOP	OTOP	Saves	OSaves
04/05	1.00	1.00	6.8	3.3	11.3	18.0	5.8	1.8	1.5	2.3	51.3	48.8	3.3	7.3
05/06	0.75	1.00	7.3	2.5	14.8	14.8	7.8	3.0	1.5	5.5	52.0	48.0	3.8	8.5

Looking at the team stats for home games (Table 12) against the top five, the Reds were unlucky not to pick up more points. The goals-against average is inflated by the 1-4 loss to Chelsea, which clearly flattered the Londoners, so the average against the other three top five teams is zero. That defeat to the Champions was a big psychological blow, although the performance was largely encouraging. Liverpool bossed the early stages, and much of the possession for the match (finishing 55%-45% in favour of the Reds), but a Djimi Traoré 'moment' killed the early momentum, and it was all uphill from then on. The other points were dropped against Man United in a dire stalemate, although Liverpool were the more likely of the two teams to break the deadlock (three shots-on-goal to United's one).

Table 13. The team statistics against the other top five Premiership teams away from home for both 2004/05 and 2005/06

Season	GFA	GAA	SOG	OSOG	Fouls	OFouls	Corners	OCorners	Offside	Ooffside	TOP	OTOP	Saves	OSaves
04/05	0.50	1.75	4.3	6.0	14.8	15.3	3.8	5.3	4.0	2.8	48.2	51.8	3.8	3.3
05/06	0.25	1.25	4.8	5.3	16.3	13.3	2.8	3.8	3.0	6.8	51.8	48.3	3.8	3.5

The statistics in Table 13 are the only team figures you will see where Liverpool were clearly bettered this year. Last year four defeats in four games are easy to spot in the statistics. Less shots-on-goal, less corners, more offsides, less possession and more saves than their opponents all indicate being outplayed in almost every away game. The statistics don't look a lot better this season on the whole, but there are signs of a swing, just like with the results. The lowering of the goals-against average is one, and recording a clean sheet away from home is another. The swing in possession back in favour of Liverpool is also encouraging. To go to the other top five clubs' own grounds and leave having had more of the ball is extremely significant. The massive increase in opposition offsides per-game is another good sign, although the lack of corners won and opposition saves forced is something Liverpool can definitely look to improve on next season.

When you further break down the three defeats and one draw away from home you see perhaps a different story. Liverpool were by far the brighter team in the first 30 minutes in their defeat at Stamford Bridge, and even ended the game with a fairly substantial edge in time of possession 53%-47% (despite being down to ten men for the final ten mintues), even if it was probably a fair result. Against Arsenal Liverpool were able to fight their way back into a game that they had been thoroughly outplayed in, only for Xabi Alonso to get sent off for accidentally slipping on the wet turf, before Steven Gerrard assisted Thierry Henry's gift of a winner. Without Alonso's farcical sending off the result would have probably been a draw, and Liverpool a point better off. The early season 0-0 stalemate with Tottenham contained disallowed goals for both sides, so with a game that could have gone either way a draw was a fair result. Then there was the Man United game at Old Trafford, with the unusual sight of the home side playing deep and trying to hit Liverpool on the counter-attack. This was a team that used to come out and score two before the away team even had time to breath. Liverpool owned the game, with seven shots-on-goal to United's four, and ended the game with an amazing 58%-42% edge in time of possession. A horror miss by Djibril Cissé and a last-minute headed winner by Rio Ferdinand were the key moments in a game the Reds should have won, and even United knew it.

Breaking down the away form against the top five, it's fair to say that the results should have been one win, two draws and one defeat — and that Liverpool should have collected four more points than was the case, in the process denying significant points to their top five rivals in these 'six pointers'.

So who is going to go the other way then if Liverpool look to be on the rise?

Table 14. Record of the top five against the top five in the Premiership in 2005/05

Team	Wins	Draws	Defeats	Points	Points-per-game	Away Wins	Clean Sheets	Failure to Score
Chelsea	7	0	1	21	2.63	3	5	1
Man United	4	3	1	15	1.88	1	5	3
Liverpool	2	2	4	8	1.00	0	4	4
Arsenal	1	3	4	6	0.75	0	1	5
Tottenham	0	4	4	4	0.50	0	1	3

Looking at the Premiership's top five teams and their records against one another (Table 14) suggests it is only Manchester United and Chelsea that Liverpool must catch, with all five teams finishing in their actual league positions in this mini-league of the elite. Chelsea put up an amazing record against the top teams, winning seven of the eight games, and losing once, away to Manchester United 1-0; their points average in these fixtures was actually in excess of their average in the remaining 30 fixtures against lesser opposition. The Champions kept five clean sheets and only failed to score in that one contest.

Manchester United also kept five clean sheets, but failed to score on three occasions, recording four wins three draws and one loss (3-0 to Chelsea away). As discussed earlier, Liverpool did manage four clean sheets but also failed to score four times. Arsenal only had one win in the top of the league contests, and recorded only one clean sheet, whilst Tottenham could not win a single game, mustering four draws and four defeats.

If Liverpool had held on for a draw, or could have pinched the game at United in January, the Reds would have finished either two or five points ahead of Ferguson's men respectively. But then had the Premiership began in October Liverpool would have been Champions, not Chelsea. Hindsight and 'what ifs' are a wonderful thing, but what is clear is that a big key to fighting for the title is putting down a marker in the away contests against the other top teams. Liverpool have not won a single away contest against the other top five finishers in the Premiership since Benítez took over and, if the team are to contest the title next season, an early season away win against Chelsea, Man United or Arsenal is a must. Liverpool did show signs this year, with the four clean sheets being a big indicator of things turning around, but the four failures to score provide the biggest concern to address. The quick attacking players introduced into the side in the summer of 2006 will help.

Table 15. The team statistics for each top five team in the Premiership from games against each other in 2005/06

Team	GFA	GAA	SOG	OSOG	Corners	OCorners	Offside	Ooffside	TOP	OTOP	Saves	OSaves
Chelsea	2.00	0.38	7.4	6.4	4.4	4.4	5.0	1.0	50.6	49.4	4.6	5.0
Man United	0.88	0.63	5.0	6.1	4.6	5.4	2.1	1.4	48.9	51.1	4.9	3.8
Liverpool	0.50	1.13	6.0	3.9	5.3	3.4	2.3	6.1	51.8	48.1	3.8	6.0
Arsenal	0.50	1.13	4.4	6.1	4.1	5.6	2.9	3.0	50.4	49.6	5.4	4.9
Tottenham	0.63	1.25	5.3	8.0	5.5	5.1	3.4	4.0	48.3	51.8	6.0	4.8

From looking at the team statistics from the top-five head-to-heads (Table 15) a few things really stand out. First is how dominant Chelsea were, scoring at a two goal rate and only conceding 0.38 goals-per-game. The Champions racked up a fantastic 7.4 shots-on-goal per-game against the other top five finishers in 2005/06. The other major thing that the team statistics indicate is that Man United were lucky to finish with four wins, three draws and one loss. United were out-shot (6.1 opponents shots-on-goal to United's 5.0), gave away more corners (5.4 for opponents compared with 4.6), saved more shots (4.9 to 3.8) and lost the possession battle 51.1% – 48.9% to their opponents. When you consider that in 1-0 wins over both Chelsea and Liverpool United were out-shot 18 to nine, second-best in possession at a significant 55% - 45%, and forced into more saves (13 to nine) it is fairly safe to say they were both stolen.

What is encouraging for Benítez is that Liverpool had the 2nd-highest shots-on-goal (6.0 per-game) of any team in the top of the table clashes, restricted their opponents to the least (3.9 per-game), drew the most offsides (6.1 per-game), and had the biggest advantage in time of possession (51.8% - 48.1%). With being the joint-lowest scorers and forcing the highest number of saves per-game it doesn't take a Harvard professor to work out that converting the many chances created is the major area that needs to be addressed. With Fernando Morientes and Djibril Cissé replaced by Robbie Fowler and Craig Bellamy — two strikers with better chance conversion rates and better goals-per-90 minutes rates — then in theory an improvement has already been made.

The most interesting point is that the final games of the season against Manchester United and Chelsea — in the FA Cup — ended in Liverpool victories. With the four league encounters against the two main challengers concluded by early February, it could be said that the timing didn't suit Liverpool, with their rivals catching them in weaker moments. When the teams met with Liverpool in form the Reds were able to run out deserved winners. (As was the case in the 2-1 victory over Chelsea in the 2006 Community Shield, at the time of this book heading to print.) Also, Robbie Fowler's late-January arrival meant he was not on the club's books for three of these four league encounters, and was excluded from the fourth, a week after he arrived, in favour of a much-needed fitness workout. Due to being cup-tied, he was also unable to face United and Chelsea in the FA Cup. Fowler still managed to score against United, in a substitute appearance for Manchester City, and has always been able to plunder goals in the biggest games. If the one thing the Reds lacked in the league games against the top teams was a ruthless finisher, it's conceivable that he could have provided the goal touch that would have made all the difference.

The 12-game Premiership unbeaten streak

The confirmation that Rafa Benítez had got to grips with the English game began one-third of the way through the season, with the start of a long unbeaten league run. Serious doubts existed after the poor league showing last season, and the disappointing start to this. In total the great run consisted of 18 games sandwiched between a Carling Cup defeat to Crystal Palace and the 0-1 heartbreaker at Man United at Old Trafford. During the 18-game span Liverpool ran up 14 wins, three draws and only the one defeat, courtesy of São Paulo in the Club World Championship; an amazing run of 78% winning football. In the Premiership during the spell the winning percentage was even higher. The run stretched between the 29th October and the 21st of January, with 11 wins (10 straight at one point) and one draw — a whopping 92% winning period that also included eight straight clean sheets, and 10 in total. Analysing the team stats here would be hopelessly one-sided in the Reds' favour. So what is there to look at? Well, there's the calibre of opposition faced. Was it against teams from the top or bottom half of the table?

Table 16. The Premiership record of the teams played during Liverpool's 12 game unbeaten streak

Opposition	Home/Away	Result	Total Premiership Record	Form Where Played	Final League Position
West Ham	H	2-0	16-7-15	7-4-8	9th
Aston Villa	A	2-0	10-12-16	6-6-7	16th
Portsmouth	H	3-0	10-8-20	5-1-13	17th
Man City	A	1-0	13-4-21	9-2-8	15th
Sunderland	A	2-0	3-6-29	1-4-14	20th
Wigan	H	3-0	15-6-17	8-3-8	10th
Middlesbrough	H	2-0	12-9-17	5-4-10	14th
Newcastle	H	2-0	17-7-14	6-2-11	7th
Everton	A	3-1	14-8-16	8-4-7	11th
West Brom	H	1-0	7-9-22	1-7-11	19th
Bolton	A	2-2	15-11-12	11-5-3	8th
Tottenham	H	1-0	18-11-9	6-6-7	5th
Totals	-	24-3	150-98-208 (33%)	73-48-107 (32%)	12th

The overall record of the teams played during the period was 150 wins, 98 draws and 208 defeats during the season. This translates into a 33% winning percentage for the teams played during the run, and indicates that these were not the most testing games.

Looking at the form of the teams depending on whether the game was played at home or away also tells a very similar story. The records tally up to 73-48-107, and a 32% winning percentage. Adding up and averaging their final league standings results in 12th position, so equating to the bottom half of the table. The final league position column, however, does also show that the run did figure five top-half teams in the 12 games played. However, the analysis does not take into account the form of those sides at the time, and obviously that can have a large bearing on the result. Either way, a 12 game unbeaten streak in the Premiership is impressive regardless of the opposition. Indeed, the Reds have slipped up too often against the lesser sides since last landing the league title. As recently as last year Liverpool lost to Southampton away, Crystal Palace away, Birmingham both home and away, drew at home to Portsmouth and drew both games with struggling Blackburn. That little lot cost Liverpool 18 points in the league, with those five teams finishing 20th, 18th, 12th, 16th and 15th respectively — an average league position of 16th.

To finish off the season Liverpool went on another fantastic 12-game run. After losing to Arsenal 2-1 away at Highbury the Reds clicked into the groove, starting with a 5-1 dismantling of Fulham at Anfield, and ending with the lifting of the FA Cup in Cardiff. On the run the Reds beat Birmingham 7-0, Chelsea 2-1 and West Ham on penalties in the FA Cup, and Fulham, Newcastle, Everton, West Brom, Bolton, Blackburn, West Ham, Aston Villa and Portsmouth in the Premiership. The nine-game Premiership winning run consisted of four home wins and five away wins, against opposition averaging out with 11th-place finishes.

The run included four top-half teams, and Liverpool outscored the nine teams by a count of 23 – six. The total 12-game run included 35 Liverpool goals, at a rate of 2.91 per-game, and only 10 for the opposition. During the run Liverpool completed doubles over Blackburn, Newcastle, West Ham, Everton, Aston Villa, Portsmouth and West Brom, finishing the season tied with Chelsea with 10 double victories over Premiership rivals.

European Form

Table 17. The European team record over the last two seasons

Season	Wins	Draws	Defeats	Points	Points-per-game	Clean Sheets	Failure to Score
2004/05	9	3	3	30	2.00	7	6
2005/06	9	3	3	30	2.00	8	6

*2005/06 stats include 3-1 win over CSKA Moscow in the European Super Cup Final

Amazingly the form in Europe was almost exactly the same this year as last. While the form was identical, the end result was far less impressive; going out at the Round of 16, as opposed to winning the trophy. This year's schedule contained fighting in all three qualifying rounds, whereas a year earlier they played the same amount of total games by competing in all of the final rounds.

The Reds easily dispatched TNS (6-0 agg) and Kaunas (6-1 agg) before repeating the efforts of 12 months earlier by winning away and losing at home to their 3rd-round qualifying opponent, this time the Bulgarian champions CSKA Sofia. The Group stages went extremely well for Liverpool, topping a group that included Chelsea, Real Betis and Anderlecht. Away wins were had in Betis and Anderlecht, whilst the Belgians were despatched 3-0 in an Anfield stroll. Two draws against Chelsea and another at home to Betis saw Liverpool finish ahead of their fellow Premiership rivals. Then Liverpool were drawn with Benfica in the first knockout stage.

Table 18. Liverpool's team statistics from both legs against Benfica in this year's Champions League

Leg	GF	GA	SOG	OSOG	Fouls	OFouls	Corners	OCorners	Offside	Ooffside	TOP	OTOP	Saves	OSaves
Away	0	1	0	3	18	17	3	7	1	1	51	49	2	0
Home	0	2	7	3	14	15	14	2	3	5	66	34	1	7

The two games against Benfica turned out to be a really big disappointment (Table 18). The away leg was played at an extremely slow tempo; it appeared that Liverpool had come away hoping to bring back a 0-0 draw for the second-leg at Anfield but Luisao's late header from a free-kick spoiled that plan. The large disappointment was that the first game was there for the taking. Liverpool went away to Portugal and finished the game with a 51%-49% edge in possession, but created nothing with that advantage — not even registering a shot on goal in the game. It was the first time since the 13th April 2005, in the 2nd leg of the Champions League quarter-final against Juventus, that the Reds had been held without a shot on target, failing to force the opposition's goalkeeper into a single save.

The second leg was completely different and, if a bit of luck had gone Liverpool's way, the run for number six in Paris would have continued. Benítez's team dominated the first 30 minutes, until Benifca gained confidence and forced their way back into the game, eventually taking the lead in the 36th minute thanks to Simao's impressive strike. It just wasn't going to be the Reds' day; a feeling confirmed by the fact a player so close to joining Liverpool struck that telling blow. The Reds registered seven shots-on-goal to Benfica's three, a whopping 14 corners to Benfica's two, forced Moretto de Souza in the Benfica goal into seven saves, had a Robbie Fowler goal harshly disallowed, and finished off the game holding a 66%-34% advantage in time of possession. The telling stat from the tie has to be that Benfica were able to convert three of six chances into goals whilst Liverpool finished the tie with zero from seven.

Table 19. 2005/06 Premiership team stats against 2005/06 Champions League team stats and 2004/05 Champions League knock-out stage stats

Comp	GF	GA	SOG	OSOG	Fouls	OFouls	Corners	OCorners	Offside	Ooffside	TOP	OTOP	Saves	OSaves
Prem 05/06	1.50	0.66	7.5	3.3	11.6	14.0	6.2	3.6	2.8	4.7	54.6	45.4	4.2	6.9
Euro 05/06	0.75	0.50	4.6	3.0	16.5	14.3	5.3	4.8	1.6	4.5	49.4	50.6	2.5	3.9
Euro 04/05	1.72	0.86	4.3	4.7	17.0	15.9	3.7	5.9	3.6	4.6	43.7	56.6	3.9	2.6

*Euro 05/06 excludes qualifiers and European Super Cup final data

Table 19 illustrates what a different beast the European game is to the Premiership. In European football you have what can be described as a 'feel out' period, similar to that seen in boxing, when two fighters who have never before faced each other are looking for potential weakness but aren't too sure when to begin the attack. Unlike domestic football, the two teams have often not played each other; if they have, it might not have been for a number of years.

Looking at the team stats from Liverpool's Premiership and European campaigns highlights the differences between the two. Both the goals-for and goals-against averages are lower in Europe, along with the saves for both teams, indicating the tighter style played in Europe. The shots-on-goal for the Reds are also much lower, as are the corners won. The opponents' shots-on-goal and offsides, however, remain the same in Europe as in the Premier League, indicating how Liverpool seem to play with more caution and not commit as many men forward.

It is often the case in Europe that the away team sets out to play very tight and defend deeper, looking to steal a goal or even the game on the counter-attack. This was best illustrated by Benifca, who played this way to perfection at Anfield, winning 2-0 but content to concede possession 34%-66% during the course of the game. The other interesting observation to be made is the significant change in time of possession. The Reds conceded more possession to their opponents (49.4%-50.6%) in Europe this season.

The different tactics deployed in Europe are perhaps best demonstrated when looking at the team statistics in the knock-out stages of last year's Champions League campaign. Liverpool dispatched Bayer Leverkusen 3-1 both home and away, then Juventus 2-1 at home and 0-0 away. The semi-finals against Chelsea finished 0-0 away and 1-0 at home, and the final finished in a 3-3 draw against AC Milan in unforgettable circumstances, with the Reds winning on penalties. Liverpool looked very much in control in the home leg of each of the first two knock-out stages, then early success against Chelsea led to defending the advantage. Away from home Liverpool easily saw off Bayer, defended resiliently in Turin against Juve, and looked the brighter team against Chelsea at Stamford Bridge. The final was the classic game of two halves. Looking at the team statistics really does show how Liverpool were able to progress to the final and win number five. The key indicator is time of possession. During last season's knock-out stages and final, Liverpool conceded possession to their opponents to the tune of 43.7%-56.6%. The Reds were also out-shot: 4.7 to 4.3. The saves-forced also went to their opponents, with Carson and Dudek making 3.9 saves-per-game and the opposition keepers only 2.6. The difference, however, lies in the fact that Liverpool were able to force home goals whilst their opponents were not. Liverpool scored at a rate of 1.72 per-game whilst their opponents only managed only 0.89.

The Reds' success in the Champions League last year was built very much on fast starts at home. In the contests against Bayer Leverkusen, Juventus and Chelsea the team were able to feed off the home crowd and fly to early leads. The first goals in those matches came after 15, 10 and four minutes respectively, all in Liverpool's favour. It was also the case in all three games that Liverpool, whether by choice or their opponents forcing the issue, played the majority of the 2nd-half in their own half defending the advantage. Away from home the tactic was to play in a cautious, more defensive style and try to pinch vital away goals. In Leverkusen this was possible, but in Turin only Milan Baros could have ended the tie, and against Chelsea the tactic almost worked to perfection, with Baros and Riise coming close to pinching a goal.

Liverpool are still able to play in their preferred style in Europe and therein lies the beauty of the system. Benítez was able to have his men fly forward last year in home ties in a 4-2-3-1 formation, but easily retreated deeper without any great change in formation when turning into a 4-5-1. The more confident and skilful the players become in the system the more Liverpool will be able to dominate in the 4-2-3-1 formation, even in Europe. These games are so important, especially in the knock-out stages, and therefore possession will always be conceded for the sake of protecting any advantage. This is perhaps even more the case at home, when conceding 'away goals' must be avoided at all costs.

Benítez's record in Europe over the last two years (three, including Valencia's Uefa Cup win) proves he is a master in this arena. The way he has diagnosed and dissected his opponents in Europe has been with the skill and steadiness of a Harley Street surgeon.

Cup form
It could be argued that it was a blessing in disguise when Crystal Palace dumped Liverpool out of the Carling Cup back in October. Had last year's finalists won through, and had good fortune in subsequent rounds, the

team could have approached 70 games for the season. The loss on the night was deserved, and in fact kick-started the 12-game unbeaten run in the Premiership through to the 22nd of January.

The key cup game within that period, with the FA Cup 3rd-round tie against Luton Town, and the events on that Sunday evening led the team to believe the cup had their name on it. Coming from 3-1 down to win 5-3 had the feel of Olympiakos, the tide-turning tie from the Champions league the season before. As with that Champions League success, some big names were beaten on the way to lifting the trophy; this was no success based on the luck of the draw.

Table 20. Liverpool's path to the final and FA Cup glory.

Round	Opponent	Score
3rd Round	Luton Town (A)	5-3
4th Round	Portsmouth (A)	2-1
5th Round	Man United (H)	1-0
Quarter-Final	Birmingham (A)	7-0
Semi-Final	Chelsea	2-1
Final	West Ham	3-3aet (3-1 pens)

No one can say that Liverpool didn't earn their place in the final, or deserve to win the trophy. In every round, other than the 3rd against Luton, Liverpool faced a Premiership side. Three of the four rounds (before neutral grounds came into play) were away from home, with only the 1-0 win against Manchester United coming at Anfield. The 4th-round saw Liverpool beat Portsmouth 2-1 on a very cold, wet and windy evening at Fratton Park, to set up the challenge of Man United at home. Peter Crouch's first half header proved the winner, and in a year of record-setting for the Reds it was the first time that Liverpool had beaten their fierce northern rivals in the competition for 85 years.

More record-setting came in the next round as Liverpool thrashed Birmingham 7-0 at St Andrews to reach the semi-finals. The win was Liverpool's largest-ever away win in the FA Cup, and the club's second largest-ever away victory in all competitions. It was the biggest win by any team in the last eight of the trophy since 1931, and the biggest FA Cup away win by any side since the 1889-90 season, which was before the club even existed. It also happened to be Liverpool's 30th clean sheet of the season, a feat that had not been achieved by any Liverpool team in the previous 22 years. For good measure, Birmingham were managed by ex-Manchester United stalwart Steve Bruce. This of course has no bearing on any record, but is nice to point out all the same.

The semi-final saw Liverpool pitted against Chelsea — the second time in 12 months the two teams met at this stage of a big competition. Last year it was the Champions League semi-final, when Luis Garcia's hotly-contested goal won the tie. This year it was a Luis Garcia goal that again settled the contest, with a goal that was every bit as beautiful as the previous year's had been scrappy.

Liverpool would meet West Ham in the final, but the Reds' work was by no means complete. The Londoners did not freeze on the big occasion, instead revelling in the freedom of being underdogs. But there was one man they just could not handle. In what turned out to be one of the best FA Cup finals of all time it was Steven Gerrard who stole the show and, arguably, the cup. The Liverpool skipper not once but twice brought his team back to tie the game, to take the game to extra-time and penalties.

If being underdogs had initially helped West Ham play without inhibition, then leading the game going into the final minutes suddenly made them nervous. As the clock ticked down they had something very precious to lose. Some scrappy defending in the 91st minute left the route open for Gerrard to thunder in a shot from almost 40 yards, and that effectively signalled the end of West Ham's belief that they could win the cup. Their subsequent penalties, after 30 minutes of extra-time stalemate, were taken with the air of a team who knew they'd had their chance and blown it.

Table 21. Liverpool's team statistics from the Premiership and their FA Cup ties in 2005/06

Comp	GF	GA	SOG	OSOG	Fouls	OFouls	Corners	OCorners	Offside	Ooffside	TOP	OTOP	Saves	OSaves
Prem	1.50	0.66	7.5	3.3	11.6	14.0	6.2	3.6	2.8	4.7	54.6	45.4	4.2	6.9
FA	3.33	1.33	5.8	5.0	12.5	14.7	5.5	5.5	2.7	3.2	55.0	45.0	6.5	3.5

Liverpool's record on the way to winning the FA Cup was quite outstanding (Table 21). The Reds scored 20 and conceded only eight goals in their six games in the competition. Remove the seven scored against Birmingham and the team still scored at a 2.6 goals-per-game rate in the remaining five games. The statistics can be compared with those seen in the Premiership, as the run included five teams from the top flight, and only Luton from the Championship. What was interesting was the increase in the oppositions' figures as the Reds took more risks to win through in the tournament; playing a more open brand of cup football.

Increased shots-on-goal by opponents did not lead to a massive increase in conceding. Liverpool's keepers were up to the task, increasing their save totals by almost two per-game. Jose Reina had some of his more mixed games in the Cup run, making a number of good saves against Man United in the 5th round but blamed by some for Didier Drogba's goal in the semi-final, when the Spaniard opted to rush out to punch John Arne Riise's poor header. The keeper himself said he had an awful final, although he still pulled off a number of crucial saves.

The team statistics and results in the FA Cup confirm the view that Liverpool can beat any team on any given day. The Reds beat both of the teams who finished above them in the league, and did so deservedly. It also gave Benítez his first domestic wins against United, Birmingham and Chelsea, having previously failed to beat them in a total of 13 combined matches in English-based competitions.

Blots on those sheets

So close, but no cigar. An inability to avoid conceding a goal in the final five games of the season meant the Reds were stuck on 33 clean sheets, one short of the club's all-time record of 34 in a single season.

The team led the Premiership standings, with 22 clean sheets, to Chelsea's 20. The total number of clean sheets was easily top amongst English teams, with Manchester United six behind and Chelsea seven. As well as 22 league clean sheets, the Liverpool keepers picked up eight in Europe and another three in cup competitions. The 33 included two against Manchester United, Chelsea and Tottenham, and one against Arsenal, to name a few of the bigger scalps in the list. It was a fantastic achievement, but what are the real benefits of keeping a clean sheet?

Table 22. The number of games Liverpool have kept a clean sheet, against not, and the number of games Liverpool have scored in, against not, in both 2004/05 and 2005/06.

	2004/05		2005/06	
	Games	Point per game	Games	Point per game
Clean Sheet	18	2.56	33	2.58
Non-clean sheet	42	1.43	29	1.59

	2004/05		2005/06	
	Games	Point per game	Games	Point per game
Scored	40	2.38	47	2.64
Not scored	20	0.20	15	0.47

Over the last two years Liverpool have averaged 2.57 points per game in contests where they have kept a clean sheet, and 1.49 points per game in those in which they have conceded a goal (Table 22). So on average, keeping a clean sheet is worth more than an extra point per game than not doing so, which clearly highlights their value. It is of course obvious, but when you deny the opposition a goal you can't lose. But rather than end in a 0-0 draw, it more often than not guarantees a win.

Rafa Benítez's first point of emphasis was to sort out and maintain a tight back line, with a team that works hard to protect each other. But for all the training ground drills, clean sheets are impossible to guarantee; any number of unforeseen events can result in the best-laid plans of mice and men going awry. So the next point of emphasis is always to begin looking at how goals can be added to increase a team's likelihood of winning, even when conceding.

Liverpool were able to increase this figure this year, as the data above shows. In the 42 games in which Liverpool conceded last year the team averaged 1.43 points per-game, whereas this season the team averaged 1.59 points per-game when breached. The team's average over the last two seasons in games in which they have scored is 2.52 points-per-game, compared with the 0.31 points-per-game when failing to beat the opposition keeper in drawing a blank.

In Benítez's first season Liverpool kept only seven clean sheets and failed to score on 13 occasions, on their way to registering 58 points in the Premiership. This season the team kept 22 clean sheets, 15 more than a year ago; we now know that a clean sheet works out to be worth roughly a point more per-game. This means, therefore, that Liverpool added 15 points to their Premiership total from 2004/05 by shutting out the opposition in 15 more games this season.

The other area in which Liverpool were able to improve was in their own failures to score. In 2004/05 the total number of Premiership games in which the Reds failed to score was 13 — just over a third of all matches; this season it was nine, an improvement of four games, and from the data above we know the difference between scoring and not scoring is worth around an extra 2.2 points each contest. From reducing the number of failures to score by four games — which doesn't sound much — Liverpool added a further nine points to their total from 2004/05. Add the benefit from keeping clean sheets to the benefit of scoring at least one goal, and that is worth an extra 25 points, the exact difference between their points totals in 2004/05 and 2005/06.

This tells us that Liverpool have only one real area that needs to be improved for the team to compete better in 2006/07. The clean sheet number is fantastic, and would be hard to beat. But the 'failure to score' figure could be improved. Manchester United only failed to score in five Premiership games, whilst Chelsea failed in six. If Liverpool could reduce their 'failure to score' figure of 2005/06 to somewhere in the region of five next season, while maintaining the total of 22 clean sheets, that should prove to be worth an additional eight points; giving a total approaching 90 on the year. Chelsea won the league this season with 91.

Set pieces and corners

Ah, zonal marking. Dear, dear zonal marking. Where would any Liverpool debate be without it? Not since the middle-ages, when the world was believed to be flat, has there been such profound misunderstanding of the way something works. It's probably the least understood thing in the history of English football (apart from a garbled Ron Atkinson co-commentary.) Man-to-man marking, as a system, does not get the blame. Zonal marking does.

Since Rafael Benítez arrived on Merseyside the Reds have implemented a zonal marking system on set pieces and corner kicks. The system does exactly what it says on the tin: the players guard zones rather than the opposition;

setting-up in danger areas in and around the six-yard box. The Reds tend to set-up to defend a corner by positioning themselves in two lines: across the six- and 18-yard boxes. Two players are stationed on either post, three (possibly four) along the six-yard box, and a further three to four in between the six- and 18-yard box. A further player is stationed between the touchline and the edge of the six-yard box, at the front post, to defend the near-post corner. The set-up is similar for a free-kick, and is geared towards defending the areas at risk of conceding goals.

The players must defend as a team, because it is the system that will work, not necessarily an individual effort. The idea is that wherever an attacking player runs, there will always be a defender within a certain distance to make a challenge. That is where this tactic really triumphs over man-to-man marking: the system in which opposition players always seem to find space through bumping, barging and blocking, or simply by losing a dozing marker. In a man-to-man system the attacking players can actually force the best defenders or headers of the ball away from the danger area, leaving a massive hole for the attacking team to flood with players. With the zonal system this is not possible, as the system sets up the best headers in the team to be in the danger areas, and they should not move unless it is to pick up a player entering their zone.

The best way to understand the whole concept is to think of an extension of what a goalkeeper does at set pieces. The keeper defends the ball; he does not mark anyone. His job is to follow the path of the ball, and intercept it when it comes into his zone — which should end at around ten yards from his goal (although some keepers still insist on flying out to the edge of the area, or in the case of David James, occasionally out of the stadium).

A goalkeeper is concerned with the ball and nothing else; after all, it is the ball that needs to be kept from the net, not the opposition players. Many often criticise the method due to it allowing the attacker to dictate the action, but on set pieces — and in fact in most situations within a game — the attacking team is always the aggressor, having developed specific set plays to predetermine where the ball will be delivered. Defence in any sport is always reactive. In basketball, a similar sport to football in that one team tries to score in another team's goal, the zone defence is highly effective. In the NBA, the top American league, the zone defence was outlawed for over 50 years — as it was felt the game would suffer and become less attractive to fans, due to lower scoring games. Ask most English football fans about zonal marking and they'd probably outline banning it from football for the reverse, given the press attention it has received. Its reputation is for being hopeless.

The statistics, however, suggest the opposite; and in cases like this, the statistics really matter, as they detail whether or not the system is working. Due to the media coverage over the last two years, and the number of football commentators who scoff at the mere thought of zonal marking, it would be easy to think that Liverpool conceded quite frequently on corner kicks. To surmise that the Reds concede on even 10% of all corners during a season would be a gross inaccuracy.

The truth is that Liverpool only conceded from two corners all season, both coming in Premiership games (Chelsea away and Everton at home). In total Liverpool faced 137 corners in the Premiership, meaning they conceded on just 1.5% of all corners. Only one team, Chelsea, have been able to come even close to that this season, allowing three goals from 127 corner attempts (2.4%), with one of those goals coming from Steven Gerrard ghosting in at the back post totally unmarked. In terms of goals conceded from free-kick crosses, Liverpool have allowed only two in the Premiership all season, one less than Chelsea in the league.

As you can see the stats suggest the complete opposite to the media myth. Nothing was said about Chelsea having problems defending corners and free-kick crosses. But why would it be? They have only allowed six goals from free-kick crosses or corners in the Premiership this year. But even that is two more than Liverpool's miserly four. The Reds are the best team at defending set-pieces in the division, even if not 100% perfect.

Liverpool conceded on just three further occasions from a free-kick cross: twice in Europe and once in the FA Cup; making a grand total of seven goals conceded from set-piece crosses (still two less than Chelsea's overall record; Manchester United conceded a whopping 15). What is apparent from analysing these stats is that four of the seven set-piece goals the Reds conceded came within a one-month span between the 22nd January and the 21st of February. During this period of the season it was apparent for all to see that the squad was extremely tired, and had hit a wall after the early start to the season, the trip to Japan and the traditionally busy Christmas programme, the effects of which had been compounded by the first two factors. The first set-piece conceded in this period was from was Rio Ferdinand's late goal for Manchester United, and the last was Benfica's late winner in Portugal. Notice word 'late' on both occasions: another sign of the tiredness of the squad; concentration being the first thing to go upon suffering tiredness, but concentration is precisely what is required on set-pieces.

No system in any sport is faultless. And it is another sport that offers the best comparison for the weaknesses of zonal marking. When implemented in basketball, the systems sees each player defend a zone around the basket, and pick up an attacking player as he enters into his zone — much like in football. This form of defence is highly effective, but can be susceptible to fast movement from side to side used to make openings for long-range shots or lanes to the basket. Even so, fantastic accuracy is required to hit the long-range shots, and quick players essential to penetrate the defence.

A similar theory holds true for the football. To attack a zonal marking system the corners must be extremely accurate, and dropped in between player's zones, directly onto the heads of the attacking players cutting quickly into or across the seams in the defence. Looking at the goals Liverpool conceded from set-pieces this season, five were in this manner. Rio Ferdinand's header at Old Trafford was from a free-kick cross placed in front of Jan Kromkamp and behind Xabi Alonso; Tim Cahill's goal for Everton at Anfield was from a corner placed perfectly behind Jamie Carragher and in front of Peter Crouch; Sean Davis' flicked header (Portsmouth FA Cup) was from a free-kick cross floated in front of Carragher, and as such almost impossible to defend against; CSKA Sofia's goal in the Champions League qualifier was scored by delivering the ball to the very front of the area, at the fringe of Josemi's zone; and finally Benfica, away in the Champions League, were able to float a ball in between Finnan and Hyypia to score.

In all five goals, therefore, the opposition were able to perfectly pinpoint the seams in the system; the ball placed at the edge of the player's zones. The goal Everton scored at Liverpool in the Premiership is perhaps the best example of this. The corner was placed to the back of Jamie Carragher's zone and to the front of Peter Crouch's, hitting the precise point where neither Liverpool player could quickly reach. Cahill darted in between their zones and was able to head home. If the ball had been played slightly shorter Carragher would have been able to get some kind of contact on the ball, to move it far enough away from Cahill; if the ball had been a fraction longer Crouch would have been able to hamper the attempt, although he was also a little slow reacting to the ball.

The final two goals were conceded in totally different manners. The first, away at Bolton, was due to Jose Reina dropping a simple cross, and as such was down to an unforeseen individual error. But the second, away at Chelsea, was due to another fault that can occur through zonal marking. William Gallas was able to spin and shoot after collecting the second-ball from a knock-down by Ricardo Carvalho. The player at fault on the goal was John Arne Riise, who was caught ball-watching. It is a common fault with all players in all systems, but when you are defending zonally it can be fatal. Riise's role on the corner was to position himself between the posts and the ball, and defend the goal in case there were any second-balls to deal with. However, he was attracted away from his position, towards a ball he stood little chance of winning, and which had drifted past his zone. The knock-down fell into the spot he had vacated, where Gallas fired home with relative ease. However, it was a tactic Chelsea used to score against other teams who don't mark zonally, including Manchester United, whose set piece defending leaves a lot to be desired. While Liverpool conceded four set-piece goals in the league, United conceded almost three times as many, with eleven.

The zonal system requires players to understand not only their roles but the roles of others, and to stick to their task until a clearance has been made. The Reds clearly had teething problems last year, but now that all the longer-serving players have got used to the system it's easy to see its benefits. It takes time to settle into, however, and it was perhaps telling that Jan Kromkamp was bypassed for Ferdinand's goal at Old Trafford, so soon after joining Liverpool.

Comparing Liverpool's own attacking production from corners this season with their opponents across the 62 games backs this up (Table 23). Liverpool scored 21 set-piece goals, whilst conceding only eight (the 8th being from a thrown-in). This works out for both sets of figures to be about 20% of all goal production. The difference comes when looking at how regularly each scored from dead-ball situations. Liverpool managed to score one set piece goal every three games, whilst their opponents only averaged one every 7.8 games.

Table 23. Set piece goals scored and conceded by Liverpool during 2004/05 and 2005/06

set pieces goals /conceded	2005/06 Liverpool	Opponents	2004/05 Liverpool	Opponents
Corner	10	2	4	4
Free-kick cross	2	5	4	6
Free-kick shot	3	0	8	4
Throw-in	5	1	0	1
Penalty miss follow-up	1	0	0	0
Total	21	8	16	15
Set piece %	20.2	19.5	19.5	26.8
Games till score/concede	3.0	7.8	3.8	4.0

The improvement from last year is fairly dramatic. The goals-for have increased, as well as the significant reduction in goals-against. Maybe the criticisms of Liverpool set-piece defending from 2004/05 was apposite, as the team conceded one goal from a set-piece every four games. But even that rate was still better than many other teams in football. The proof that the system is now working comes in the fact that it now takes teams on average four more games before they score a goal from a dead-ball situation against Liverpool. However, while Liverpool scored 10 set-piece goals in the league, Chelsea notched a phenomenal 21.

Another statistic of note from the table above was that not one of Liverpool's keepers was beaten from a direct free-kick shot on goal all season. That is an amazing fact, and can only be down to good goalkeeping and superb organisation of the wall.

From where were the goals scored?
Before the Fulham game an the 15th March, some 50 games into the 2005-06 season, Liverpool had only scored a grand total of five goals within the six-yard box. If you take this further you find that Liverpool actually scored three of the five in one game: against CSKA Moscow in the European Super Cup Final. That, therefore, left two six-yard box goals in 49 games.

While the obituaries of the Reds' strikers were being written the real problem was about getting deeper into the box, and poaching some goals. With Peter Crouch the perfect ball-holding target man, Fernando Morientes dropping deep to link play, and Djibril Cissé playing on the right wing, very few goals were coming from close range. Strikers weren't getting into poaching positions, and none could be called a natural poacher, so they weren't necessarily the most effective when they did get in there.

Enter Robbie Fowler. Even though Fowler only scored five goals, his opening strike against Fulham at Anfield really did open the floodgates for the rest of the team. It was Fowler at his best, reacting to a flick-on in the six-yard box and heading home. With the other players following from his example, Liverpool experienced a massive increase in close-range goal production from that point onwards.

Up until the Fulham game five of Liverpool's 69 goals had come from inside the six-yard box, for a paltry 7% of all goals scored. Nine of the next 18 goals Liverpool scored (including four of the five against Fulham and three of the seven against Birmingham in the FA Cup) where from inside the six-yard box. The team finished up with 17 goals (16%) from close range, but it was still down on last year's total of 19 (23%).

As mentioned at the beginning of this chapter, shots-on-goal were up nearly one a game from last year, but the goal production remained similar. Logic suggests that the further you are from the goal the less likely you are to score; the shot will need to be more accurate and powerful, given that the goalkeeper will have more time to judge its flight and move into position to save. The only real advantage in striking from long distance is that there's the likelihood of the keeper being unsighted due to bodies in the way; while, of course, you often don't need to work as hard to force a clear shooting attempt, given the opposition may be prepared to stand off and happily let you shoot (how often do you see teams retreat to the edge of their area, only for a shot to be fired in while they're backpeddling, followed by a look of 'Oh...'?).

But clearly Liverpool are a potent force from further out. Last year the Reds scored a number of spectacular long-distance efforts, including Steven Gerrard's goals against Olympiakos and Middlesbrough, and Luis Garcia's sweet volley against Juventus at Anfield. The Reds lashed in 20 goals from outside the box in 2004/05, and conceded only four from such a distance. The same thing occurred this season, with the Reds firing in 26 goals from further out than the 18-yard box. This equates to a quarter of all the goals Liverpool scored this season. It's clear, however, that no team should rely on long-range efforts. Closer-range chances need to be created. To increase the chances of success every possible form of goalscoring should be in your armoury.

Table 24. The areas where Liverpool scored and conceded goals during 04/05 and 05/06

Goal distance	2005/06		2004/05	
	Liverpool	Opponents	Liverpool	Opponents
PEN	6	3	5	1
Inside 6 yard box	17	15	19	21
Inside18 yard box	55	24	38	30
Outside 18 yard box	26	2	20	4
Total	104	44	82	56

The other thing to note from Table 24 is how the opponents score their goals against Liverpool, as it holds a key as to how the Reds now operate. As previously discussed, under Gérard Houllier Liverpool defended much deeper than they now tend to, and as a result kept a lot of the action in front of them. What these statistics show is that the number of close-range goals conceded by Liverpool is quite high, and last year the total conceded even outnumbered those scored by the Reds themselves inside the six-yard box.

Playing with the defensive line higher up the pitch has enabled Liverpool to dominate more games in terms of possession, and allow the defence to support the midfield and the midfield to support the attack. It also leads to the opposition attempting to get in behind the defence, and that is why it is so important to have a well-implemented offside trap. As we have seen Liverpool have made massive strides this year in increasing the number of opposition offsides, but the tactic also comes with its risks. The ball over the top, through the middle, or out to the wing has been a common theme on goals conceded by the Reds this year.

This type of action invariably leads to tap-ins or one-on-ones with the keeper for the opposition. Three of Chelsea's four goals at Anfield were tap-ins after getting behind the Liverpool defence. More were scored: São Paulo, Portsmouth away, Bolton's second at the Reebok, Thierry Henry's first at Highbury, Fulham at Anfield, West Ham's first in the cup final, and CSKA Moscow's goal in the Super Cup Final: all scored by beating the offside trap in some way.

Perhaps a lack of blistering pace in defence adds to the risk; however, when the offside trap has been played to perfection there have been no such concerns, and even the number of close-range goals conceded this season is less than a year ago. Speed at the back is not a necessity, providing you see danger quickly and have an uncanny understanding within the unit. Think of the great Arsenal teams of the '80s, with Lee Dixon, Nigel Winterburn, Steve Bould and Tony Adams. What pace would give Liverpool is a little extra insurance policy, should the trap fail; someone capable of getting back in double-quick time to clear the danger. But it's pointless introducing a quick player if he cannot synchronise with the others on the offside trap — and cause more openings as a result — and his reading of the game is suspect. Djimi Traoré was the best recovery tackler at the club since Mark Lawrenson, but the Frenchman's overall game just did not develop (in the way his long legs clearly did).

By pushing up and holding a higher line, Liverpool's defence and midfield press the ball with great aggression, meaning the opposition often don't have time and space on the ball to pick out their desired killer passes. Defending the edge of the area, as Liverpool used to under Houllier, means there's less space in behind the back line; but it gives more space for the opposition to have the ball in front of the area, to look to make something happen or to simply fire in a shot.

With a two– or three– man combination from Xabi Alonso, Momo Sissoko, Steven Gerrard or Didi Hamann employed to guard the defence, this area was in very good hands; so much so that the German was allowed to leave the club. The effectiveness of this system is probably best illustrated with how many goals the Reds allow — or don't allow, for that matter — from long range. During the 60 games played in 2004/05, Benítez's team only conceded four goals from shots outside the area. Even that impressively parsimonious figure was bettered this season, with Liverpool conceding just two goals from longer than 18 yards, and one of those was an outrageous fluke: Simao's brilliant (if telegraphed) effort for Benfica and Paul Konchesky's over-hit looping cross for West Ham in the FA Cup Final. When you take into account that Liverpool have scored 46 goals in the last two seasons from this distance the low figures for the opposition become even more eye-opening. While the space in behind leaves the back four susceptible from a canny pass, they face little chance of an opponent lamping one in from 25 yards (not to be confused with *Lamparding* one in, which involves a minimum of two deflections).

Post-Christmas fade

January, the darkest time of the year. With Christmas and New Year out of the way, depression often sets in; suicide rates rise to their highest point (no, we won't provide the stats to prove it). And if you were a Liverpool fan at the beginning of 2006, you were probably dreaming of balmy Istanbul evenings, or even cold but happy nights at Goodison Park and the Stadium of Light. With good reason. During Rafael Benítez's reign a worrying trend has occurred in each of the two seasons that could be called the 'January 15th slide'.

Table 25. Teams performance before and after January 15th the last two seasons

Season	Comp	Before 15th Jan			After 15th Jan		
		Games	Points	PPG	Games	Points	PPG
2004/05	Total	34	60	1.76	26	39	1.50
2004/05	Prem	22	37	1.68	16	21	1.31
2005/06	Total	37	80	2.16	25	51	2.04
2005/06	Prem	20	44	2.20	18	38	2.11

Before 15th January in Benítez's first season, the Reds had been performing pretty well in all competitions. They had 37 points from 22 games in the Premiership and before Christmas had won through to the Champions League knock-out stage. On the 15th of January they were defeated 1-0 at home to Manchester United, and then the winter blues descended. Liverpool then went on to lose eight more times in the remaining 25 games, being dumped out of the

FA Cup by Burnley and losing the Carling Cup final to Chelsea in the process. The Reds only managed to pick up 21 points (including three points for a cup win) from their final games of the season; an anaemic total during any period, especially when competing for that final Champions League spot at the time. But there were exceptional circumstances: a new manager, injured players and a squad that couldn't spread itself across a number of competitions.

The strange thing was that not only did a similar winter fade occur this season but it was again United who precipitated the slide. As you can see in Table 22, after Liverpool were able to beat Tottenham at home on 14th January their form for the rest of the season did dip, starting with that 0-1 heartbreaker at Old Trafford. It could have been so much worse, however, because in the first 13 games after the 15th January (between playing Man United away and before playing Fulham on the 15th March at Anfield) the Reds only secured 17 points, or a 1.30 per-game average. The form was even worse in the Premiership, where the Reds only gathered 11 points in the first nine games from that point in the year. The form took a dramatic turn for the better with a big 5-1 win over Fulham, and the great Merseyside Prozac shortage was averted (which was important, given the annually high need of Evertonians).

From being down in the dumps it was suddenly all smiles for Liverpudlians, with 18 goals in four matches, on the way winning the final 12 games of the season, nine of those coming in the Premiership. Even with such a strong finish the effect of any sustained period of poor form is easy to see, as Liverpool produced less points-per-game from the date the dry spell began than they had before it.

It could be coincidental that the slump occurred at the same point two years running. Alternatively, it could be more scientific, and be down to the training schedule. In 2005/06 it was almost certainly due in part to the late finish to the previous season, because of success in the Champions League, followed by the ludicrously early beginning to the new campaign, with the added burden of a trip to Japan right before the extremely hectic English festive programme. With the end to the season in sight and spring in the air, the Reds found their second wind, as well as their very best form.

When were the goals scored?

Table 26. Timings of goals during the 2005/06 season

	0-15	16-30	31-45	46-60	61-75	76-90	90+
Liverpool	11	19	19	13	15	25	2
Opponents	1	10	11	5	9	8	0

Table 26 shows some interesting facts as to when Liverpool scored and conceded goals. The Reds were able to get a fast start in nine games this year for a total of 11 goals, scoring twice within the first 15 minutes away at both Real Betis in Europe and Birmingham City in the FA Cup. Benítez's men were able to fire home a further 38 of their 104 goals this season in the 30 minutes before the break. The 15 minutes before half-time was also the worst for conceding goals. Liverpool scored the biggest percentage (24%) of their goals, however, in the last 15 minutes of the match, easily scoring the greatest number of goals of any team in the Premier League during this stage of a game; testament to Pako Ayestaran's gruelling training regime. The Reds were quite balanced for most of the season, scoring 47% of their goals before half-time and 53% after, whilst the goals the team conceded were split 50-50 between before and after the break.

Breaking these goal timings down to periods of the season adds further evidence to the theory that during Liverpool's worst run — the 13 game stretch from the middle of January to the middle of March — the players were simply exhausted and worn down from the backlog of fixtures. As mentioned during the set-piece section in this chapter, concentration is the first thing to wane through tiredness, and this is the skill required the most nearing half- or full-time, as fatigue sets in. It is no coincidence, therefore, that during the 13-game downturn in form this season Liverpool conceded nine of their 12 goals (75%) in the two periods 10 minutes before the end of each half. The players were simply exhausted during this phase of the season, mentally as well as physically. It's credit to all concerned that they rallied so effectively in the last two months of the campaign.

Where in the goal?

This is a light-hearted note on which to end the chapter: looking at where exactly in the goal the Reds placed the ball to score, and the same for opposition goals.

Table 27. Position the ball entered the goal from the players view point during both 2004/05 and 2005/06

2005/06

Liverpool

8	5	0
8	1	6
28	22	26

Opponents

1	1	3
3	0	4
10	11	11

2004/05

Liverpool

10	3	2
2	1	8
30	13	13

Opponents

4	3	2
4	1	1
13	12	16

These type of charts are interesting for individual players in particular, as they show his placement tendencies on goals; when adding all the players together you'd expect a more even spread. What these charts do show is that whether Liverpool worked on it or not, the scoring chart this year is far more even than last season. Last year 30 of Liverpool's 82 goals (37%) were scored in the bottom left-hand corner of the goal, with Milan Baros scoring eight of his 13 goals in that segment.

This year there is a fairly consistent spread on where the ball has entered the goal, primarily amongst the three bottom sections, making Liverpool's tendencies harder to predict. The other interesting point is that when you add up all the goal positions charted here 72% of all goals scored are in the bottom three positions. It just shows that the modern coaching theory of hitting it hard and low is most effective. When on form and confident, however, most strikers should be able to place the ball in any section of the net with some regularity.

Chapter Four
Formations and Line-ups

Football is a fluid game, built upon the movement and interaction of players — and with it the subsequent creation of space on the pitch — and yet we are obsessed with adding extra boundaries that force players into set formations and systems; assessing the tactics as if the players are rigidly stuck to the metal bar in table football. (Not to be confused with the suggestion that "Player X needs a rod up his arse".)

During a game no team's formation will remain rigid, with players moving forward, backward, inside or out, depending on occurrences during the game; and all this without even resorting to the Dutch brand of 'total football' — the *Karma Sutra* of footballing formations. However, some teams will obviously employ greater attacking movement than others; these tend to be the more expansive and ambitious sides, the best British example of which in recent years has been Arsenal.

Defending is usually the only time a team will resemble its on-paper formation: two banks of four, and depending on their workrate, two strikers either dropping back in, or standing around up front. There will still be players who have to move to close down the ball, and in so doing distort the team's shape, but the basic positions will be there. However, when on the attack, a team's players can be scattered all over the pitch; runners drifting left and right, midfielders bursting past forwards, forwards dropping deep or heading towards the byline. The key is that once the ball is lost the shape of the team resorts as quickly as possible to its on-paper formation, like an animal retreating into its protective shell.

A problem during Gérard Houllier's tenure was that the Reds never emerged far enough from this shell; they were always in a half-defensive stance, with one eye on what the opposition might do if they just happened to win back the ball. The wide midfielders did not push opposing full-backs towards their own goal, and few of the four midfielders ran ahead of the strikers. There wasn't a great deal of movement between positions; instead, the protective shell was in place for 90 minutes. It as if that shell was a barricade, and rather than risk the messy intricacies of hand-to-hand combat, long-range missiles were sent 'over the top' from behind the safety of this protective platform. It was down to Michael Owen and Emile Heskey to chase down these missiles and make sure they reached the target (perhaps more of a suicide mission in combat than in football, although still a thankless task at times). There is certainly far greater tactical flexibility in the Reds' armoury in 2006.

In this chapter we have assigned team statistics to formations and groups of players, to analyse their effect on the overall performance of the team, and to look at their interaction with each other. For each subset of data we have been able to calculate a goals-for average, a goals-against average, a clean sheet percentage and an average points won. We have adjusted these figures by the minutes that each group have played together, so all averages are over 90 minutes rather than games, and added in an overall difference figure from the team mean for the four statistics.

Team Formation

No one can accuse Rafa Benítez of sticking to tried and tested methods. One of the most impressive things about the Spaniard has been the way in which he has adapted to the demands of Premiership football, and changed his systems to better fit the English game. Before his arrival his preferred formation was most definitely 4-2-3-1, which he had used to win two *La Liga* titles and a Uefa Cup with Valencia, and which worked perfectly for continental football. In his first season with Liverpool Benítez looked to implement his preferred style, but English football proved a difficult arena for the formation (although clearly, once again, the tactics were spot-on in Europe). A big part of the problem was down to the personnel Benítez inherited, whereby he was forced to improvise with players rather than use those who perfectly suited the system. And of course there's the fact that implementing a new system and style takes time in any industry, let alone with a football team.

The system itself must also take some of the blame for the poor results. The 4-2-3-1 formation is conducive to possession football. It provides a solid defensive platform, with two midfielders sitting deeper protecting the back four, and relies on the three more advanced midfielders to get forward and support the lone striker, who will be looking to bring them into play.

The problem Benítez found was that many English clubs will come out hard in the first 30 minutes, to try and gain an advantage; on the continent there is often more sparring, with both teams playing in fits and starts, brief bursts and blasts. Rather than slow, slow, quick quick slow, English football is often quick, quick, quick quick *even quicker*. The more aggressive style of the Premiership saw Benítez's players harried and harassed, and forced into mistakes before they could get a firm foothold in the game. Players could not get forward to support the lone striker, and moves broke down as a result. When done well, 4-5-1 can help a team control a midfield, and if you control the midfield you control the game.

On the other hand, in its most traditional sense 4-4-2 can be less spectacular, but more 'steady' in all areas of the pitch. A lot of responsibility falls onto the strikers, as the midfield can be matched or outnumbered, so the ball needs to stick with them. And depending on where the second striker plays, 4-4-2 can easily be seen as 4-4-1-1.

Table 1. The percentage of playing time in 4-2-3-1 and 4-4-2 formations in 2004/05 and 2005/06

2004/05

% of Playing time

4-2-3-1	Competition	4-4-2.
78%	Europe	22%
72%	FA Cup	28%
53%	League	47%
32%	Carling Cup	68%
57%	Total	43%

Games Started

4-2-3-1	Competition	4-4-2.
12	Europe	3
1	FA Cup	0
19	League	19
1	Carling Cup	5
33	Total	27

2005/06

% of Playing time

4-2-3-1	Competition	4-4-2.
39%	Europe	61%
46%	FA Cup	54%
33%	League	67%
0%	Carling Cup	100%
50%	World Club	50%
36%	Total	64%

Games Started

4-2-3-1	Competition	4-4-2.
5	Europe	10
2	FA Cup	4
11	League	27
0	Carling Cup	1
1	World Club	1
19	Total	43

In 2004/05 Liverpool spent 57% of all playing time, and started 33 games, in the 4-2-3-1 formation, compared with 43% and 27 games respectively in 4-4-2 (Table 1). This split was even greater in Europe, where the Reds started 12 of their 15 games, and played 78% of all playing time, in the 4-2-3-1 formation on their way to winning the competition.

The figures for 2005/06, however, are radically different. They go to show how Benítez has adapted his thinking to the Premiership. In 2005/06 Liverpool started 43 games with the 4-4-2 formation and only 19 with the 4-2-3-1 line-up. The percentage of playing time was also one-sided, with the team playing 64% of the total number of minutes in the season in 4-4-2; a 21% swing away from 4-2-3-1. The changes from major playing style was even seen in Europe, where the team made only five starts in the 4-2-3-1 compared with

10 in the standard 4-4-2.

Although the 4-2-3-1 formation was no longer the most common formation it was still used in the majority of key games. Of the 11 league starts with the formation six were against the top sides, including both league games against Chelsea, Manchester United at home and Arsenal away; games where the Reds could not afford to lose the midfield battle. In fact, in all 10 games against Chelsea over the last two seasons in league, cup and Europe Liverpool have started the game in the 4-2-3-1 system.

When Liverpool play the 4-4-2 system it is often not in the traditional way; the second striker will drop into midfield areas to link the play. This '4-4-1-1' can easily become 4-5-1 when defending, and blur the lines of distinction between the two formations. Under Benítez Liverpool have always played with two central midfielders protecting the defence, making it important for one of the strikers to drop deeper to collect the ball, and play in the wider midfield two to support the attack. Another way at looking at these systems is to see how the team has performed with one striker, and compare it with how two forwards fared (Table 2).

Table 2. Team statistics when Liverpool play with one forward and two.

2005/06

Team Statistics						
Forwards	GFA	GAA	MINS	CS%	PPG	Difference
2 upfront	1.57	0.70	3610	55.7	2.19	0.04
1 upfront	1.82	0.71	2030	47.3	1.91	-0.08

2004/05

Team Statistics						
Forwards	GFA	GAA	MINS	CS%	PPG	Difference
2 upfront	1.62	0.73	2334	38.0	1.95	0.89
1 upfront	1.14	1.05	3166	23.1	1.41	-0.60

In 2004/05 there was no contest — the team statistics were far better when the team employed two up front. It has to be taken into consideration that the strikers — all of whom Benítez inherited (until Fernando Morientes arrived in the January) — were almost certainly more used to playing in pairs, so breaking from that routine was always going to present teething problems; having said that, Djibril Cissé was used as a lone striker at Auxerre, although in a different system (one where the wide men quickly made it a front three), and he had his own issues settling into English football and, of course, the five months out with a broken leg. With two strikers Liverpool scored more often, conceded less frequently and won more games as a result.

Part of the problem with the single striker formation was that 40% of the time it fell to Milan Baros to perform the role. Baros is a fine striker, who can score goals and certainly give defenders headaches, but he is not a target man. Rather than lay the ball to midfielders so the team could advance as one, and in so doing get numbers in the box, the Czech's first instinct was often to spin away towards goal, making it a case of him against the defence. At times he was successful, and it could be exciting for fans to witness his swashbuckling style, but it was usually a case of him losing to odds that were stacked distinctly in the opposition's favour. Djibril Cissé, who accounted for 15% of the lone striking time, was also happier facing the opposition goal than with his back to it. Florent Sinama-Pongolle played a further 13% of the spearhead minutes, and his inexperience made it a tough ask; lacking any kind of physical presence he could not make the most of his fine control. So almost 70% of the time it was a striker not really suited to the role who was trying to make the system work; these were all fast, counter-attacking strikers brought to the club by the previous manager.

The remaining 32% were shared by Neil Mellor and Fernando Morientes, two players better equipped to hold up the ball and play people in. In the case of Morientes, Benítez had felt he was more than capable of excelling in the role, given he was good in the air, of a decent size and possessed both an assured touch and a fine footballing brain, but the Spanish striker never settled into the pace and brutality of the English game, and would never prove 100% effective in the role. Within six months Benítez knew he needed another solution.

Looking at the lone striker statistics this season (Table 2) it is clear to see the improvements made. The single striker system in fact produced the considerably better scoring rate, 1.82 goals-per-game (compared with 1.57), and managed to maintain the same goals-against average (0.71) as the two-up formations. The team, however, was not quite as effective overall, winning less frequently. The closeness of the team statistics for two different formations — to each other, and to the overall team averages — shows how effectively Benítez has tweaked each system to get it to work. The personnel was a better fit to the Valencia system, with Peter Crouch (54%) and Fernando Morientes (28%) playing the vast majority of the lone striker minutes; the improvement apparent in the 0.68 goals-per-game hike for the team on 2004/05.

Liverpool will continue to use a combination of 4-2-3-1, traditional 4-4-2 and a mixture of the two next season, and perhaps even reprise the 3-5-2 'wingback' formation seen two years running at Newcastle, but as the quality of the personnel continues to improve to match Benítez's wishes it's fair to expect better results from the formation with which he made his name in Spain.

Defensive Line-ups

With the Reds becoming famous for their defensive meanness under Rafa Benítez there was one group of players who stood out as an outstanding unit. The Reina/Riise/Carragher/Hyypia/Finnan quintet was remarkably effective this season, (Table 3), and you can only wonder how many more clean sheets could have been garnered had they spent more time together on the pitch.

Did Benítez's rotation of his defenders, in particular his full-backs, deny the team even better results, or were these periods of rest crucial to the overall success of the team in 2005/06? As ever with rotation, the alternative scenario can never be played out.

Table 3. Team statistics of Liverpool 'back-fives' during the 2004/05 and 2005/06 seasons (minimum 135 minutes)

2005/06

Back-Five	Team Statistics					
	GFA	GAA	MINS	CS%	PPG	Difference
Reina/Riise/Carragher/Hyypia/Finnan	1.78	0.37	1716	71.4	2.39	0.94
Reina/Warnock/Carragher/Hyypia/Finnan	1.37	0.53	1185	62.7	1.95	-0.16
Reina/Traore/Carragher/Hyypia/Finnan	1.14	1.14	394	59.1	0.99	-2.00
Reina/Traore/Carragher/Hyypia/Josemi	1.74	0.58	311	52.1	2.43	0.53
Dudek/Riise/Carragher/Hyypia/Finnan	1.67	0.33	270	66.7	3.00	1.43
Reina/Riise/Carragher/Hyypia/Josemi	1.27	1.27	212	5.7	2.28	-1.24
Reina/Riise/Agger/Hyypia/Finnan	1.03	0.51	175	48.6	1.97	-0.60
Reina/Traore/Carragher/Hyypia/Kromkamp	2.00	0.67	135	33.3	2.33	0.42
Team	1.66	0.70	5640	52.7	2.09	-

2004/05

Back-Five	Team Statistics					
	GFA	GAA	MINS	CS%	PPG	Difference
Dudek/Traore/Carragher/Hyypia/Finnan	1.36	1.06	1187	28.6	1.61	-0.14
Kirkland/Traore/Carragher/Hyypia/Josemi	1.07	1.31	755	23.8	1.30	-1.04
Dudek/Riise/Carragher/Hyypia/Josemi	1.54	0.78	584	43.5	1.78	0.64
Dudek/Riise/Carragher/Hyypia/Finnan	2.32	1.16	311	38.3	2.12	1.33
Kirkland/Riise/Carragher/Hyypia/Finnan	2.13	0.85	211	0	2.20	1.15
Team	1.34	0.92	5490	29.5	1.62	-

The Reina/Riise/Carragher/Hyypia/Finnan quintet was an aggregated 0.94 better than the team averages for goals-for, goals-against, clean sheet percentage and points won per-contest. To put in bluntly, they were a ruthlessly efficient unit.

The team averaged a healthy 1.78 goals-per-game (0.12 above the team mean) in games played by the best back five, and collected 0.3 more points-per-contest. The greatest benefits, however, were in the defensive numbers, where the team averaged a minuscule 0.37 goals against a game — entering the FA Cup final this figure was 0.23, with only four goals conceded. Over the course of the season the unit kept a clean sheet 71.4% of the time. Didier Drogba's headed goal in the FA Cup semi-final, Liverpool's 58th game of the season, was the first goal the quintet conceded in open play all season. The run consisted of 1576 minutes (over 17.5 games) of football, with the other three goals coming on set pieces against Manchester United, Benfica and Everton. Rio Ferdinand's headed goal at Old Trafford, in Liverpool's 38th game, was the first conceded by the unit, arriving after 966 minutes of football, or the equivalent of nearly 11 full games. When the statistics for the group were so good it begs the question: why didn't they play more often? It is one that only Rafa Benítez and the Liverpool coaching staff know the answer to. It is hard to believe that with figures like that the unit only played a total of 30% of the season's minutes.

Further evidence of the brilliance of this quintet was that the removal of any one of these players from the line-up had negative consequences. The least unrest was caused when Dudek replaced Reina behind the best back four, as the team won all three games and posted an even lower goals-against average. (Dudek's overall figures in the season were less impressive than Reina's, but the Pole was only on the losing side when the defence in front of him was not at its strongest.)

While Dudek's three games didn't prove radically different to the overall pattern, when a defender was removed from the equation it was a different story. The team performed to some of its averages when Riise was replaced by Warnock, with the team posting another good goals-against average (0.53) and clean sheet percentage (66%), but had more trouble scoring (1.37) and thus winning games (1.95 points). The biggest differences came in games when either Riise was replaced by Traoré or Finnan was replaced by Josemi, where the team averaged goals-against figures of 1.14 and 1.27 respectively.

In 2004/05 the inclusion of Traoré alongside the best trio of Carragher, Hyypia and Finnan completed the most-used defensive line-up, with Dudek in goal. The signs regarding Riise's affect on the defence were in the figures last season, because any line-up that included him rather than Traoré performed better overall than the team's average, whilst every line-up that didn't performed below. There were signs, as well, of the possibility that the back line of Riise, Carragher, Hyypia and Finnan could be a very good one in the future, but not quite to the extent that we witnessed in 2005/06 (Table 4).

Table 4. Team statistics of Riise/Carragher/Hyypia/Finnan back line in 04/05 and 05/06.

2005/06

Team Statistics						
Best Back-Four	GFA	GAA	MINS	CS%	PPG	Difference
Riise/Carragher/Hyypia/Finnan	1.87	0.48	2075	67.7	2.50	0.99
Team	1.66	0.70	5640	52.7	2.09	-

2004/05

Team Statistics						
Best Back-Four	GFA	GAA	MINS	CS%	PPG	Difference
Riise/Carragher/Hyypia/Finnan	2.21	1.02	529	22.5	2.13	1.21
Team	1.34	0.92	5490	29.5	1.62	-

In 2004/05 the four defenders only played 529 minutes together, but did put up some good figures. The numbers were mainly impressive in an attacking sense — which one might expect due to Riise being a more attacking full-back than the alternatives. The team averaged 2.21 goals-per-game with them as the back four, and won at a rate of 2.13 points-per-game.

Conversely, the goals-against average of 1.02 was actually worse than the team's average of 0.92 for the season, and the clean sheet percentage was also lower than average. Whether it was the addition of Reina, the extra work on Riise's defensive skills or through playing more regularly with each other (529 minutes together in 2004/05 compared with 2075 minutes in 2005/06), the unit improved in every statistical category. The fact that the best quintet was able to get off to that 966 minute goal-free streak to open the season was made all the more amazing by the fact that the four defenders had only played the equivalent of barely six games together the year before, and with the exception of pre-season matches had never played a moment with their new Spanish goalkeeper. To build up that kind of trust and understanding usually takes years, so to start off with almost 1000 minutes without conceding is some achievement.

Central midfield pairs

Knowing when to go forward and when to stay back; knowing when to jump in and tackle and when to hold off and jockey; knowing who picks up which runner: all essential elements of understanding in the central midfield partnership. At the heart of the team, the central midfielders control much of the side's equilibrium.

As with the defensive unit, the central midfield area had to deal with the arrival of a new player, and needed to gel quickly to perform to the required level.

Table 5. Team statistics of Liverpool's central midfield pairs in 2004/05 and 2005/06

2005/06

Central Midfield 2	Team Statistics					
	GFA	GAA	MINS	CS%	PPG	Difference
Alonso and Sissoko	1.67	0.74	2422	51.8	2.22	0.09
Alonso and Gerrard	2.32	0.50	894	61.3	2.41	1.27
Sissoko and Hamann	0.88	0.33	820	55.9	1.90	-0.57
Alonso and Hamann	0.70	1.16	773	48.3	1.61	-1.94
Gerrard and Hamann	2.43	0.57	630	47.3	1.97	0.73
Gerrard and Sissoko	4.89	0.98	92	42.4	2.38	3.14
Team	1.66	0.70	5640	52.7	2.09	-

2004/05

Central Midfield 2	Team Statistics					
	GFA	GAA	MINS	CS%	PPG	Difference
Alonso and Sissoko	1.37	0.96	1317	22.8	1.24	-0.46
Gerrard and Hamann	1.54	0.58	933	38.7	1.56	0.57
Alonso and Gerrard	1.56	1.56	634	18.9	1.84	-0.31
Team	1.34	0.92	5490	29.5	1.62	-

The trust between the two players who play this position appears to take at least a year to develop (Table 5). Last year the best pair were Gerrard and Hamann, two players who had played countless games and minutes together since 1999, whilst this year the best pair statistical were Alonso and Gerrard, just 12 months after putting up below-average figures following the Spaniard's arrival. In 2004/05 the team scored above average when Gerrard and Alonso played together, as one might expect. But the Reds also conceded at a very high rate. Every single statistic has improved this season, but the latter has been completely reversed as the two have grown accustomed to each other's way of playing. The goals-against average for the team fell by over a goal-per-game, from 1.56 last season to 0.5 this season. The team's goals-for average was 0.76 per-game higher this season compared with last, and won at a rate of 0.57 points-per-game higher in their games.

If this theory holds true it will be good news for Liverpool, given the hugely promising relationship already built up between 2005/06 new-boy

Momo Sissoko and Xabi Alonso. Just like the best defensive quintet, the pair put up amazing numbers early on, being on the field only four times when the team conceded during their first 1046 minutes together (0.34 goals-against average). Overall the young pair, whose radically different skills combine to make a very effective whole, put up figures that were an aggregate 0.09 above the team's averages this season; given their ages, and the fact that both are still relatively new to English football, they can still improve — both as individuals and as a duo. The two played 43% of the total minutes for the unit, usually with Steven Gerrard either covering on the right wing or playing as a more advanced central midfielder.

Wide men and wingers

Unlike the previous units in this chapter, these two positions require no real relationship; knowledge of each other's style of play is not a necessity. The pair are not relying on one another for help, but do have a relationship with the team. First, each has a defensive responsibility to his flank, and must build up a relationship with the full-back and central midfield. Second, the pair must be able to provide an attacking thrust, but not at the expense of their defensive duties — although some wide players (such as Jan Kromkamp) were in the midfield mainly for the their defensive stability, while someone like Djibril Cissé was there primarily to go forward.

Table 6. Team statistics of Liverpool's wide midfield pairs in 2004/05 and 2005/06 (minimum 150 minutes)

2005/06

Wide Midfield 2	Team Statistics					
	GFA	GAA	MINS	CS%	PPG	Difference
Kewell and Garcia	1.89	0.74	856	41.7	1.90	-0.11
Kewell and Gerrard	1.10	0.77	821	50.1	2.25	-0.50
Riise and Garcia	1.33	0.67	540	60.4	1.80	-0.51
Kewell and Cisse	2.21	0.81	447	49.0	2.03	0.34
Zenden and Garcia	1.71	0.28	316	59.8	2.34	0.79
Riise and Gerrard	2.51	0.62	287	47.7	2.36	1.15
Garcia and Gerrard	1.31	0.99	274	91.2	2.72	0.38
Kewell and Kromkamp	1.58	0.79	228	57.0	2.83	0.61
Zenden and Potter	3.58	0.45	201	68.7	2.99	3.23
Zenden and Cissé	2.29	0	157	100.0	2.58	2.29
Riise and Cissé	1.80	0.60	150	50.0	3.00	1.12
Team	1.66	0.70	5640	52.7	2.09	-

2004/05

Wide Midfield 2	Team Statistics					
	GFA	GAA	MINS	CS%	PPG	Difference
Riise and Garcia	1.52	0.99	1539	25.0	1.78	0.23
Riise and Nunez	1.38	0.61	586	38.6	2.17	0.99
Kewell and Garcia	2.71	0.90	199	18.6	1.80	1.46
Team	1.34	0.92	5490	29.5	1.62	-

Far and away the best pair in 2004/05 were Harry Kewell on the left and Luis Garcia on the right. The two put up a goals-for average of 2.71 per game in their 199 minutes together. So it was no wonder that a year later, after Kewell overcame his injury and rediscovered his form, the two spent the most time out of any pair (15%) on the flanks. The overall results though were not as good as in 2004/05, although the first season was based on less than 200 minutes of football. In Benítez's second season the pair did inflate the team's goals-for average to a healthy 1.89 per-game, from the overall team average of 1.66, whilst averaging out at the same goals-against average. But Liverpool only won at a 1.90 points-per-game rate with the pair in tandem; a figure 0.19 points-per-game lower than the team average of 2.09 in the season.

In fact the three most used pairs all posted team statistics with aggregated totals below that of the overall averages for the team, to the tune of 0.5 for both Kewell/Gerrard and Riise/Garcia. The three pairs who performed the best (out of those with decent playing time) were the Kewell/Cissé, Zenden/Garcia and Riise/Gerrard line-ups.

Perhaps it just goes to show the inconsistency in this area, due to injuries and the lack of a genuine right winger, but there was no other unit this season that saw as much game-to-game or in-game changes. It is also true that Benítez, like most managers, looks to get defensive late in games when his side has a lead to protect; as such he will substitute attacking wide players for more defensive ones — often full-backs — to hold onto a result. The best of the pairs in terms of team stats — out of those with greater than 200 minutes played — was the Riise/Gerrard pairing, which adds further evidence to the type of season Riise had. In 2004/05 he was actually part of the two most-used pairs with Luis Garcia and Antonio Nunez respectively. These were also two of only three pairs to have above-average numbers across the board. His 'partnership' with Gerrard this season, however, generated 2.51 goals-per-game for the Reds while conceding at a rate of only 0.62. The next of those to put up good numbers was the attacking pairing of Harry Kewell and Djibril Cissé; with them together on the flanks the team put up the second-highest goals-for average (2.21). However, as might be expected, the team also conceded at a high rate as a consequence; but still well below the one per-game mark, at 0.80 per-contest.

Striking pairings

Hunt and St John; Toshack and Keegan; Rush and Dalglish; Beardsley and Aldridge: Liverpool have had some memorable and enduring strike partnerships down the years. There have also been those, as seen with the unisons of Robbie Fowler and Stan Collymore and Michael Owen and Emile Heskey, that burned brightly at times but, for one reason or another, were not as consistent or devastating as might have been the case.

Often it's about balance rather than pitting two out-and-out scorers alongside one another. Fowler and Owen never really clicked, while in 1989 Rush and Aldridge were deemed too similar, and the latter sold to Real Sociedad. Normally one partner has to be prepared to drop into midfield, or to drift wide and run the channels. The last successful two-pronged strikeforce was Alan Shearer and Chris Sutton of Blackburn in 1995: two target-men who stayed in advanced central positions and fed off the service from two old-fashioned wingers.

The role of the forward is to score for the team, but it is to also create chances and to play his part in the collective effort. How many goals he needs to score depends on how many the team needs to score, and how many others chip in with. If the team works with him in it, then he is good for the team, even if he doesn't contribute what would traditionally be seen as 'enough' goals.

Forwards need to have a good relationship with each other, but also with the midfielders around them. These are not isolated units in a team, but converging elements. In sides that play with two forwards the pair must instinctively know where to run to receive a cross or a pass, and also appreciate each other's tendencies, so as to not both run into the same space. Invariably you see a new pairing go after the same ball; a sixth sense develops between the best, and that can only add to the performance of the team. Little in football can top the power that comes from the understanding between two players; the moment when two individuals meet on the same wavelength, so that it's almost like the same player is both giving and receiving the ball. In the time it would take Kenny Dalglish to hit an inch-perfect 40-yard through-ball to Ian Rush — and for Rush to have known where to run, and in so doing left the defender for dead — the opposition would be cut to ribbons before they knew what hit them. It would take the world's most-gifted dribbler five times as long to cover that distance with the ball at his feet, and his chances of successfully taking on an entire defence would be far slimmer.

Forwards are also relied upon to be the first line of defence; something that's been commonplace at Liverpool for decades. To overlook the defensive work undertaken by forwards, and their influence on a team's defensive record, is to miss one piece of the puzzle; even if no striker would be selected merely for his ability to track back. In a year where Liverpool's defensive record was tighter than Scrooge on Christmas Eve, some forwards must have contributed a significant amount. Just check out the partnerships that Fernando Morientes was a part of and the team's corresponding goals-against average for each pair (Table 7). Morientes might have had trouble scoring and creating goals this year but his defensive work did not go unnoticed, and he was rewarded by being in the winning team more often than any other Liverpool forward.

Table 7. Team statistics of Liverpool's forward playing pairs in 2004/05 and 2005/06

2005/06

Centre-Forward 2	Team Statistics					
	GFA	GAA	MINS	CS%	PPG	Difference
Morientes and Crouch	1.61	0.59	1062	66.6	2.12	0.23
Crouch and Cissé	2.03	1.08	753	56.8	2.26	0.20
Morientes and Cissé	1.61	0.54	672	37.5	2.12	-0.01
Gerrard and Crouch	1.53	0.97	649	42.7	1.36	-1.23
Fowler and Morientes	1.23	0.46	585	37.4	2.38	-0.05
Fowler and Crouch	1.32	0.66	273	80.6	2.01	-0.10
Gerrard and Morientes	1.80	0	250	77.2	1.85	0.85
Garcia and Morientes	1.44	0.72	250	32.4	1.74	-0.79
Garcia and Crouch	2.05	0	219	58.0	2.28	1.33
Garcia and Cissé	2.86	0.71	126	60.3	3.00	2.18
Team	1.66	0.70	5640	52.7	2.09	-

2004/05

Centre-Forward 2	Team Statistics					
	GFA	GAA	MINS	CS%	PPG	Difference
Cissé and Baros	1.49	0.69	785	40.6	1.95	0.82
Morientes and Baros	1.22	1.10	734	21.0	1.61	-0.40
Gerrard and Baros	1.98	1.10	409	32.8	1.40	0.27
Team	1.34	0.92	5490	29.5	1.62	-

The pairings given in Table 7 are of the two most advanced players in each contest. As discussed at the beginning of this chapter, Liverpool played most of the season in either a 4-4-2 or 4-2-3-1 system. In both systems there was always someone responsible for supporting the main striker, even if his primary role would have him considered as a midfielder.

The Morientes/Crouch pair was the most-used, playing 19% of the total season minutes, with the team putting up above-average aggregated numbers in their appearances together. The goals-for was slightly lower than average, as might be expected given neither proved prolific, but the goals-against was fantastic, at only 0.59 goals conceded per-game, and a clean sheet percentage of 66.6%. The pair scored seven of their combined 22 goals (32%) when paired together, at a steady-if-unspectacular goals-per-90 minutes rate of 0.60. With neither being the quickest, they were not a duo who would run in behind defenders, and thus presented some limitations.

There were no speed concerns in the second-most used front line, with the inclusion of the lightning-quick Djibril Cissé alongside Crouch. On paper this would appear a logical partnership, with the fast Cissé feeding off Crouch's flicks and knock-downs. Statistically that proved the case, in an attacking sense at least. The Reds scored at a rate of 2.01 goals-per-game, easily the best rate of any pair playing more than 250 minutes together. The problem was that the team also averaged 1.08 goals-per-game conceded in their 753 minutes in tandem, the worst of any pair in the team. Crouch and Cissé scored a total of nine goals when together as a front two, at a fantastic rate of 1.08 goals-per-90 minutes. But it's a partnership that will not be seen again, as is the case with the first pair mentioned, with both Cissé and Morientes offloaded in July 2006. The next line-up was the Morientes/Cissé pair, which produced figures fairly similar to the Morientes/Crouch partnership. The team's goals-for average was fair-to-middling, but it was the team's goals-against that stands out again; the inclusion of Morientes made Liverpool harder to score against. The pair scored seven goals together, at a good rate of 0.94 per-90 minutes.

What is interesting about the next pair — Gerrard and Crouch — is that the team statistics say the team didn't fare too well when they were together, but the two players did. In fact the team statistics of the pair were the worst of any — with the team scoring 0.13 below average at 1.53 goals-per-game, conceding at an average 0.27 more at 0.97 per-game, and winning 0.73 points less per-contest than the overall team marks. The pair scored five goals in their 649 minutes together, at a rate per-90 minutes of 0.69. Gerrard in fact scored four of his five goals in attacking midfield/forward positions with Crouch as his partner, highlighting how well the two dovetailed. But this was a partnership usually reserved for the tougher fixtures, with Gerrard slipping back into midfield to bolster numbers, so that may well skew the figures slightly.

The next two most-used partnerships include Robbie Fowler, and both performed at around the team averages. Like Morientes, his partner in the first of these pairings, Fowler is a fantastic defensive forward who works hard to close off space for the opposition as they look to start moves; evinced by the pair's goals-against average (0.46 per-game) — the best of any attacking unit of the season. Fowler's rate with Peter Crouch was also impressive in this respect. Fowler and Morientes' partnership might have been under the team's goal-scoring average, but that low goals-against helped the pair to be the partnership with the highest points won per-game, averaging at a whopping 2.38 (over a 38 game campaign that rate would garner 90 points).

The pair were also far more prolific later in the season, having begun to establish that sixth sense discussed in the opening to this section. In their last four games together the pair played a total of 238 minutes, with the team scoring 1.89 goals-per-game, conceding only 0.38 and winning every contest (Table 8). Fowler scored twice and Morientes once in the spell, at a combined rate of 1.13 goals-per-90 minutes. Morientes was also the provider of Fowler's two goals, picking up the primary assist on both occasions: when he squared from Riise's throw-in against Blackburn, and flicked to Fowler to score at Portsmouth with a deft touch. The pair also combined to release Cissé to score his second against West Ham at Upton Park.

Table 8. Team statistics of Robbie Fowler and Fernando Morientes in their last 4 games together

Last 4 games	Team Statistics					
	GFA	GAA	MINS	CS%	PPG	Difference
Fowler and Morientes	1.89	0.38	238	26.5	3.00	1.20

The next four striking pairs in the list are all attacking midfielders combined with out-and-out strikers, and you can see the benefit the team received from these partnerships. Luis Garcia had two fantastic partnerships up front, one with Peter Crouch and one with Djibril Cissé. The partnerships were worth

2.05 and 2.86 goals-per-game in 219 and 126 minutes respectively — admittedly a small sample period. Steven Gerrard's partnership with Fernando Morientes was also a good one, with the team not conceding a single goal and scoring five times in their 250 minutes together. Of those five goals three came from the pair, with Morientes scoring twice and Gerrard once.

The best full team

From analysing the separate units of the team individually, would it be possible to put them together into a full team, and if so, did they play together in 2005/06?

The best defence was clearly the Reina/Riise/Carragher/Hyypia/Finnan quintet, with the best central midfield two being the Gerrard and Alonso combination. But then it starts to get complicated, given the versatility of certain players, and the current inability to clone human beings. On the wing it is harder to determine the best, but in terms of playing a good number of minutes and performing above average a Riise/Gerrard combination would be the best selection. However, that's impossible since we already have Riise and Gerrard in the team. So the consistent and balanced pairing of Harry Kewell and Luis Garcia would make most sense. Up front it comes down to a toss-up between the steady and defensively-sound pairing of Crouch and Morientes, or the impressive attacking production of the Crouch/Cissé pair.

Looking at the data, a team comprising of Reina, Riise, Carragher, Hyypia, Finnan, Gerrard, Alonso, Kewell, Garcia, Crouch and Morientes played just once, as did Reina, Riise, Carragher, Hyypia, Finnan, Gerrard, Alonso, Kewell, Garcia, Crouch, and Cissé. The first started and played 67 minutes against Newcastle at Anfield, scoring twice and conceding nothing, whilst the latter started and also played 67 minutes against West Brom at home, scoring once before the line-up was changed.

The fact that the combination of the best units played so few minutes just goes to show how the different sets of players play and interact with each other. It is fair to assess smaller groups of players with each other, given they play together regularly as part of a specific unit, but the line-up around them often changes. For example the best back five played together for 1716 minutes, but only played 286 minutes together with the best central midfield two, who in turn played a total of 412 minutes with the best wide midfield two, and played 469 minutes with the front pair of Crouch and Morientes.

Altogether though, the best two sides 'on paper' played only 67 minutes on grass. What is clear is that very good relationships, with the exception of the wide midfield two, need to be made between players in close proximity, or those with similar roles in similar areas. The defensive unit needs to work as a team to hold the right positions, mark the opposition and foil them with an offside trap. In addition to that they need to share good communication. The central midfielders and the strikers need to possess a good understanding. How players react and play within their separate units is crucial, because no individual plays in isolation. With new players arriving ahead of 2006/07, it will be interesting to look back in a year's time to see how this picture has changed.

Chapter Five
Player Statistics

We've seen how the Reds have been able to improve in almost every attacking and defensive team statistic this season, but who were the players contributing most to the improvements seen across the board? Every year some players will improve, a number will remain consistent and others will decline in some way. The key for any manager is to put together a team which gels, where the sum of the parts improves year on year. This chapter details the specific contributions of those in the squad.

The changes in Liverpool's style (indeed, *styles*) of play under Rafa Benítez are also very apparent in the player statistics. Under Benítez Liverpool have become much more flexible, and it's clear to see how many different players had a fairly major input on the results. While Steven Gerrard was clearly the star man, there was a pleasing consistency in terms of the key contributions from the majority of the squad.

Table 1. Liverpool's assists-per-goal during 2004/05 and 2005/06

Season	Games	Goals	Assists	Assists per goal
2004/05	60	82	113	1.38
2005/06	62	104	176	1.69

As can be seen in Table 1, Liverpool scored 22 more goals this year than a year ago, despite playing just two additional games. However, it is the assist total that catches the eye, increasing by a massive 63 this season. The Reds have recorded 0.31 more assists-per-goal this season than last, upping the average to 1.69 assists-per-goal from 1.38. This tells us that more goals were created with at least two Liverpool passes, suggesting increasingly intricate build-ups were involved, rather than profiting from the opposition conceding the ball directly to the goalscorer.

Goals, assists and points

Table 2 provides the total points recorded by each player who registered either a goal or an assist during the 2005/06 season. It is given as a pure count form, to clearly show who scored or assisted in the most goals during the season, and is sorted by total points.

Table 2. The top goal, assist and point scorers for Liverpool in 2005/06

Rank	Player	Starts	Goals	Assists	Points
1	Gerrard	49	23	28	51
2	Crouch	42	13	18	31
3	Cissé	29	19	11	30
4	Garcia	28	11	15	26
5	Alonso	47	5	15	20
	Morientes	33	9	11	20
7	Finnan	51	0	17	17
	Riise	42	4	13	17
9	Kewell	30	3	9	12
10	Hamann	23	0	8	8
	Hyypia	58	2	6	8
12	Zenden	11	2	5	7
	Carragher	57	1	6	7
	Fowler	10	5	2	7
15	Reina	53	0	4	4
	Sissoko	37	0	4	4
17	Pongolle	4	3	0	3
18	Le Tallec	2	0	2	2
	Warnock	23	1	1	2
20	Kromkamp	7	0	1	1
	Own goals	62	3	-	3
-	TEAM TOTAL	62	104	176	280

The numbers show just how important Steven Gerrard was for Liverpool this season. His 23 goals were the most registered by a Red, as were his 28 assists, both of which combine for a total of 51 attacking points. Gerrard was, therefore, involved in some way — by either scoring or setting up — 51 of Liverpool's 104 goals scored in 2005/06. Put another way, Gerrard had a direct involvement in exactly 49% of all goals the Reds scored this season. Last year a lot was written about how Liverpool were very much a one-man team; when Gerrard was either rested or injured the Reds struggled.

Working with the same system, it's possible to compare Gerrard with the top players at rival clubs. Wayne Rooney was Manchester United's top points scorer, with just 39, although Ruud van Nistelrooy was one behind on 38, to make them a potent pairing. Frank Lampard was top for Chelsea, with 44 points, ahead of Didier Drogba who racked up 31, the exact same number as Peter Crouch; interesting, given they mirror each other's role to some extent. Thierry Henry was the second-highest points scorer overall, with 50; one less than Gerrard, and over twice as many as Jose Antonio Reyes, the next highest points scorer at the north London club.

In 2004/05 Steven Gerrard accounted in some way for 30 of the 82 goals Liverpool scored (13 goals and 17 assists), or 36.6% of the team's total attacking production. It must be noted here that Gerrard missed two months of Benítez's first season with a broken foot, sustained at Old Trafford. Gerrard's production soared a year later, but so did that of the team, and fewer articles about a one-man team have been written as a result.

A contributing factor in Gerrard's improvement was the addition of Peter Crouch. Hopefully by now it is apparent that the purchase of the tall forward was a shrewd move by Rafa Benítez. Crouch is the perfect striker to complement a forward-thinking midfielder like Gerrard. He is the type of striker that world-class players love to play alongside, and more evidence of his effectiveness can be found in England's record when the Liverpool No. 15 makes an appearance. He makes things happen.

Of Steven Gerrard's 23 goals this season, 19 were scored from open play (four penalty conversions) and six of them (or 26.1%) were assisted by Crouch. Crouch found the favour returned by Gerrard, as seven of his 13 goals (or 54%) were assisted in some way by the Liverpool captain. Crouch himself finished second in the team in total attacking points for the 2005/06 season. The 6'7" forward managed to score 13 goals and assist on a further 18. The 18 assists were easily the highest total observed for a striker over the last two years, as last season the highest total by an out-and-out forward was Milan Baros, with only eight.

Djibril Cissé was another player who had a good year as a scorer and creator, despite limited time in his natural position up front. The Frenchman finished third with 30 total attacking points. For a good portion of his playing time this season Cissé was used in wide midfield, which perhaps explains to some extent the higher number of assists (11) he picked up this season compared with a year ago (three). The French striker also contributed 19 goals, but four came in the early stages of the Champions League and a further two in the Super Cup final; also, a fair few of his goals were scored in the final ten minutes of games, with the result already decided. On the other hand, his goal in the FA Cup final was very valuable. Still a 30 point season (19 goals, 11 assists) is a good return, especially when being played out of position, and drawing the short straw in the rotation system up front.

Next in the list is Luis Garcia, another figure who comes under heavy criticism at times, primarily for giving the ball away too frequently. Despite his flaws he remains an important creative force. The little Spaniard might try too hard at times, often failing with little flicks and step-overs that bring groans from the Kop, but he continues to make things happen, and help the Reds win important games. The Spaniard scored 11 goals this season, and with 15 was joint 4th in the team for assists, making a grand total of 26 attacking points on the year.

Tied for 5th in the team in total points were Xabi Alonso and Fernando Morientes, who both managed 20-point seasons. Alonso picked up his 20 by scoring five goals and assisting on another 15, whilst Morientes' 20 were comprised of nine goals and 11 assists. Alonso is perhaps the player whose creative brilliance has least impact on these particular stats. As mentioned in the team statistic chapter of this book, Alonso is the first link between defence and midfield. He is often the first player that his team-mates look to for a pass out of defence, or to begin an attack. He is often not one of the last two players to carve out an attacking move, but has played a key role at some stage. The Spaniard possesses an amazing ability to create space for himself off the ball with a canny economy of movement. He has a knack of being able to drift off his opponent and pick up the ball, often in very deep positions, and see the whole pitch ahead of him. He is always looking for the ball and, not only that, nearly always does something useful with it when in possession. His numbers are actually a little down on last year, as will be discussed later, but he has still been extremely effective this season. Morientes, on the other hand, actually spent most of the year in 8th place in this category, trailing both Steve Finnan and John Arne Riise. A late flurry of points in his last six appearances, where he picked up one goal and five assists, meant the Spaniard leapfrogged the two full-backs to draw level with Alonso for the season.

Tied for 7th in the list were Riise and, more surprisingly perhaps, Finnan. Many fans and pundits would have put quite a few other Liverpool players above Finnan this season, and who could blame them, as the Irish international didn't score a goal all year or grab any headlines. However, Finnan assisted in 17 goals, and was extremely valuable crossing from the right; unlike a lot of top-level players, he was always happy to cut inside to centre with his 'weaker' foot if a route outside the full-back was blocked. With the lack of a natural right-sided midfielder — especially one who would hog the touchline — Finnan was asked to get forward and make things happen, and possibly found more space with Gerrard's tendency to drift inside and draw opponents infield with him. Finnan's assist total was 3rd in the team, and leads nicely into Peter Crouch's impact on the overall attacking production.

The Crouch effect

Table 3. Defender and goalkeeper assists in 2004/05 and 2005/06

2004/05			2005/06		
Player	Assists	Assists per 90	Player	Assists	Assists per 90
Riise	3	0.15	Riise	7	0.24
Finnan	1	0.03	Finnan	17	0.35
Carragher	4	0.07	Carragher	6	0.10
Hyypia	1	0.02	Hyypia	6	0.10
Troare	1	0.03	Warnock	1	0.05
Kirkland	1	0.07	Reina	4	0.07
Josemi	2	0.11	-		
Whitbread	2	0.46	-		
Total	15	0.07	Total	41	0.15

As Table 3 above clearly shows, the assists from defensive positions increased a huge amount this year. Last year the defence accounted for a total of only 15 assists, at a rate of 0.07 per-90 minutes. The figure was lower than it might otherwise have been, due to both Riise and Finnan picking up only four of their combined 16 assists from defensive positions. The reverse is true this year, however, with five defenders and Jose Reina recording a combined total of 41 assists, at a rate of 0.15 per-90 minutes. Unlike a year ago, both Riise (seven of his 13) and Finnan (all of his 17) picked up the vast majority of their assists from defensive positions. In total Riise picked up four more assists than a year ago when playing at left-back, whilst Finnan increased his total by a massive 16 assists, finishing with 17 at the end of the season.

Finnan was not the only defender to increase his assist production this season, with both Hyypia and Jamie Carragher doing likewise. Carragher was able to increase his total from four last year to six this season, whilst Hyypia increased his total from only one a year ago to also claim six assists this year. The assist increase from defensive players has not just been confined to defenders, and can also be observed in the goalkeeper assists. Last year the only goalkeeping assist went to Chris Kirkland, whilst this season Reina was able to collect a total of four. Defenders have definitely been much more involved in attacking play, primarily through being better placed to support the attack. In addition to that, Liverpool have also implemented a longer-ball style that unlike hit-and-hope is capable of maintaining a good amount of possession, with defenders hitting longer diagonal balls to the forwards. Peter Crouch is a true target man, a focal point for the Liverpool attack, but also offers a lot more skill on the floor than the majority of tall centre forwards

The flexibility of Liverpool's attacking football was perhaps best displayed in the Merseyside derby at Anfield in March, even after being reduced to ten men. Liverpool's first goal came from sustained attacking football that led to a corner for the Reds; Xabi Alonso expertly curled the ball to the near post where Everton's Phil Neville glanced the ball in his own net. The second was scored from a huge kick by Reina, flicked on by Crouch and finished by Garcia. The third was scored by Harry Kewell, who was found in front of the area with a tidy square ball from Finnan, who had found his way forward on the right. As you can see from the description of the goals the first was scored from good set piece delivery, the second from a long ball, and the third from a more gradual passing move finished off with an accurate long range strike. Two of the three goals in the game involved defensive players in some way, while the goal from the corner could easily have done, had Neville not been so generous in doing Hyypia and Carragher's job for them.

This is just an indication of how Benítez is trying to build a unit that not only defends as team, but also attacks as a team, with defenders asked to not only play the first ball of an attacking move but sometimes also the last.

Total Points-Per-90 Minutes

Table 4. Points-per-90 minutes rate of Liverpool players during the 2005/06 campaign (minimum 360 minutes)

Rank	Player	Points	Points per 90 mins
1	Gerrard	51	1.08
2	Cissé	30	0.94
3	Crouch	31	0.85
4	Garcia	26	0.80
5	Fowler	7	0.73
6	Morientes	20	0.61
7	Zenden	7	0.58
8	Pongolle	3	0.50
9	Alonso	20	0.44
10	Kewell	12	0.39
11	Riise	17	0.39
12	Finnan	17	0.34
13	Hamann	8	0.32
14	Hyypia	8	0.14
15	Carragher	7	0.12
16	Kromkamp	1	0.12
17	Sissoko	4	0.11
18	Warnock	2	0.09
19	Reina	4	0.07
-	TEAM TOTAL	280	4.47

Steven Gerrard finished the season in the number one spot in this category (Table 4) as he did in the total points field, finishing the season with an average of 1.08 attacking points-per-90 minutes. That means that on average he either scored or assisted in a goal once every 83 minutes, a phenomenal rate. What might surprise a few people is the second name in the list. Many criticised Djibril Cissé during the season but the French striker did a good job overall, even if it ultimately proved insufficient to remove the doubts of Benítez, with the striker loaned to Marseilles for a year in the summer of 2006, following a second horrific leg-break.

Cissé actually spent 36% of his playing time on the flank, and he still put up numbers that many forwards would be happy with. He finished the season averaging an assist or goal at a rate of 0.94 per-90 minutes. Put another way, the forward had a hand in a goal in just under every 96 minutes of football he played this season. His numbers far outweigh those put up by Milan Baros last season, when the Czech Republic star managed 13 goals and eight assists for 21 points at a rate of 0.60 points-per-90 minutes, and he played all his minutes in a forward position. When Cissé's points and performances are broken down further there is some possible evidence as to why he was criticised, as is discussed in his player section later in the book, but when looking over the whole season his numbers are actually very good.

Third and 4th are Peter Crouch and Luis Garcia, with 0.85 and 0.80 points-per-90 respectively. Three of the next four players in the list, however, might not be exactly who people would have thought. Fifth in the team in points-per-90 was Robbie Fowler, who posted a figure of 0.73, primarily due to the five goals he scored in his short spell after arriving in the January transfer window. On the total points list Fowler was way down, tied for 12th place, due to his limited appearances; further evidence of how rate statistics should be used to determine a player's true performance in any given time frame.

Another indication of this comes with the player in 7th place in points-per-90 minutes, Bolo Zenden. Zenden made only 11 starts this season but did manage to score twice and assist on a further five goals before his season was ended by a knee injury. Zenden's seven total points position him tied for 12th with Fowler and Carragher for overall points, but worked out at an impressive rate of 0.58 per-90 minutes, which placed him in 7th place in the squad. Zenden began the season well, especially in the Champions league, picking up three assists in the two games against Kaunas and another in Liverpool's first game of the group stage away at Real Betis on the 13th September, albeit without ever really playing his best football. Then just before he got injured he discovered his best form, registering three points, including both of his goals in the season, in a four game span in November. Zenden was also incredibly effective defensively on the left of midfield, an indication of which was seen when Rafa Benítez chose a left side of Riise and Zenden against Real Betis at Anfield in an attempt to negate the skillful Joaquin, a mission which was accomplished in a 0-0 draw. Zenden's experience as a full-back with Barcelona told in such situations.

A comparison with Harry Kewell's points-per-90 rate shows Zenden's to be far greater. As we have already seen, the Dutchman's seven points came in 1095 minutes, for a rate of 0.58 per-90 minutes, whereas Kewell's 12 points came in 2752 minutes at a rate of 0.39. As you can see there is quite a difference between them; for every point Zenden scored last season it took Kewell almost 73 minutes longer to match. Kewell clearly played well in the second half of the season, once he had overcome his groin injury and found his match fitness, but his best work was in the overall passing moves; more is still required in terms of cutting edge. The individual team statistics are actually an eye-opener for a player like Kewell, who underachieves when it comes to individual statistics, but the team actually performs much better, and scores more frequently, with him in the line-up. His biggest value over the last two seasons, however, appears to be in giving the team great balance and giving the opposition a potential problem — one that needs addressing prior to the game, thus taking a lot of the opposition's focus, with two players often assigned to him to close him down — for example, Chelsea's tactic to play Geremi and Ferreira to negate Kewell in the FA Cup semi-final; and, on the basis of what transpired, one of the least-successful opposition tactics in the entire season.

The 8th player in the list was Florent Sinama-Pongolle, who produced at a rate of 0.50 points-per-90 minutes. All his points were picked up with goals, posting three in his 538 minutes with the Reds. What is interesting is that going into the last few weeks of the season Fernando Morientes was actually lower than Sinama-Pongolle, with a point production rate just below 0.5 per-90 minutes. The Spaniard's six points in his last six appearances pushed him up the list, to overtake the loaned-out Sinama-Pongolle and injured Zenden. When 'Flo' was loaned out to Blackburn in the January transfer window many pundits wondered why Liverpool were happy to do without the young French striker due to his immense speed and his ability to score important goals, even when not playing regularly. It seemed a reasonable question at the time and even more so as Liverpool began to struggle to score over the following 4-5 weeks. But the young Frenchman was not going to feature as often once Robbie Fowler was brought back to the club, and that little extra bit of class told. As already discussed, Fowler's points per-90 rate was actually 5th in the team, whilst Sinama-Pongolle rate placed him 8th, which indicates a clear improvement. At that time in the season Fernando Morientes, despite a similar points-rate to Pongolle, offered more experience to the side; while Morientes would be sold to Valencia at the end of this season, he ended the campaign with some valuable contributions, and Fowler, in particular, linked well with the Spaniard as they helped each other to goals and assists.

While neither Sinama-Pongolle nor Morientes scored as often as they should have, there was a big difference in their creative impact. Over the last two seasons Sinama-Pongolle picked up only two assists in 1655 minutes, whilst Morientes picked up 15 in 4126 minutes. 'Nando' may have had some trouble in front of goal this season, netting only nine times, but when you combine his assists he had an involvement in a goal once every 147 minutes, compared with Pongolle's involvement once every 179 minutes. The last point to note from Table 5 is the slide down the standings of Alonso, Riise and Finnan compared with the total point numbers. The three players moved from being either tied for 5th or 7th place in the team to 9th, 11th and 12th position respectively. All three collected high point totals on the year but also played more minutes than most, hence bringing down their points-per-90 minutes averages.

Premiership Points-per-90 minutes

Table 5. Premiership points-per-90 minutes rate of Liverpool players during the 2005/ 06 campaign (minimum 360 minutes)

Rank	Player	Points	Points per 90 mins
1	Garcia	16	0.91
2	Cissé	16	0.84
3	Fowler	7	0.82
4	Crouch	18	0.76
5	Gerrard	21	0.69
6	Morientes	14	0.69
7	Zenden	3	0.60
8	Alonso	14	0.49
9	Kewell	10	0.45
10	Finnan	9	0.28
11	Hamann	3	0.24
12	Riise	5	0.20
13	Hyypia	6	0.17
14	Kromkamp	1	0.15
15	Warnock	2	0.14
16	Carragher	4	0.11
17	Reina	3	0.09
18	Sissoko	1	0.05
-	TEAM TOTAL	155	4.08

What often happens when looking at this category over all games played in a season, and comparing with those just played in the Premiership, a drop off — or preservation in rate at best — is often observed for most players. The Premiership has become more defensive in the last five years, with a greater number of tight games taking place; it's far tougher to score goals, and gone are the days in the '90s when Alan Shearer, Robbie Fowler and Andy Cole could rack up 30-40 goal seasons, or the '80s when both Ian Rush and Clive Allen came close to 50. Looking at the points-per-90 minutes for the Liverpool squad during the 2005/06 Premiership campaign (Table 5), this downward trend can been seen for most players. It is, therefore, even more amazing to see Luis Garcia actually prove *more* productive in the league when compared with his overall figures. This, from a player believed by many to be far more effective in Europe than in the hurly-burly of the English league.

Garcia actually picked up attacking points at a rate of an additional 0.11 per-90 minutes when playing in the Premiership than his overall figures — leading the team in the league with a rate of 0.91. Djibril Cissé again finished second, but with a slightly less impressive figure of 0.84 points-per-90, compared with his 0.94 in all competitions. Robbie Fowler was third, and was one of only a handful of players to show a significant increase in Premiership play. With Fowler cup-tied in the FA Cup, and joining the club at the knockout stage of Champions League — which lasted just two fruitless games against Benfica — there were very few opportunities for Fowler to impress outside of the league campaign. His league figures weren't helped initially by the fact he was returning from a long lay-off at Manchester City, and he was patently off the pace early on; after finally opening his account against Fulham with a goal and an assist he went on to add a string of three game-winning goals in three straight games in early April, to prove the old instincts were still present.

One more player stands out: Steven Gerrard. His overall production in the season was phenomenal, at well over the one point per-90 minutes. However, in the Premiership his rate fell to 0.69, down into 5th place. His Premiership form was actually fairly similar to last season, posting the same assist rate but upping his goal rate. With supreme form in Europe and other domestic competitions, Gerrard is definitely capable of delivering more in the Premiership. If he had scored at his overall season rate in the league this season, which he is arguably capable of doing, he would have actually tallied five more goals in the Premiership, taking him close to the all-competitions 30-goal mark reserved for the country's best centre-forwards. When you dig deeper into Gerrard's goals, however, you discover that nine came against so called 'lesser' opposition: five against TNS, two against Kaunas, and one apiece against Crystal Palace and Luton. Excluding those games and goals, Gerrard scored 14 goals against top-class opposition in 3798 minutes, for a goals-per-90 minutes rate of 0.33; the same rate as he scored in the league.

Total goals-per-90 minutes

It's probably fair to say that an average rate for a forward is around 0.4 goals-per-90 minutes (e.g. Mark Viduka, Premiership rate of 0.38), an above-average rate is 0.5 per-90 (e.g. Darren Bent, Premiership rate of 0.51), a very good rate is 0.6 per-90 (e.g. Robbie Keane, Premiership rate of 0.63), and the world- or top- class level are those strikers with rates above the 0.7 per-90 minutes level (Thierry Henry, Premiership 2005/06 0.91).

Table 6. Goals-per-90 minutes rate of Liverpool players during the 2005/06 campaign (minimum 360 minutes)

Rank	Player	Goals	Goals per 90 mins
1	Cissé	19	0.60
2	Fowler	5	0.52
3	Pongolle	3	0.50
4	Gerrard	23	0.49
5	Crouch	13	0.35
6	Garcia	11	0.34
7	Morientes	9	0.27
8	Zenden	2	0.16
9	Alonso	5	0.11
10	Kewell	3	0.10
11	Riise	4	0.09
12	Warnock	1	0.05
13	Hyypia	2	0.03
14	Carragher	1	0.02
-	TEAM TOTAL	104	1.66

Even though Steven Gerrard was the top goal scorer in total this season for the Reds, the skipper actually finishes 4th in terms of goals-per-90 minutes. The top player in this category was actually Djibril Cissé, which is even more amazing when you consider he played considerable minutes on either flank and often drew the short straw in regards to the teams rotation system up front. His rate of 0.6 goals-per-90 minutes is actually very prolific, and had he played more regularly for the Reds in 2005/06 he could have easily totaled 25-30 goals this season. Even so, it wasn't enough to convince Rafa Benítez that the Frenchman fitted with his varied tactical needs.

In 2nd-place for this statistic is Robbie Fowler, despite a slow start. There is usually an acclimatisation period for any new player, even one who once knew the club inside-out. Once you factor in the unfamiliar management, different team-mates, alterations in playing style, changes in training and the different daily routines a professional footballer has to go through when swapping teams, it is a wonder that they ever properly acclimatise when moving mid-season. If Fowler were to replicate his end-of-season form over the whole of next season he would register somewhere in the region of 15-20 goals; a successful pre-season fitness regime, and he could conceivably get even more.

Florent Sinama-Pongolle was third, following his limited minutes. Having scored four goals at a rate of 0.31 per-90 minutes in 2004/05, he managed three at a rate of 0.50 this season. The increase, and the combined rate of the last two seasons (seven goals at 0.38 per-90 minutes) suggests he has a future in top league football. His high rate at Liverpool this season was not maintained at Blackburn, however, where he managed only one goal in his 708 minutes, for very low rate of 0.13 per-90 minutes, although his performances were widely praised. His combined Liverpool/Blackburn season rate was 0.29, but the young forward is definitely capable of more.

Fourth in the team was Steven Gerrard, who scored his 23 goals at a rate of 0.49 goals-per-90. That he played 37% of this time on the right-wing makes it more impressive, although he was rarely restricted to staying out wide. The 0.49 goals-per-90 minutes figure was actually greater than Frank Lampard, another high scoring midfielder, and the player with whom Gerrard is most often compared. Over the course of the season Lampard scored 20 goals in 4290 minutes, for a rate of 0.42 goals-per-90 minutes, some 0.07 goals-per-90 below Gerrard's rate this season. This is not even taking into account the fact that Lampard scored six penalties this season (Gerrard scored four) and had a much lower rate of scoring from open play than Gerrard: 0.40 compared with 0.29. (No stats are available as to who has eaten the greater number of pies.)

Next in the list were Crouch, Luis Garcia and Morientes in 5th, 6th and 7th place, with similar rates of 0.35, 0.34 and 0.27 goals-per-90 minutes respectively. Of the three, Garcia's rate is the one that stands out, as he plays the vast majority of his minutes in midfield positions, whilst only occasionally playing behind the main striker. You could say that all three players score at about the same rate as each other, but where Crouch and Garcia proved more valuable to the team was in setting up goals. As you'll see in the assists-per-90 minutes section, both Crouch and Garcia assist at over twice the rate of Morientes. There is then quite a drop off between 7th place in the team and those in the group 8th, 9th, 10th and 11th. This group is made up of three midfielders and one part-time midfielder/defender, and perhaps shows a weakness or area that could be improved in the 2006/07 season. Zenden comes in 8th place with a rate of 0.16, Alonso in 9th at 0.11, Kewell at 10th at 0.10 and Riise at 11th with a rate of 0.09. After analysing goalscoring rates per-90 minutes by position all but Zenden's rate are below the average (0.14) observed for goalscoring midfielders, and therefore need to be improved upon next season, with the clear exception of Alonso, whose role is more concerned with starting moves than finishing them. When you look at the number of goals from midfield this season the overall total does look impressive (see Table 7), but there is not a lot of scoring in depth.

Table 7. Liverpool's goals from midfield position in 2005/06

Player	Goals	Goals per 90 mins
Gerrard	23	0.49
Garcia	11	0.34
Cissé	7	0.61
Alonso	5	0.11
Kewell	3	0.10
Riise	2	0.10
Zenden	2	0.16
Warnock	1	0.92
Total	54	0.27

The overall total of 54 midfield goals is an impressive total, and works out as 51.9% of all the goals the Reds scored in 2005/06, similar to a year earlier. Steven Gerrard and Luis Garcia, however, account for 63% of this total and removing their goals leaves very little. Additionally, Riise played more left-back this season than left-midfield, as did Steven Warnock, and if the stats are anything to go by both will continue to spend most of their playing time at the deeper position.

Looking further into the midfield scoring production, Alonso scores at a good rate for a midfielder who sits so deep, while Sissoko never did open his account. The real problem appears to be goals from wide midfield positions, with 44% of midfield scoring coming from central midfielders — and in Benítez's systems they are not necessarily the most ambitious players. After scoring only three goals all season Harry Kewell must add more next year, having finally found his form in a Red shirt; he is easily capable of 10-15, although increased options on that flank might limit his chances. Additionally, a fully fit Zenden throughout 2006/07 would be expected to yield more goals, but he's another who might struggle for considerable playing time. Luis Garcia actually scored all but two of his goals from wide midfield positions, and Djibril Cissé contributed seven of his 19 from either flank, although one was a penalty, the taking of which has little to do with where the player is actually deployed in the system.

Premiership goals-per-90 minutes

A lot was made this season as to whether Liverpool possessed a consistent 20–25 goals-a-season striker, and whether it is something that is needed in the squad. The arrival of Craig Bellamy, who registered 17 goals in 32 games for Blackburn, will help matters, but the chances are that the 20-goal mark is his upper-limit. Dirk Kuyt's arrival in August 2006, however, means the Reds now have a recognised goal-poacher going into next season, while Robbie Fowler will always score goals if he gets enough minutes on the pitch.

It's hard to know if people mean 20-25 goals in just the Premiership, or across all competitions, when expressing the need for high-scoring forwards. Michael Owen's scoring record at Liverpool was always up there with the very best, but his highest league tally was 19; his highest overall was 28. In this age of striker rotation, it is surely as important to have four strikers who can all score at a steady rate all season, rather than rely on one über-striker through whom all the tactics are dictated. If you have Thierry Henry, then sure, you're onto a winner if he stays fit, but few players in world football are as reliable.

Only five times since the inception of the Premiership has the eventual Champions boasted a top scorer with 20 league goals or more. It's actually been far more common for teams to win the title with 12-18 from their top striker, as seen with Mark Hughes, Eric Cantona, Teddy Sheringham and Ole Gunnar Solskjaer at Manchester United in the 1990s, as well as Dennis

Bergkamp in 1998 for Arsenal; all within that bracket — with Hughes in 1992 and Cantona in 1993 scoring as few as 12 and 13 goals respectively. In the last two years, Chelsea's main striker Didier Drogba scored a very modest 12 and then 10 goals, and even Frank Lampard, the club's top scorer in both those campaigns, peaked at 16 goals.

With four main strikers on the books at top clubs, not to mention at least one goalscoring midfielder, it is the *rate* of their goals that is most important. For the Premiership season, the lowest rate per-90 minutes required by a player in order to score 20 goals would be around 0.53. To score 25, the lowest rate required would be 0.66. Looking at the scoring rates from Liverpool players over the course of 62 games (Table 6 from the previous section), Liverpool didn't have a single player who scored at the 25 goals-a-season Premiership rate. But they did have two in the 20 goals-a-season Premiership rate: Djibril Cissé and Robbie Fowler. Cissé has subsequently been moved on, and in his stead we have Craig Bellamy, who also possessed a goals-per-minute rate which put him into the 20 league goals-a-season bracket. While Peter Crouch suffered a difficult start to his first season at Anfield, his later scoring rate was more in keeping with his final season at Southampton, where he scored in the 20 league goals-a-season bracket. While he's not a player who can be relied upon for lots of goals, he is capable of scoring at a healthy rate. At the start of September 2006, for club and country Crouch had scored 26 goals in nine months — or seven months, if you remove the summer breaks before and after the World Cup; however, only nine of those were in the Premiership. Dirk Kuyt's figures in Dutch football (discussed in detail in the final chapter of the book) put him up there with the very best finishers in world football, but it's difficult to compare a striking rate from another league. His tally of 71 league goals in 101 games was virtually identical to Djibril Cissé's record with Auxerre, and the Frenchman proved less successful than anticipated once imported to England; however, as we've seen, his overall scoring *rate* was actually fairly impressive.

Table 6 shows the players' goalscoring rates in all games this season, not just those in the Premiership. So what were the Liverpool players' goalscoring rates per-90 minutes in league games only?

Table 8. Premiership goals-per-90 minutes rate of Liverpool players during the 2005/06 campaign (minimum 360 minutes)

Rank	Player	Goals	Goals per 90 mins
1	Fowler	5	0.58
2	Cissé	9	0.47
3	Zenden	2	0.40
4	Garcia	7	0.40
5	Crouch	8	0.34
6	Gerrard	10	0.33
7	Morientes	5	0.25
8	Kewell	3	0.13
9	Alonso	3	0.11
10	Warnock	1	0.07
11	Riise	1	0.04
12	Hyypia	1	0.03
-	TEAM TOTAL	57	1.50

Quite a few players can be seen to maintain their overall rates in the season. The changes seen for Crouch, Morientes, Kewell, Alonso, Warnock and Hyypia are all either nothing or so small to be significant. The rates seen for Cissé and Gerrard, however, are significantly lower, and as explained earlier in the case of Gerrard, were perhaps inflated in the first place through early season Champions League qualifiers against limited opposition. Cissé's rate of 0.47 goals-per-90 was second in the team and placed him 17th in the whole of the Premiership. It is just below a 20-goal rate of 0.53. In the case of Zenden the rate is inflated due to both his goals coming in his short minutes in the Premiership, while his overall rate of 0.16 is more in line with his rates of a year ago at Boro. As we saw earlier, Luis Garcia had a significantly increased points-per-90 rate in the Premiership, and that is also reflected in his goals rate.

The most interesting figure is Robbie Fowler's. His Premiership rate with Liverpool — 0.58 goals-per-90 minutes — actually placed him 7th in the entire Premiership in this category, one place ahead of new recruit Craig Bellamy. Add to Fowler's figures his goal in 61 minutes of Premiership action with Man City (against Manchester United, deliciously enough), and Fowler has a combined figures of six goals in 834 Premiership minutes. That equates to 0.65 goals-per-90, a rate that would push up Fowler into 5th place in the league behind Thierry Henry, Jimmy Floyd Hasselbaink, Ruud van Nistlerooy and Michael Owen.

Whichever way you look at it, Fowler was fantastic in his trial spell back with Liverpool, and really did give the team expert finishing; enough to earn that new contract. Fowler is easily capable of maintaining a scoring rate around 0.6 goals-per-90 minutes; the only question is whether or not he can maintain his level of fitness for a full year. It certainly did look like he was approaching a good level of sharpness by season's end, and if he could maintain that level he could possibly start 20 games for the Reds in the Premiership next season. If that were the case, then with added substitute appearances, Fowler could quite easily score between 15-20 goals, and vastly improve Liverpool's strike rate.

The 25-goal mark in the Premiership is actually incredibly difficult to reach. Since the 2001/02 season, a striker has only registered 25+ goals four times during a Premiership campaign. In fact only two players have completed this feat. They were Thierry Henry (thrice) and Ruud van Nistlerooy, the two top strikers in English football this decade. The numbers are not even that much more impressive when you look at the number of 20-plus goal scorers in recent seasons.

Table 9. Number of Premiership goal scorers scoring 20 or more goals

Season	Number of players scoring 20+ goals
2001/02	4
2002/03	4
2003/04	4
2004/05	2
2005/06	2

As can be seen in Table 9, in each of the last two seasons only two players in each campaign have scored within the 20-25 goals bracket. There may be many reasons for this, such as rotation systems, increased squad sizes, and greater organisation in most defences, but it does suggest that top forwards should not necessarily be assessed on a 20-25 goals-a-season level, but more on a 15-20 goals-a-season range. This is further evidence that total goals are no longer the best way to judge a player's performance, and that goalscoring rates (excluding those with very few minutes' playing time) would be a better indicator.

Table 10. The goalscoring rates of the top 10 Premiership scorers

Player	Goals	Goals per 90 mins
Henry	27	0.91
van Nistelrooy	21	0.73
D. Bent	18	0.51
Keane	16	0.63
Lampard	16	0.46
Rooney	16	0.47
Harewood	14	0.44
Bellamy	13	0.58
Yakubu	13	0.45
Camara	12	0.49

Looking at the pure goal numbers alone does not give the true picture of how good a striker really is. Darren Bent scored 18 goals this season in the Premiership, only three behind Ruud van Nistelrooy. When looking at the two players rate of goalscoring, however, we see Bent scored his at a rate of 0.51 per-90 minutes and van Nistelrooy scored his at 0.73 per-90. This is a significant difference, much greater than the three goal variance in the season. In fact for every goal van Nistelrooy scored Bent had to play just over 52 minutes more to match him. If both had played every minute of every game in the Premiership the goalscoring difference between the two players would have been nine goals, van Nistelrooy with 27 and Bent 19, only one more than he actually did score on the year. It's also clear that Craig Bellamy scored more frequently in his playing time than Bent. Strikers at top clubs have to sit out a lot of playing minutes, but while they are 'resting' the man in their place is likely to be scoring goals himself.

Some players cannot last the pace of every minute of every single game of a season, and this is especially true of older strikers whose legs need to be saved. Meanwhile, some players are incredibly effective impact substitutes, scoring a goal every time they enter the fray with five minutes to go, but somehow fail to come even remotely close to matching their scoring rate when starting games.

Looking at the Liverpool forwards and those of their Premiership rivals, we see that Djibril Cissé matched or bettered the rates of Lampard, Rooney, Harewood, Yakubu and Camara, but just did not have the playing time to register more than his nine goals on the year. We also see that Robbie Fowler would have easily been near the top had he played all year with the Reds, and played significant minutes.

As you can see, looking at the player's goalscoring rates as well as their goal totals adds a dimension to assessing a player's season. It also appears unfair to put midfielders in with strikers, and defenders in with both, as all three groups of players have different goalscoring responsibilities. A more sensible analysis would be to look at top scorers and goalscoring rates by position. From looking at the scoring rates of the top goalscorers in the Premiership you may think that 'lesser' players (or players who had short spells of good form) top the rate rankings, but this is not the case. As you'll see in Tables 11, 12 and 13 (below), ranking players by goalscoring rates actually appears to bring out the better goalscoring players and push them nearer to the top.

Looking at the top twenty forwards in terms of goalscoring rate (see Table 11) it is hard to argue with any of the top 10, or even the top 20 for that matter. It was interesting to see Jimmy Floyd Hasselbaink climb into the second spot by season's end, as van Nistelrooy's rate dropped through irregular playing time after falling out with his manager. As you can see Fowler finished 7th with his Liverpool form, but add to that his Man City form and the returning hero actually moves above Robbie Keane and into 5th place in the league. Djibril Cissé finished the season in 16th position, ahead of Wayne Rooney, Andy (sorry, *Andrew*) Cole and Mido — although when you breakdown the Frenchman's scoring by position played the story changes.

In Premiership play Cissé only scored three goals when playing in a centre forward position in 897 minutes, for a rate of 0.301 per-90 minutes. This rate would actually see him finish 40th in the league, below Peter Crouch in 36th place, and below the average rate for the position. Liverpool's other regular first team striker, Fernando Morientes, finished even lower than this, in 47th place in the table for forwards. Another point of note is that Marlon Harewood doesn't even make the top 20 strike rates, but did finish the season 7th in the league in total goals with 14.

Table 11. Top twenty Forwards in goals-per-90 minutes in the league in 2005/06 (minimum 630 minutes)

Rank	Team	Player	Position	Starts	Goals	Goals per 90 mins
1	Arsenal	Henry	F	30	27	0.908
2	Middlesbrough	Hasselbaink	F	12	10	0.814
3	Man United	van Nistelrooy	F	27	21	0.727
4	Newcastle	Owen	F	10	7	0.713
5	Totenham	Keane	F	25	16	0.625
6	Fulham	Collins John	F	15	11	0.606
7	Liverpool	Fowler	F	9	5	0.582
8	Blackburn	Bellamy	F	22	13	0.581
9	Man United	Saha	F	12	7	0.548
10	Chelsea	Drogba	F	20	12	0.541
11	Chelsea	Crespo	F	20	10	0.536
12	Fulham	Helguson	F	15	8	0.518
13	Charlton	D. Bent	F	36	18	0.512
14	Wigan	Camara	F	24	12	0.488
15	Aston Villa	Moore	F	16	8	0.485
16	Liverpool	Cissé	F	19	9	0.471
17	Totenham	Mido	F	24	11	0.469
18	Man United	Rooney	F	34	16	0.468
19	Man City	Cole	F	20	9	0.458
20	Middlesbrough	Yakubu	F	29	13	0.452

Table 12. Top twenty Midfielders in goals-per-90 minutes in the league in 2005/06 (minimum 630 minutes)

Rank	Team	Player	Position	Starts	Goals	Goals per 90 mins
1	Chelsea	Lampard	M	35	16	0.456
2	Liverpool	Garcia	M	15	7	0.399
3	Man United	Ronaldo	M	24	9	0.355
4	Chelsea	Cole	M	26	8	0.340
5	Liverpool	Gerrard	M	32	10	0.330
6	Bolton	Stelios	M	29	9	0.318
7	Chelsea	Robben	M	21	6	0.302
8	Arsenal	Robert Pires	M	23	7	0.289
9	Blackburn	Pedersen	M	34	9	0.288
10	Birmingham	Jarosik	M	19	5	0.271
11	Bolton	Nolan	M	35	9	0.259
12	Newcastle	Solano	M	27	6	0.242
13	Chelsea	Geremi	M	8	2	0.231
14	Portsmouth	Mendes	M	14	3	0.220
15	Sunderland	Le Tallec	M	12	3	0.219
16	Tottenham	Jenas	M	30	6	0.209
17	Wigan	Scharner	M	14	3	0.206
18	Everton	Cahill	M	32	6	0.196
19	Man City	Barton	M	31	6	0.195
20	Newcastle	N'Zogbia	M	27	5	0.194

In terms of midfielders (see Table 12), it was Frank Lampard who led the league with a rate of 0.456, as well as being the midfielder who scored the most total goals as well. His rate was actually 21st in the league overall. Had he played enough minutes to qualify, Andreas Johansson of Wigan would actually have led the league as the Swede scored four goals in his six Premiership starts for a rate of 0.581, which in any short spell is a fantastic rate, but not necessarily one he could maintain over the course of a season.

Next in the list was Liverpool's very own Luis Garcia. Over the last two seasons Garcia has scored a total of 24 goals, with 15 coming in the Premiership, and none from free-kick shots or penalties. His Premiership rate this year was better than Joe Cole of Chelsea (4th) and Ronaldo of Manchester United (3rd), and even out-did Liverpool's Steven Gerrard, who finished in 5th place for all midfielders in the league.

It goes to show that Liverpool do have two of the very best scoring midfielders in the league, who easily compete with Joe Cole and Frank Lampard for the best pair. The Chelsea duo, thanks mainly to Lampard, managed 24 goals this season in the Premiership, at a rate of 0.41 per-90 minutes, compared with the Liverpool pair's 17 goals at a rate of 0.36. The advantage that Chelsea had in 2005/06 was that they also had Robben in the top ten, scoring six goals at a rate of 0.3 per-90. It is possible, if a little unlikely, that had Zenden remained fit he could have matched his fellow Dutchman's total, but even if this was true Chelsea still possessed more scoring depth from midfield. In fact, had Bolo Zenden played enough minutes to qualify, his goals rate in the Premiership was higher than Luis Garcia's, at 0.4 per-90, due to both his goals coming in the league. His rate, however, was artificially high, and on his form of the last few years he scores at a rate somewhere above average for the position at around the 0.17 – 0.2 mark, which is lower than the rate Robben tends to score at. It is interesting to note that of Djibril Cissé's nine Premiership goals, six came from wide positions during 821 minutes. That is a rate per-90 minutes of 0.658, well above Lampard's league-leading rate for a midfielder.

One of the other names to stand out is Liverpool's Anthony Le Tallec's, in 15th place, ahead of noted midfield poacher Tim Cahill. That Le Tallec scored *any* goals in a season-long loan at Sunderland, in a side bereft of any attacking momentum, is little short of miraculous. However, he spent time in a number of positions, although even when stationed up front, as a nominal striker, he spent much of his time in his own half fighting fires.

How different it might have been had the Reds' procured either Stelios Giannakopoulos or Nolberto Solano, both summer targets in 2005. Both finished in the top twenty in the league in midfield scoring rate, netting nine and six goals respectively. Had Liverpool secured Stelios to play right-midfield the team would have had more balance, allowing Gerrard to play more centrally, which almost certainly would have upped his goal tally; when combined with Garcia, theoretically the trio could have eclipsed Chelsea's best three of Lampard, Cole and Robben. Add to that Mark 'Speedy' Gonzalez, had his permit come through, and Liverpool would almost certainly have scored more than 57 goals in the Premiership, and put more pressure on the eventual Champions.

The other two Liverpool midfielders to score during the season, Harry Kewell and Xabi Alonso, both finished below the average rate for the position, ending in 41st and 54th position respectively. In the case of Alonso, however, he did score at a better rate than the defensive central midfielders of the Reds' rivals, such as Cesc Febregas, Michael Essien, Gilberto and Michael Carrick.

In 2005/06 Liverpool did not have a single defender in this category (see Table 13). In fact the Reds only had three defenders who actually scored goals, and both Warnock's and Riise's came whilst they were playing in midfield roles. It is an area that can definitely be improved on, although the primary role of the unit is to prevent the opposition from scoring — and that is the area where Liverpool's group excelled. Clearly the purchase of Fabio Aurelio, an attacking and skillful left-back, is designed to help in this area.

Table 13. Top twenty Defenders in goals-per-90 minutes in the league in 2005/06 (minimum 630 minutes)

Rank	Team	Player	Position	Starts	Goals	Goals per 90 mins
1	Bolton	Jaidi	D	15	3	0.219
2	Bolton	Campo	D	8	2	0.208
3	Arsenal	Cygan	D	11	2	0.193
4	Portsmouth	Taylor	D	32	6	0.189
5	Aston Villa	Ridgewell	D	30	5	0.165
6	West Ham	Collins	D	13	2	0.158
7	Chelsea	Gallas	D	33	5	0.153
8	Man City	Sommeil	D	14	2	0.150
9	Middlesbrough	Queudrue	D	26	3	0.125
10	Totenham	King	D	26	3	0.116
11	Chelsea	Terry	D	36	4	0.111
12	Middlesbrough	Parnaby	D	19	2	0.109
13	Arsenal	Senderos	D	19	2	0.107
14	Arsenal	Campbell	D	20	2	0.103
15	Blackburn	Todd	D	20	2	0.102
16	Man City	Dunne	D	31	3	0.096
17	Newcastle	Bramble	D	21	2	0.092
18	Aston Villa	Delaney	D	12	1	0.083
19	Man United	Ferdinand	D	37	3	0.082
20	Birmingham	Clapham	D	13	1	0.075

Defending is something that Chelsea do extremely well as well — finishing second in the league with 20 clean sheets, and top in terms of the fewest goals conceded — but they also have two defenders in the top twenty in terms of goals rate and goals total. William Gallas was tied for second in the league with five goals, and John Terry finished fourth with four, making a total of nine from only two defenders. Add to that the goals scored by Ricardo Carvalho and Assio Del Horno, and Chelsea racked up 11 goals from defence — far superior to Liverpool's solitary strike. (However, going into the new season William Gallas' future looks in doubt, while Del Horno has been sold. Could this cost the Blues?)

Table 14. Comparison between the Premiership goalscoring rates of the two teams in 2005/06

Player	Position	Goals	Goals per 90 mins	Player	Position	Goals	Goals per 90 mins
Hyypia	D	1	0.03	Del Horno	D	1	0.04
Riise	D	1	0.04	Carvalho	D	1	0.05
Warnock	D	1	0.07	Gallas	D	5	0.15
Kewell	M	3	0.13	Terry	D	4	0.11
Gerrard	M	10	0.33	Essien	M	2	0.07
Garcia	M	7	0.40	Lampard	M	16	0.46
Alonso	M	3	0.11	Cole	M	8	0.34
Zenden	M	2	0.40	Duff	M	3	0.17
Cissé	F	9	0.47	Geremi	M	2	0.23
Fowler	F	5	0.58	Robben	M	6	0.30
Crouch	F	8	0.34	Crespo	F	10	0.54
Morientes	F	5	0.25	Drogba	F	12	0.54
-	-	-	-	Gudjohnsen	F	2	0.12
Total	-	55	1.45	Total	-	72	1.89

In terms of the breakdown of where the goals are coming from, Chelsea actually only got 24 goals out of players with a primary position of striker (Drogba, Crespo and Gudjohnsen, the latter two having since been offloaded); Liverpool managed a less consistent but bigger total of 27. If you look at rates, Fowler had the best of all forwards but Chelsea got a consistent rate of 0.54 goals-per-90 from both Crespo and Drogba. Djibril Cissé was just too inconsistent when playing as a striker. However, Crouch and Morientes combined easily eclipsed both Gudjohnsen's total and rate. So, honours even.

A big difference between the two teams can be seen in midfield. As discussed earlier in the chapter, Gerrard and Garcia are a match for Lampard and Cole in terms of production and total goals, while Alonso just edges it over Essien. The real difference comes in the other wide midfield scorers for both teams. Chelsea got six goals from Robben, three from Duff (another to since leave Stamford Bridge) and another two from Geremi, for a total of 11, whilst Liverpool got three from Kewell and two from Zenden, who was injured most of the year.

Total assists-per-90 minutes

Table 15. Assists-per-90 minutes rate of Liverpool players during the 2005/06 campaign (minimum 360 minutes)

Rank	Player	Assists	Assists per 90 mins
1	Gerrard	28	0.59
2	Crouch	18	0.49
3	Garcia	15	0.46
4	Zenden	5	0.41
5	Cissé	11	0.34
6	Morientes	11	0.34
7	Finnan	17	0.34
8	Alonso	15	0.33
9	Hamann	8	0.32
10	Riise	13	0.30
11	Kewell	9	0.29
12	Fowler	2	0.21
13	Kromkamp	1	0.12
14	Sissoko	4	0.11
15	Carragher	6	0.10
16	Hyypia	6	0.10
17	Reina	4	0.07
18	Warnock	1	0.05
-	TEAM TOTAL	174	2.81

Another statistic, another table for Steven Gerrard to top. The Liverpool skipper led the assists-per-90 minutes category, with an amazing 0.59 per-90 rate on 28 assists. The rate is 0.17 higher than the figure of 0.42 he posted last season, which placed him second in the team. Xabi Alonso was the player who led last year's figures, with a rate of 0.44 per-90 minutes with his 12 assists. From the table you can see that in total three players bettered that rate this year, with Bolo Zenden also coming extremely close, at 0.41 per-90 minutes. Peter Crouch (0.49) and Luis Garcia (0.46) came closest to matching their captain's involvement in the creation of goals. As we saw when we looked at goals-per-90 minutes earlier, both players posted similar rates in this category as well. Statistically speaking their games are very similar, even if their style and appearance differs wildly.

There are many ways to skin a cat, as the saying goes, and these two players epitomise that on a football field. Crouch scored 13 goals and assisted in a further 18 for 31 attacking points, at rates per-90 minutes of 0.35, 0.49 and 0.85 (in total), whilst Garcia scored 11 and assisted in 15 for 26 attacking points, at rates of 0.34, 0.46 and 0.80. Despite criticism aimed at both, they remain extremely effective in their own way, and very valuable for Liverpool.

In 5th place was Djibril Cissé, picking up a surprising 11 assists in the season. Four were accumulated whilst playing wide on the right of midfield, whilst the remaining seven came when playing in his more natural forward position.

Down in 8th in the list was Xabi Alonso. As mentioned earlier, the Spaniard's production did decrease this season; however, his role and influence in attacking moves did not. Alonso managed 15 assists this season, compared with 12 a season ago, but while the number increased the rate decreased. Last year Alonso topped the team at 0.44 assists per-90 minutes, whereas this year his 15 assists rated at 0.33. Alonso was more closely marked this season, but it was still a very impressive campaign for the playmaker. However, there where times when teams didn't set out to stop the Spaniard, and they paid the price. Two such games were the FA Cup tie with Luton, where the Spaniard scored two of the longest goals of the season, and the away Premiership tie with West Brom, where he twice played long balls, comparable to a quarterback in American Football, to pick out Djibril Cissé on the right wing, with both leading to Liverpool goals. The long diagonal ball out wide is a favourite pass of Alonso's, and Benítez with two new wingers arriving will be looking for Alonso to hit them in these positions in 2006/07.

Ninth in the squad, and perhaps a surprise given his defensive positioning and nature, was Didi Hamann, with a rate of 0.32 per-90 minutes on his eight assists. For most of the season Hamann's assist rate actually had him 5th in the squad, until Morientes, Alonso and Cissé had bright finishes. Six of Hamann's eight assists this season came via the last touch before a goal was scored, indicating then that it was he who put through the killer ball for someone else to finish. The biggest surprise was that Kewell, at 11th in the list, was on form this season but still didn't register many assists this year, finishing below the defensive-minded Hamann.

The last point to mention from this table is that Jamie Carragher led the central defenders in assists rate (0.105), although only he and Hyypia (0.104) really qualified, with Agger sure to contribute next season after displaying a brilliant range and accuracy of passing in his few appearances. In goal Jose Reina almost matched the two centre-backs, posting an assist rate of 0.07 per-90 minutes, and used the ball far better than Liverpool's goalkeepers from a year ago.

Premiership Assists-per-90 minutes

Table 16. Premiership assists-per-90 minutes rate of Liverpool players during the 2005/06 campaign (minimum 360 minutes)

Rank	Player	Assists	Assist per 90 mins
1	Garcia	9	0.51
2	Morientes	9	0.44
3	Crouch	10	0.42
4	Alonso	11	0.39
5	Cissé	7	0.37
6	Gerrard	11	0.36
7	Kewell	7	0.31
8	Finnan	9	0.28
9	Hamann	3	0.24
10	Fowler	2	0.23
11	Zenden	1	0.20
12	Riise	4	0.16
13	Kromkamp	1	0.15
14	Hyypia	5	0.15
15	Carragher	4	0.11
16	Reina	3	0.09
17	Warnock	1	0.07
18	Sissoko	1	0.05
-	TEAM TOTAL	98	2.58

Luis Garcia was the team's most potent creative weapon in the Premiership in 2005/06, leading the team in assists (see Table 16) and points-per-90 minutes in the league, and coming 4th in goals rate in that competition. Fernando Morientes' assist rate in the league was helped massively by those five assists in his last four Premiership appearances. Most of the year he was at a rate of about 0.23 assists-per-90 minutes, but his final rate of 0.44 is closer to reflecting the player's natural ability. Peter Crouch was amazingly consistent putting up similar assist rates in whatever competition he played in.

The Premiership was actually Xabi Alonso's best competition in terms of assist production, picking up 11 of his 15 in the league, for a better rate at 0.39 per-90 minutes. As we saw with his decline in goals-per-90 minutes rate, Steven Gerrard also picked up assists less regularly in the Premiership, and another indication that the Liverpool skipper could deliver more in the league. Another player who had his best assist production in the Premiership was Harry Kewell, picking up seven of his nine assists on the year in the league, leading to a rate of 0.31 per-90 minutes.

Improvement and decline in attacking production

As already explained, by adding goals and assists together we arrive at an overall attacking production measure that we've called points. In this section we will look at the difference in the points of Liverpool players over the last two seasons, and also if the new arrivals offered an improvement over those who left the Reds in 2005.

Table 17. Improvement and decline measured in changes in points-per-90 minutes for players in the Liverpool squad between 2004/05 and 2005/06.

Player	Points per 90 minutes			
	2004/05	2005/06	Change	%
Gerrard	0.73	1.08	0.35	44
Cissé	0.53	0.94	0.41	70
Garcia	0.53	0.80	0.27	45
Morientes	0.53	0.61	0.08	14
Pongolle	0.47	0.50	0.03	6
Alonso	0.55	0.44	-0.11	-18
Kewell	0.35	0.39	0.04	11
Riise	0.39	0.39	0.00	0
Finnan	0.11	0.34	0.23	185
Hamann	0.33	0.32	-0.01	-2
Hyypia	0.08	0.14	0.06	66
Carragher	0.07	0.12	0.05	67
Warnock	0.19	0.09	-0.10	-46
Team	3.13	4.47	1.34	39

Table 17, above, shows that of the 14 players who registered a point for the team in both 2004/05 and 2005/06, only three showed a decrease in attacking production this season. The greatest of these declines was from Stephen

Warnock, whose attacking production dipped by 46% from a year ago. This was primarily from playing more left-back this season than in 2004/05, and also the greater minutes giving a truer representation of the player. Xabi Alonso's production also went down this season. The only other player to show any kind of a decline was Didi Hamann, although a 2% reduction is hardly worth noting. John Arne Riise managed to exactly match his production from a year ago; impressive, seeing as his playing time between left-back and left-midfield was totally reversed: spending only 33% of his time in midfield this season compared with 61% a year ago.

The greatest increase in production was seen from Steve Finnan, even though the right-back failed to score this season, and played only 3% of his playing time in right-midfield, compared with 29% in 2004/05. The right-back's attack production rose by over 185%, which is a phenomenal increase. Two of the next three greatest percentage increases were also from defenders, Jamie Carragher (67%) and Sami Hyypia (66%), primarily due to reasons already discussed in the 'Crouch Effect' section of this chapter.

The second biggest increase in production was by Djibril Cissé, who returned to form after missing most of 2004/05 to a broken leg sustained at Blackburn. Cissé's production was fairly good a year ago, especially when you consider that it takes time to recover performance on the field even after recovering in the weights room. This season Cissé's production was far greater, and added up to a 70% improvement on his attacking production from a year ago. Other attacking players who showed a notable improvement were Luis Garcia (45%), Steven Gerrard (44%), Fernando Morientes (14%) and Harry Kewell (11%).

The fact Gerrard was able to increase an already high points-per-90 minutes figure by 44% just goes to show what a force he is on the pitch, and he is only just entering his prime playing years. Even though Harry Kewell's figures weren't what one might have expected from such an outstanding talent they were still an 11% improvement on last season. In 2004/05 Kewell was often playing with injuries just to maintain a place in the side. This season Kewell was finally fit and able to work his way back to form, especially since his main rival for playing time on the left of midfield, Bolo Zenden, went down early with a knee injury, and Mark Gonzalez, another rival for the role, needed to wait another 12 months to secure a work permit. An injury sustained at the World Cup, following his best display in a number of years, wrote-off yet another pre-season ahead of the new season, and an uphill battle awaits Kewell once again.

Having looked at the improvements and declines for players who were at the club in both 2004/05 and 2005/06, what were the changes in attacking production between those joining, and those who left or were loaned out? As can be seen in Table 18, below, almost man-for-man the new player has been an upgrade. The table attempts to pair up like-for-like wherever possible.

Table 18. Comparison of players In against those Out in terms of attacking points production

OUT 2004/05			IN 2005/06		
Player	Points	Points per 90 mins	Player	Points	Points per 90 mins
Baros	21	0.60	Crouch	31	0.85
Nunez	5	0.32	Zenden	7	0.58
Josemi	2	0.11	Kromkamp	1	0.12
Kirkland	1	0.07	Reina	4	0.07
Mellor	6	0.63	Fowler	7	0.73
Biscan	5	0.23	Sissoko	4	0.11
Smicer	1	0.18	Agger	0	0
Diao	1	0.11	-	-	-
Total	42	0.30	Total	54	0.34

The biggest difference is of course at the top of the table, with Peter Crouch coming in and Milan Baros exiting, and where the production change has been pronounced. Crouch scored as many goals as had Baros in 2004/05 (13), but it is in the assists and team play that the real difference is felt. Crouch picked up 18 assists on the year, whilst in 2005/06 Baros only collected eight.

Further down the list we see the improvement Zenden was over both Smicer and Nunez combined; even when playing only just over 1000 minutes on the year he still managed a point more than the two wide midfielders had in 2004/05. Kromkamp appeared a significant upgrade over Josemi defensively, although the difference in their points-per-90 rate was marginal. Fowler was an obvious upgrade over Mellor, even though the younger man's productivity was very healthy in Benítez's first season. Sissoko was a defensive upgrade over Biscan, clearly, but is still a little raw on the attacking front. Overall the total production of the seven players purchased before or during 2005/06 was 54 points, at rate of 0.34 per-90 minutes. The departing eight players only managed 42 points a year ago, at a rate of 0.30 per-90 minutes, although the main impact of Reina, Sissoko and Kromkamp was seen at the other end of the pitch.

Mistakes leading to goals and Mistake percentages-per-90 minutes
As discussed in an earlier chapter, assigning mistakes within a game can become biased. But by setting parameters, and monitoring mistakes over a full season, it does give a great indication as to those players who are erring most frequently. When you combine these figures with things like the team's goals-against and clean sheet average, you are able to build up a good picture of how well a certain player performed in any given year. In Table 19, the mistakes leading-to-goals and mistake percentages of every player who made a costly mistake is given. There is no team ranking of this statistic because those who make the least mistakes are obviously midfielders and attackers, many of whom did not record a single error that cost a goal. It is sorted by mistake percentage, and is more of a comparison for defenders and goalkeepers.

Table 19. Mistakes leading to goals and mistake percentages of Liverpool players during the 2005/06 campaign (minimum 360 minutes)

Player/situation	Mistakes leading to goals	MLG % (adjusted over 90 minutes)
Crouch	1	2.7
Gerrard	2	4.2
Alonso	2	4.4
Carragher	3	5.2
Riise	3	6.9
Reina	5	9.3
Team Marking	6	9.6
Kromkamp	1	11.8
Finnan	6	11.9
Hyypia	10	17.3
Warnock	5	23.2
Agger	1	25.0
Josemi	3	32.5
Dudek	2	39.4
Whitbread	1	41.5
Traore	7	45.1
Total	58	-

A year ago Liverpool players committed 66 goal-costing mistakes, in 60 games; this season that figure was cut to 58, whilst playing two additional games. As discussed previously it really is a measure primarily for defenders, since it is very rare for a midfielder or forward to even pick up a mistake. Often balls given away higher up the pitch don't lead to defensive errors; if the ball is given away this Liverpool team always has players flying in to regain possession, and covers for each other in an admirable manner. There are occasions, such as Alonso's underhit pass in the FA Cup Final that led to West Ham's first goal, but they are few and far between.

The defender least likely to make a mistake in any 90 minutes of football was Jamie Carragher. His three mistakes work out to a percentage of 5.2%. That means that in only 5.2% of the total games Carragher played during the season he made a mistake that led to an opposition goal; or one costly mistake every seventeen full games. That is a phenomenally low rate.

Next in the list for defenders is John Arne Riise, who put in a surprisingly consistent season at left-back. Riise also only made three mistakes that led to goals, but at a slightly higher percentage than Carragher of 6.9%, or one every 13 full games. Next amongst defensive players was goalkeeper Jose Reina, who only committed five mistakes all season, for a mistake percentage of 9.3%, or roughly one every tenth match. This was a massive improvement on a year ago, when the Liverpool goalkeepers combined to commit 18 costly errors. Reina was able to improve this stat by 13 on the combined total of a year ago — meaning 13 less goals conceded due to Reina's reliability alone. When we discussed clean sheets in the Team Statistics chapter of the book we discovered than the difference in points between conceding and not conceding was in fact one point; we can, therefore, surmise that Reina added 13 points to the team through reduction of costly errors.

Next in the list are team mistakes: assigned when there is no single individual to blame. It is a situation where the whole team was at fault, such as not being ready for a free-kick and all reacting late, or several players being pulled out of position. There were six team mistakes in total this year, at a percentage of 9.6%. That was a vast improvement on the year before, when the team committed 10 errors at 16.39%.

Next comes Jan Kromkamp, who picked up one mistake in his short spell with the club after January. Kromkamp was a vast improvement over Josemi, as you can see from the table. Josemi was near the bottom based on his form in the first half of this season, committing three mistakes, but at a percentage of 32.5%. This percentage could be said to be artificially high due to low playing time — but it's actually in keeping with his torrid time in England; the Spaniard registered a sizeable seven mistakes, at a percentage of 36.8%, in 2004/05. Steve Finnan and Sami Hyypia were next in the team, posting mistake percentages of 11.9% and 17.3% respectively. Stephen Warnock put up a concerning mistake percentage of 23.2% on his five mistakes — one of which was a flying-headed own goal. He did prove to be much more reliable than Djimi Traoré, though, who posted the worst mistake percentage in the team: 45.1% on his seven mistakes. When he played the Reds struggled.

Premiership Mistakes leading to goals and Mistake percentages-per-90 minutes

In direct contrast to attacking production, most players' mistake and mistake percentages improved in Premiership play when compared with those seen overall in the season. This gives a further indication of the tighter, more defensive nature of the Premiership this season; cup football, and domestic cup football in particular, tends to be more strewn with errors.

The most impressive thing when looking at the mistake table for Premiership play (see Table 20) is that Jamie Carragher did not record a single costly error. It was not like he didn't play very much either — he made 36 of a possible 38 starts, and played 3240 of a possible 3420 minutes. In fact, going back to 2004/05, it's 4275 minutes since Carragher committed a mistake that led to the opposition scoring. That works out to be the equivalent of 47.5 total games without an error, and just goes to show the amazing consistency of the vice-captain.

Table 20. Premiership mistakes leading to goals and mistake percentages of Liverpool players during the 2005/06 campaign (minimum 360 minutes)

Player/situation	Mistakes leading to goals	MLG % (adjusted over 90 minutes)
Carragher	0	0.0
Gerrard	1	3.3
Alonso	1	3.5
Riise	1	4.0
Crouch	1	4.2
Team Marking	3	7.9
Reina	3	9.1
Finnan	4	12.3
Warnock	2	13.7
Hyypia	5	14.5
Kromkamp	1	14.9
Agger	1	25.0
Josemi	1	34.4
Dudek	2	39.4
Traore	6	66.8
Total	32	-

Overall the team committed 32 mistakes that led to opposition goals in the 2005/06 Premiership campaign, which is a significant improvement on the 47 committed a year ago. As you can see from the table, along with Jamie Carragher, those defensive players who had improved rates were John Arne Riise, Jose Reina, Sami Hyypia and Stephen Warnock.

In the case of Warnock this was a very encouraging sign, since he played 68% of all his minutes in the league, and this is where he recorded the best mistake percentage. Overall his percentage was 23.2%, but in Premiership play this was reduced to 13.7%. The gap between himself and Traoré also grew much wider in the league. Six of Traoré's seven mistakes occurred in the Premiership, taking his percentage out to a whopping 66.8%; in other words, errors that led to the opposition scoring twice in every three full games he played.

Improvement and decline in mistake percentage

Table 21. Improvement and decline measured in changes in mistake percentage for players in the Liverpool squad between 2004/05 and 2005/06.

Player	Mistakes leading to goals %		
	2004/05	2005/06	Change
Finnan	2.2	11.9	-9.70
Carragher	7.1	5.2	1.90
Hyypia	14.4	17.3	-2.90
Josemi	36.8	32.5	4.30
Riise	3.9	6.9	-3.00
Traore	23.1	45.1	-22.00
Whitbread	23.1	41.5	-18.40
Dudek	19.1	39.4	-20.30
Gerrard	4.9	4.3	0.60
Reina	29.5*	9.3	20.20

* Mistake % for all Liverpool goalkeepers combined in 2004/05

Table 21 details the changes in mistake percentage between 2004/05 and 2005/06. As can be seen, there was a mixture of improvements, declines and sustaining of the previous year's form. Neither Alonso nor Warnock are included in the list, as neither player committed an error that led to a goal in 2004/05.

In the case of Steve Finnan this is an occasion when an unbelievably good season in 2004/05 meant the only way was down. Finnan was seen to decline in mistake percentage this season, but after posting only one mistake in 4015 minutes last year, it would have been almost impossible for him to improve. The other point to remember in the case of Finnan is that he only played 3% of his time on the right of midfield this season, compared with 29% in 2004/05. Since mistakes leading to goals are far more likely to picked up by defenders than midfielders, given their proximity to their own goal (and less scope for others to bale them out), this has a large effect. Finnan remains an extremely solid defender, but as suggested by his incredible assist rate, he was pushing forward more often, which will always lead to being caught out of position.

Amazingly, Jamie Carragher was actually able to improve his mistake percentage to 5.2%, from just 7.1% a year earlier. It just goes to prove that Carragher is still improving in what is still a fairly new role to him, as he enters his prime playing years. For Sami Hyypia the slight decrease in performance is perhaps indicative of the big Finn being on the downside of his career. His percentage is still a very respectable 17.3%, and is under the 20% level that is expected of a top defender. Hyypia has always been prone to errors, and vulnerable to quick strikers, but more often than not makes up for it with incredible consistency; in 2005/06 he featured more than any other player, at a time in his career when he was expecting more rest periods. Despite mistakes, you know with Hyypia that you will get eight very good games out of every ten.

For John Arne Riise the slight decline is due in the most part to a similar change in playing time in midfield, as explained for Steve Finnan. Riise played 67% of his minutes at left-back this season, compared with only 39% a year ago, and the change can mostly be attributed to this. The fact that it was only a 3% change — from 3.9% last year to 6.9% this season — goes to show how reliable Riise was at left-back.

The biggest positive change was seen for Jose Reina when compared with the Liverpool goalkeepers of a year ago. Dudek, Carson and Kirkland combined committed 18 errors last year, at a mistake percentage of 29.5%. Reina improved on that by 20.20%, finishing with only five mistakes at a rate of 9.3%.

Table 22. Comparison of players IN against those OUT in terms of mistakes leading to goals and mistake percentage.

OUT 2004/05			IN 2005/06		
Player	Mistakes	%	Player	Mistakes	%
Pellegrino	6	54.0	Agger	1	25.0
Josemi	7	36.8	Kromkamp	1	14.9
Kirkland	9	64.3	Reina	5	9.33
Total	22	49.80	Total	7	10.6

When you look at the mistakes — and more importantly the mistake percentages — of the defenders who left the club in 2005, and those who joined in 2005/06, you can see the vast improvement made in this area (see Table 23). The change is startling.

Mauricio Pellegrino arrived in the January 2005 transfer window, and although he played extremely well in a couple of games, it was largely a baptism of fire. It usually takes time to settle into the Premiership, and had Pellegrino been a couple of years younger Benítez might have persevered for another season, to allow the Argentine time to adapt. But time wasn't on Pellegrino's side (and in one game it was reported that he was overtaken by a comatose snail). Josemi was another who never settled, struggling with the speed of the Premiership, having initially looked more than capable of being a success. Still, he got to dance on the podium in a Spanish flag in Istanbul, having featured en route to the Champions League final, so he can't have too many regrets.

Individual 'team' statistics: Goals-for average

Players' individual stats give one type of picture about how they performed, but what about the effect a player's presence has in the team? After all, he will not have been playing the opposition on his own, and it's pointless a player putting in good 'point scoring' performances if his inclusion in the side creates even greater problems.

As an example, while both Djibril Cissé and Steven Gerrard were very productive from a right-wing position this season — with the Frenchman actually just shading it in terms of goals and assists-per-90 minutes in the role — the Reds won significantly more games when the captain was stationed out there. The all-round abilities of Gerrard gave strength at both ends of the pitch, while Cissé was clearly good going forward but less interested in tracking back, which is part of the role in modern-day football.

To get a better handle on the impact that different players have on the overall team play, we developed the 'Individual Team' statistics. How does the inclusion of each player affect the team statistics, such as goals-for average, goals-against average, clean sheet percentage, points won, and the total 'goal-effect' of each player on the whole season? What you have to take into consideration with these statistics is that the more a player plays, the more he will approach the overall average of the team. It's logical: if a player played every minute, he'd obviously match the overall average. The beauty is that no player plays 100% of a season, so this is very unlikely to happen. The player who played the most minutes was Sami Hyypia, but even he sat out 436 minutes (almost five whole games). The best way to view these tables is to look at those players at either extreme. Who were the players in the squad whose inclusion boosted the team average, and who were the players that dragged it down? All figures have again been adjusted for the minutes played by each player and are, therefore, averages over 90 minutes of football.

The first one we will concentrate on is the goals-for average of the team for each individual player (see Table 23). The table is broken into two samples: one for the average from all the games played in 2005/06, and one from the Premiership campaign.

Table 23. The Team's goals-for average for each individual player overall and in the Premiership in 2005/06 (minimum 360 minutes)

Overall

Premiership

Player	Starts	Goals For average	Player	Starts	Goals For average
Agger	4	2.50	Agger	4	2.50
Potter	5	2.48	Zenden	5	1.80
Zenden	11	2.05	Kromkamp	6	1.79
Carson	4	2.00	Crouch	27	1.72
Kromkamp	7	1.88	Hamann	13	1.65
Cissé	29	1.82	Garcia	15	1.65
Gerrard	49	1.81	Kewell	22	1.61
Crouch	42	1.75	Gerrard	32	1.58
Kewell	30	1.70	Traore	9	1.56
Carragher	57	1.69	Morientes	20	1.53
Riise	42	1.68	Carragher	36	1.53
Reina	53	1.66	Reina	33	1.52
Hyypia	58	1.66	Warnock	15	1.51
Team	62	1.66	Finnan	33	1.50
Garcia	28	1.65	Team	38	1.50
Alonso	47	1.63	Hyypia	35	1.43
Finnan	51	1.60	Cissé	19	1.41
Morientes	33	1.56	Fowler	9	1.40
Sissoko	37	1.55	Dudek	5	1.38
Warnock	23	1.53	Riise	24	1.35
Pongolle	4	1.51	Sissoko	21	1.34
Josemi	9	1.51	Alonso	29	1.30
Traore	16	1.42			
Dudek	5	1.38			
Fowler	10	1.26			
Hamann	23	1.26			

What is interesting with these statistics is they reinforce ideas about which players are good in an attacking sense, but also bring out some other very revealing results. In the overall goals-for average for the whole season you can see names like Djibril Cissé, Steven Gerrard and Harry Kewell above the team's average, which is what you might expect. But you also see Jamie Carragher. In fact Carragher is above-average in both the overall and Premiership table. Peter Crouch is another who is well above average in both tables. He has the third highest goals-for average overall, and the highest goals-for average in the Premiership for regular players (those who made over 10 starts). When he plays, the Reds score more regularly.

As you'd expect, the inclusion of more defensive midfielders tends to pull the average down. It appears that when they play the games are much tighter, with less goals scored by either team. Xabi Alonso and Momo Sissoko both finish below the team's overall and Premiership goals-for average. The last point to make about this set of figures is where Fernando Morientes sits on both charts. In his Premiership appearances the team finished with average figures; however, overall on the year the team's goals-for average was below average, indicating the team scored less often when the Spaniard was in the team. This was also the case for Robbie Fowler, but his average was hampered by a small sample size, and by joining the team at a time when it couldn't even locate the farm, let alone hit the proverbial barn door.

The interesting correlation here is that Liverpool won an above-average number of points when either Fowler and Morientes was playing; the Reds keeping it extremely tight at the back when they lined-up, and scoring precious few goals in the process. These were often the games won by a solitary goal.

Individual team statistics: Goals-against average

Table 24. The Team's goals-against average for each individual player overall and in the Premiership in 2005/06 (minimum 360 minutes)

Overall

Player	Starts	Goals Against average
Zenden	11	0.25
Morientes	33	0.52
Fowler	10	0.52
Riise	42	0.58
Reina	53	0.63
Sissoko	37	0.63
Finnan	51	0.65
Hyypia	58	0.67
Hamann	23	0.69
Team	62	0.70
Carragher	57	0.70
Garcia	28	0.70
Gerrard	49	0.72
Warnock	23	0.74
Agger	4	0.75
Alonso	47	0.77
Cissé	29	0.78
Dudek	5	0.79
Kromkamp	7	0.82
Kewell	30	0.82
Pongolle	4	0.84
Crouch	42	0.87
Josemi	9	0.87
Potter	5	0.90
Traore	16	0.90
Carson	4	1.50

Premiership

Player	Starts	Goals Against average
Zenden	5	0.00
Morientes	20	0.44
Fowler	9	0.47
Riise	24	0.48
Finnan	33	0.58
Gerrard	32	0.59
Sissoko	21	0.60
Warnock	15	0.62
Cissé	19	0.63
Reina	33	0.64
Hyypia	35	0.64
Team	38	0.66
Carragher	36	0.67
Alonso	29	0.67
Kewell	22	0.67
Agger	4	0.75
Dudek	5	0.79
Garcia	15	0.80
Crouch	27	0.84
Hamann	13	0.86
Kromkamp	6	0.90
Traore	9	1.23

While admittedly a small sample size, Bolo Zenden's team stats are fantastic in the 11 starts overall, and even better in the five Premiership matches he started (see Table 25). His team goals-for averages were near the top, but his team goals-against averages are superb. His overall figures might be artificially high due to a number of starts in early qualifying rounds, but his Premiership ones — the real litmus test of a player's quality — speak for themselves. Zenden never did see the ball enter his own net in his 451 minutes of Premiership action in 2005/06, finishing the year with a zero goals-against average. Meanwhile, Fernando Morientes might have had a disappointing team goals-for average, but he did have the best team goals-against average in the squad. His work on the pitch, both with and without the ball, clearly contributed to the improvement seen this season, but it still wasn't enough to convince Rafa Benítez, who felt the former Real Madrid player hadn't lived up to his expectations.

The no.1 defender in the list was John Arne Riise. The Norwegian had an overall team average of 0.58, which was 0.12 better than the team mean, and an average of 0.48 in the Premiership appearances, an 0.18 improvement in the team mean in the league. Combine these figures with Riise's low mistake numbers (and percentage) and everything indicates it was a very successful season at the back for the Reds' no.6. Other players above the team average on both tables include Jose Reina, Steve Finnan, Momo Sissoko, Sami Hyypia, Jamie Carragher and Steven Gerrard. Peter Crouch comes out below average for both tables, and adds further evidence as to why he was often substituted late in games. On the below-average side, Josemi and Traoré were the two defenders with the worst figures. In the case of Traoré he had the second worst team goals-against average overall, and the worst in the Premiership, where the team averaged 1.23 goals-against per-game in his appearances in the competition, some 0.57 goals-per-game below the team mean.

Individual team statistics: Clean sheet percentage

Table 25. The Team's clean sheet percentage for each individual player overall and in the Premiership in 2005/06 (minimum 360 minutes)

Overall

Player	Starts	Clean sheet %
Zenden	11	66.2
Riise	42	59.4
Finnan	51	59.0
Reina	53	56.0
Gerrard	49	55.9
Garcia	28	54.3
Hyypia	58	54.1
Crouch	42	53.8
Sissoko	37	53.7
Carragher	57	53.4
Alonso	47	53.2
Morientes	33	52.8
Team	62	52.7
Cissé	29	52.6
Fowler	10	51.1
Hamann	23	50.8
Potter	5	50.5
Warnock	23	46.9
Kewell	30	44.2
Traore	16	43.0
Dudek	5	39.4
Josemi	9	31.5
Kromkamp	7	30.6
Pongolle	4	30.5
Agger	4	25.0
Carson	4	25.0

Premiership

Player	Starts	Clean sheet %
Zenden	5	84.9
Riise	24	68.1
Morientes	20	65.0
Finnan	33	64.1
Garcia	15	62.3
Cissé	19	61.5
Alonso	29	61.4
Gerrard	32	61.2
Reina	33	60.8
Hyypia	35	59.7
Carragher	36	58.3
Team	38	57.9
Sissoko	21	57.4
Warnock	15	57.3
Fowler	9	56.8
Crouch	27	54.7
Kewell	22	50.0
Hamann	13	43.9
Dudek	5	39.4
Kromkamp	6	37.5
Traore	9	27.0
Agger	4	25.0

Riise again stands out here, posting team clean sheet percentages of 59.4% and 68.1% overall and in the Premiership respectively. Also excelling is Steve Finnan, who had comparable figures to Riise of 59.0% and 64.1% in the two splits. Fernando Morientes also had above average figure in both categories, adding further weight to the notion that even though he struggled in front of goal he helped the team defensively by frequently dropping into midfield positions.

Another player with above average results in both splits was Luis Garcia, with an overall figure of 54.3%, and a Premiership figure of 62.3%. This appears strange, as he is a player seen by many as a 'luxury', who offers extravagant skills going forward — often resulting in lost possession — and nothing at the other end of the pitch. However, tracking back and getting stuck-in were bigger parts of his game in his second season in England, even if he was never going to shoulder-charge Alan Shearer or Jason Roberts off the ball. Even so, his figures are still surprising. Upon investigating this in more detail, Garcia played a large majority of his minutes during Liverpool's long clean sheet streak through November and December. Did he contribute significantly to this record with hard work, or was the sky-high confidence of the team able to compensate on those 'loose flicks' days? In all likelihood it was a bit of both.

Individual team statistics: points won

Table 26. The Team's average points won for each individual player overall and in the Premiership in 2005/06 (minimum 360 minutes)

Overall

Player	Starts	Pts per game
Agger	4	2.50
Zenden	11	2.39
Kromkamp	7	2.38
Dudek	5	2.36
Fowler	10	2.26
Riise	42	2.26
Cissé	29	2.23
Sissoko	37	2.17
Alonso	47	2.15
Carragher	57	2.14
Morientes	33	2.13
Reina	53	2.11
Hyypia	58	2.11
Team	62	2.09
Finnan	51	2.08
Gerrard	49	2.07
Josemi	9	2.03
Garcia	28	2.01
Kewell	30	1.98
Crouch	42	1.98
Potter	5	1.98
Warnock	23	1.93
Hamann	23	1.82
Traore	16	1.74
Pongolle	4	1.67
Carson	4	1.50

Premiership

Player	Starts	Pts per game
Fowler	9	2.51
Agger	4	2.50
Morientes	20	2.47
Kromkamp	6	2.41
Dudek	5	2.36
Zenden	5	2.30
Riise	24	2.25
Cissé	19	2.24
Finnan	33	2.23
Sissoko	21	2.20
Carragher	36	2.17
Team	38	2.16
Gerrard	32	2.16
Kewell	22	2.15
Hyypia	35	2.14
Reina	33	2.13
Alonso	29	2.11
Warnock	15	2.08
Garcia	15	2.07
Hamann	13	2.02
Crouch	27	1.99
Traore	9	1.65

All that defensive work Fernando Morientes put in was not in vain, as the team won above-average points with him in the line-up overall; while in the Premiership the Reds averaged 2.47 points per-game when he featured, 0.31 per-game higher than the team mean.

Other players whose presence resulted in above-average points hauls were John Arne Riise, Robbie Fowler, Djibril Cissé, Momo Sissoko, Xabi Alonso, Jamie Carragher and Sami Hyypia. Steven Gerrard was around the team average overall, as was Jose Reina. Players who didn't fare as well were Djimi Traoré, Didi Hamann and Peter Crouch. The tall forward was fantastic in attacking production — individually and for the team — but defensively the team figures were not so good, meaning that Crouch finished below the team's average on points won overall as well as in Premiership appearances.

Individual team statistics: Total goal-effect in the season

Table 27. The total goal-effect in the team of each individual player overall and in the Premiership in 2005/06 (minimum 360 minutes)

Overall

Player	Starts	Goals against	Goals for	Total goal effect
Zenden	11	5.5	4.7	10.2
Gerrard	49	-0.9	7.1	6.1
Riise	42	5.2	0.9	6.1
Reina	53	3.8	0.0	3.8
Agger	4	-0.2	3.4	3.2
Morientes	33	5.9	-3.3	2.6
Cissé	29	-2.6	5.1	2.6
Hyypia	58	1.7	0.0	1.7
Carragher	57	0.0	1.7	1.7
Kromkamp	7	-1.0	1.9	0.9
Garcia	28	0.0	-0.3	-0.3
Finnan	51	2.5	-3.0	-0.5
Sissoko	37	2.7	-4.2	-1.5
Pongolle	4	-0.8	-0.9	-1.7
Carson	4	-3.2	1.4	-1.8
Dudek	5	-0.5	-1.4	-1.9
Fowler	10	1.7	-3.8	-2.1
Kewell	30	-3.7	1.2	-2.4
Crouch	42	-6.2	3.3	-2.9
Josemi	9	-1.6	-1.4	-3.0
Warnock	23	-0.9	-2.8	-3.7
Alonso	47	-3.2	-1.4	-4.5
Traore	16	-3.1	-3.7	-6.8
Hamann	23	0.2	-9.9	-9.6

Premiership

Player	Starts	Goals against	Goals for	Total goal effect
Morientes	20	4.5	0.6	5.1
Zenden	5	3.3	1.5	4.8
Gerrard	32	2.1	2.4	4.5
Agger	4	-0.4	4.0	3.6
Finnan	33	2.6	0.0	2.6
Kewell	22	-0.2	2.5	2.2
Reina	33	0.7	0.7	1.3
Crouch	27	-4.3	5.2	1.0
Fowler	9	1.6	-0.9	0.8
Riise	24	4.5	-3.8	0.8
Warnock	15	0.6	0.1	0.7
Carragher	36	-0.4	1.1	0.7
Kromkamp	6	-1.6	1.9	0.3
Garcia	15	-2.5	2.6	0.2
Hamann	13	-2.5	1.9	-0.6
Cissé	19	0.6	-1.7	-1.1
Dudek	5	-0.7	-0.6	-1.3
Hyypia	35	0.7	-2.4	-1.7
Sissoko	21	1.3	-3.5	-2.2
Traore	9	-5.1	0.5	-4.6
Alonso	29	-0.3	-5.7	-6.0

The total goal-effect of each player (Table 27) takes into consideration the team's goals-for and goals-against averages. It compares them with the team's average, and then adjusts them according to how many minutes each player played, to give the total goals a player added or took away from the team when he appeared over the whole season.

To give an example, if Player X has a goals-for rating of -5 having played ten games, that means that in those ten games the Reds scored five goals fewer than would be expected. As the average goals-per-game was 1.66, in a ten game spell the Reds' would have amassed 16.6 goals at the season's scoring rate. With a rating of -5, Player X's presence in the team resulted in just 11.6 Liverpool goals. So his presence on the pitch had a detrimental effect on the goals-for column. A goals-for rating of +5 adds five to that total.

A goals-against rating of +5 for Player X, however, would mean that in the games he played the Reds conceded five fewer goals. As the Reds' goals-against average was 0.7 per-game, a ten game run would normally result in seven goals conceded; with a rating of +5, Player X's involvement on the pitch would have coincided with just two goals conceded.

So looking at the figures of Bolo Zenden, who tops the table, you can see that in all his playing time the Reds scored 4.7 goals more than the average over 62 games. Zenden started 11 games and featured in six more, making a total of 1095 minutes in a red shirt. Therefore, in those 1095 minutes (which works out at fractionally over 12 full games), rather than score approximately 20 goals, the Reds scored closer to 25. The same applies to his impact on the Reds' defence. During a 1095-minute portion of the season, the Reds could have been expected to concede 8.4 goals. Instead, his presence coincided in the conceding of just three goals. Therefore the swing in Liverpool's goal difference in Zenden's time would be approximately +10, with almost five goals added to the goals-for column and just over five taken away from the conceded column. Much of this may have been coincidental, due to the quality of the opposition or the form of other players in the team — after all, a midfielder could have a stinker, but if his striker scores four goals from four half-chances, everyone will share in the credit. The goal-differential of +10 coincides with Zenden's time on the pitch, but he isn't the one making all the saves and scoring all the goals. Despite that, it's an interesting indication all the same.

The more minutes a player plays, the closer he will be to the average. But by the same token, anyone who has played 30-50 games and is significantly above the average can either be looked upon as the luckiest of lucky tokens, or someone who really does influence proceedings.

Both the overall and Premiership table show how valuable Steven Gerrard is to the team. In the season overall, when Gerrard played his attacking skills were worth seven additional goals to the team, and whilst his defensive skills coincided with the conceding of an extra goal, his total goal-effect in the team was worth six extra goals to the Reds. In the Premiership he actually improved upon the team's defensive average by two goals, which placed him just behind Riise, Morientes, Zenden and Finnan.

While double-positive effects in both goals-for and goals-against show that a player adds goals to his team while denying them to the opposition, double - negatives in both show that the player takes goals away from Liverpool and adds them to the other team (Traoré -3.1 goals against, -3.7 goals for). The total goals effect of the Liverpool forwards makes interesting reading because both Cissé and Crouch had a positive effect in the team's scoring in the season — 5.1 and 3.3 goals respectively — but had a combined effect of adding 8.8 goals to what the team conceded. Morientes was completely the other way around, improving the defence by a total of 5.9 goals in the season, but taking away 3.3 goals from the attack. Xabi Alonso doesn't come out well in this category, which is somewhat surprising. Overall the team conceded three goals more than average and scored one goal less than average in games in which he played, for a total goal-effect of -4.5 goals. However, Alonso tended to be saved for the tougher games, while being rested in the more routine encounters.

Didi Hamann was another who didn't do too well here, and it's hard to say why two 'holding' midfielders suffer by comparison; logically they should be in the middle of the table, helping the team to concede less but also not getting forward to influence attacks — and that's certainly true of the German. His defensive skills were actually a 0.2 goals improvement on the average, but the team scored an incredible total of almost 10 goals below average in games in which he played. This made Hamann a very valuable defensive player, but apparently at a great cost to the attacking production of the team.

Chapter Six
Player-by-Player tables

Goalkeepers

Scott Carson No.20									Age: 19	Height: 6'3"				Goalkeeper	
Season	Individual											Team			
YEAR COMP	GS	MINS	ASSISTS	POINTS	ASSIST (90)	POINTS (90)	GA	SAVES	SAVE%	MLG	MLG % (90	CS	CS %	GFA	GAA PTS
2005-06 Total	4	360	0	0	0	0	6	13	68.4	0	0	1	25	2.00	1.50 1.50
2005-06 Euro	2	180	0	0	0	0	1	7	87.5	0	0	1	50	1.00	0.50 1.50
2005-06 Cups	2	180	0	0	0	0	5	6	54.5	0	0	0	0	3.00	2.50 1.50
2005-06 Total	9	810	With Sheff Weds				5	44	89.8	-	-	5	55.5	1.33	0.56 2.00
2004-05 Total	5	450	0	0	0	0	4	20	83.3	1	20.00	1	20	1.00	0.80 1.80
2004-05 Prem	4	360	0	0	0	0	3	15	83.3	0	0	1	25	0.75	0.75 1.50

Scott Carson's Liverpool career began in 2004/05, after he joined from Leeds in the January transfer window. He lost on his debut, 1-0 away to Newcastle, but had a steady game. His biggest test was against Juventus in the Champions League, where he pulled off some excellent saves, but also let the softest of headers elude his grasp.

Carson posted an extremely impressive 83.3% save percentage in his five total starts in 2004/05, and exactly the same figure in his four Premiership outings that season. In 2005/06 Carson was only given four starts in total in the Liverpool goal — none in the Premiership — where he recorded two wins and two defeats and picked up one clean sheet. Carson's save percentage in his two Champions League qualifiers, the Carling cup loss at Crystal Palace and the FA Cup win over Luton was only 66.6%, although he was left exposed to a greater percentage of 'unsaveable' shots in those latter two games, while having precious few saves to make in the former two.

After joining Sheffield Wednesday on loan in the January transfer window the young England keeper recorded a sizzling 89.8% save percentage, and picked up four clean sheets in his eight starts with the Championship side, who, understandably, wanted Carson to return for 2006/07. Their hopes were dashed when he signed a new five-year deal at Liverpool, just months after attending the World Cup with England as a late replacement in the third-choice goalkeeping role. His potential remains immense, but he is competing with Pepe Reina, who is vastly more experienced and only three years older. In August Carson joined Charlton on loan for the season, where he'll hopefully gain the first-team top-level experience he needs.

Jerzy Dudek No.1										Age: 32 Height: 6'2"						Goalkeeper
Misc	Individual											Team				
YEAR	COMP	GS	MINS	ASSISTS	POINTS	ASSIST (90)	POINTS (90)	GA	SAVES	SAVE%	MLG	MLG % (90)	CS	CS %	GFA	GAA	PTS
2005-06 Total	5	457	0	0	0	0	4	20	83.3	2	39.39		2	39.4	1.38	0.79	2.36
2005-06 Prem	5	457	0	0	0	0	4	20	83.3	2	39.39		2	39.4	1.38	0.79	2.36
2004-05 Total	41	3780	0	0	0	0	37	162	81.4	8	19.05		14	33.3	1.40	0.88	1.64
2004-05 Prem	24	2160	0	0	0	0	25	96	79.3	5	20.83		5	20.8	1.46	1.04	1.58

Fresh from his Istanbul heroics, Jerzy Dudek's luck over the following 12 months could not have contrasted more starkly. First, Jose Reina arrived from Villarreal in the summer, and became the clear first choice custodian. Shortly after, with a move away from Anfield looking a certainty, Dudek broke his elbow in training. Just five starts would follow in 2005/06 for the Pole, all in the final third of the season. He would also suffer the burglary of all his medals (later recovered), and was bizarrely omitted from Poland's World Cup squad, having been his country's undisputed No.1 for several years. It was a season to forget, although nothing can take away the memories of May 25th, and the place he secured in the club's history.

His first action of 2005/06 was to replace Jose Reina after the Spaniard 'struck' Arjen Robben at Stamford Bridge. Dudek came on as a sub with the score at 2-0, and with just ten minutes left. He finally made his first start of the season — a Premiership away game against Charlton on 8th February — but gave away a penalty and let another goal through his legs as Liverpool suffered a 2-0 loss. He managed to settle after that, however, and picked up two wins (against Wigan and Arsenal) with clean sheets before Jose Reina returned from suspension. Another start in a midweek fixture against West Ham and another in the last Premiership game of the season away at Portsmouth took Dudek's appearances to six for the season — recording an improved 83.3% save percentage compared with a figure of 79.3% a year ago, but from a far lower sample.

Chris Kirkland No. n/a										Age: 24 Height: 6'5"						Goalkeeper
Misc	Individual											Team				
YEAR	COMP	GS	MINS	ASSISTS	POINTS	ASSIST (90)	POINTS (90)	GA	SAVES	SAVE%	MLG	MLG % (90)	CS	CS %	GFA	GAA	PTS
2005-06 Total	12	1080	With West Brom					22	55	71.4	-	-		1	8.3	1.00	1.83	0.75
2004-05 Total	14	1260	1	1	0.07	0.07	15	37	71.1	9	64.29		3	21.4	1.29	1.07	1.50
2004-05 Prem	10	900	1	1	0.07	0.07	13	27	67.5	8	80.00		1	10	1.40	1.30	1.40

Chris Kirkland was another Liverpool keeper to have a miserable year. After a horror-show season in the Liverpool goal in 2004/05 — with nine mistakes leading to goals in only 1260 minutes, as he battled to overcome a chronic back problem — the former England U21 keeper was loaned out for the year to West Brom. After starting well at the Hawthorns and even earning a recall into the England squad, Kirkland was hit by another injury in October, forcing him out till December, and he had to wait till January to start another game. In March the injury jinx struck again, ending the big keeper's season with only 12 starts, and a save percentage of just 71.4% at The Hawthorns.

Kirkland has tremendous talent — a superb shot-stopper — but he just can't stay fit. With a maximum of only 15 starts in any year for the last five seasons, installing Kirkland as first choice remains a risk for any manager, but at only 25 years of age (when 2006/07 starts), time is still on his side. Any fresh injuries, however, and the doubts will only grow. Wigan's Paul Jewell felt it was a risk worth taking, and Kirkland joined the Latics on loan in the summer of 2006, with a view to a permanent move, and was instantly called up to Steve McLaren's first England squad. Before he played a competitive game for Wigan he finally got his first England cap, which won his father and some friends £10,000 from a bet, but cost Liverpool £250,000 as part of the original deal that took him from Coventry. However, should he eventually be sold to Wigan, as could well be the case, his new-found status as a full international can help recoup that money.

As well as the injuries, another reason Kirkland will probably be sold is his slowness off his line; with the Reds defending such a high line the keeper to act as the sweeper. Not only is Pepe Reina far swifter out of his area when needed, he is also far better at distributing the ball.

Jose Reina No.25							Age: 22	Height: 6'2"					Goalkeeper		
Misc		Individual										Team			
YEAR	COMP	GS	MINS	ASSISTS	POINTS	ASSIST (90)	POINTS (90)	GA	SAVES	SAVE%	MLG	MLG % (90	CS	CS %	GFA	GAA PTS
2005-06 Total		53	4823	4	4	0.07	0.07	34	210	86.1	5	9.33	30	56	1.66	0.63 2.11
2005-06 Prem		33	2963	3	3	0.09	0.09	21	141	87.0	3	9.11	20	60.8	1.52	0.64 2.13
2005-06 Euro		13	1200	1	1	0.08	0.08	7	28	80.0	0	0.00	7	52.5	1.58	0.53 2.03
2005-06 Cups		7	660	0	0	0.00	0.00	6	41	87.2	2	27.27	3	40.9	2.45	0.82 2.18
2004-05 Total		-	-	-	-	-	-	-	-	-	-	-	-	-	-	-
2004-05 Prem		-	-	-	-	-	-	-	-	-	-	-	-	-	-	-

Sky TV's Andy Gray, amongst others, commented that any goalkeeper could play behind Liverpool's defence, they were that reliable. This was poor analysis; a team's defensive record is never a product of just the defence, goalkeeper or midfield — it is a combination of all areas of the team. Liverpool's defensive improvement has been substantial this season, and Reina clearly played a crucial role. He was not merely the beneficiary of others' efforts. The synergy between a goalkeeper and a back four is something all teams look to build. The increased confidence in the Liverpool defence was directly related to the confidence held in their goalkeeper's ability. Statistics such as clean sheets, goals-against average and even mistakes made by goalkeepers can be influenced by outfield players, so when comparing goalkeepers, the best stat to look at is the one thing goalkeepers are clearly responsible for — stopping the ball from entering the net.

The table below, Table 1, gives the top 15 save percentages of Premiership goalkeepers in 2005/06 Premiership games. As you can see Reina actually came second in the league in this statistic — only bettered by Chelsea's Petr

Cech by a fraction of one percent.

Table 1. Top 15 Save percentages of Premiership goalkeepers in 2005/06

Rank	Player	Team	Age	Starts	Ten+ Saves	Save %
1	Cech	Chelsea	23	34	0	87.42
2	Reina	Liverpool	23	33	2	87.04
3	Niemi	Fulham	33	10	2	85.25
4	Van der Sar	Man United	35	38	0	84.65
5	Myhre	Charlton	32	20	3	84.56
6	Filan	Wigan	36	15	1	84.52
7	Lehmann	Arsenal	36	38	2	84.50
8	Sorensen	Aston Villa	29	36	6	82.47
9	Taylor	Birmingham	34	34	5	82.11
10	Crossley	Fulham	36	13	0	80.72
11	Friedel	Blackburn	35	38	2	80.37
12	Kuszczuk	West Brom	24	28	3	80.30
13	Given	Newcastle	30	38	4	80.09
14	Robinson	Tottenham	26	38	3	80.00
15	James	Man City	36	38	3	79.75

Other goalkeepers might have saved more total shots — because they had more to save — or had higher 'double figure' save games, but Jose Reina was second in the league by saving 87.04% of goalscoring chances that came his way. Analysing the numbers further reveals that even with the protection of the Liverpool defence, the Liverpool keeper had to save more chances than Petr Cech, while the Spanish international also had more 'double figure' save games, when Liverpool's defence had an off-day.

Table 2. Reina vs Cech

	GS	Mins	GAA	GFA	Save %	Clean Sheets	CS %
Reina	33	2963	0.64	1.52	87.04	20	60.6
Cech	34	3015	0.60	1.94	87.42	18	52.9

Looking further at the seasons the two young goalkeepers had (see Table 2) it is amazing how comparable the two were. Both played roughly 3000 minutes in the Premiership, posted goals-against averages of 0.6 goals-per-game, and had 87% save percentages. Both keepers were born in the same year and had their 23rd birthdays during the season, which is amazing when you consider that the average age of the other 13 goalies in Table 1 is actually 32.4 years, almost a full decade older.

The only differences between the two were that Reina kept 20 clean sheets compared with Cech's 18, thus meaning the Spaniard won the Premiership's golden gloves award in his first season, and that Cech's team were able to score more goals for him (1.94 per-game, compared with Liverpool's 1.52 per-game) when he was between the sticks.

This shows where the gap between Liverpool and Chelsea still exists. With Reina equalling Cech's performance in goal and the Liverpool defensive work having improved to a point where it is on a par with Chelsea's (25 goals to Chelsea's 22, and 20 clean sheets to the Blues' 18), it is the gulf of goals scored that still separates the two teams. Chelsea scored 72 goals in the 2005/06 Premiership campaign, whilst the Reds scored only 57.

The purchase of Reina was a definite factor in Liverpool closing the gap on Chelsea, and will be major factor in any future challenges as well. The improved goalkeeping Reina has provided the club is not only visible in the greater number of clean sheets but also in the reduction in goals conceded. Liverpool's goalkeepers of a year ago posted a combined save percentage of 77.1% in the Premiership, a good 10% below Reina's 87% this season. This means that during the course of the Premiership campaign Jose Reina prevented 16 goals with the improved save percentage, when compared with the save percentage posted by Liverpool's trio of goalkeepers a year earlier.

When you consider the findings in the clean sheets piece in the Team Statistics section — that a goal conceded produces a point less per-game than a clean sheet — Reina was almost certainly responsible for increasing Liverpool's Premiership points tally by 16 points. Liverpool were able to cut the gap between themselves and Chelsea in the Premiership from 37 points to nine this season — a total swing of 28 points in the Reds' favour. It could therefore be surmised that Jose Reina was responsible for 57% of the Premiership turnaround.

Defenders

Daniel Agger No.5										Age: 21	Height: 6'3"			Centre-Back	
Misc		Individual										Team			
YEAR	COMP	GS	MINS	GOALS	ASSISTS	POINTS	GOALS (90)	ASSISTS (90)	POINTS (90)	MLG	MLG % (90)	CS	CS %	GFA	GAA	PTS
2005-06 Total		4	360	0	0	0	0.00	0.00	0.00	1	25.00	1	25	2.50	0.75	2.50
2005-06 Prem		4	360	0	0	0	0.00	0.00	0.00	1	25.00	1	25	2.50	0.75	2.50
2004-05 Total		-	-	-	-	-	-	-	-	-	-	-	-	-	-	-
2004-05 Prem		-	-	-	-	-	-	-	-	-	-	-	-	-	-	-

After a longstanding association with Carlsberg, Denmark's most famous export, the Reds added the Scandinavian country's most expensive footballing export: Daniel Agger, bought for £5.8m in January 2006. In his four starts after joining the Reds from Brondby the young Danish centre-back displayed impressive composure, a good positional sense, able athleticism and an expansive passing range.

It was, however, a rare off-pass that led to his only mistake. A loose cross-field ball against Fulham was intercepted and resulted in Collins John equalising at Anfield. That blip aside, Agger's short passing was crisp and his long passing accurate. But what was especially apparent was the confidence in his own ability, which is very rare for a 21-year-old centre-back. Agger, who was touted by a Danish magazine as the country's No.1 prospect in all sports, oozed composure and assurance, and was not shy in bringing the ball out of defence. Indeed, he led the break for Liverpool's second goal against Newcastle at St James' Park, when he played on the left side of a middle three. If he can overcome some niggling injuries he should feature more heavily in 2006/07, but as with fellow new-boy Gabriel Paletta, his first *full* season at Anfield will be more about navigating a steep learning curve.

Antonio Barragan No.36						Age: 18 Height: 6'1"								Right-Back	
Misc	Individual										Team				
YEAR COMP	GS	MINS	GOALS	ASSISTS	POINTS	GOALS (90)	ASSISTS (90)	POINTS (90)	MLG	MLG % (90)	CS	CS %	GFA	GAA	PTS
2005-06 Total	0	11	0	0	0	0.00	0.00	0.00	0	0.00	0	0	0.00	0	3.00
2004-05 Total	-	-	-	-	-	-	-	-	-	-	-	-	-	-	-
2004-05 Prem	-	-	-	-	-	-	-	-	-	-	-	-	-	-	-

Antonio Barragan played just 11 minutes during the season, making his Liverpool debut as a replacement for Fernando Morientes in the Reds 3-1 win away at CSKA Sofia in the Champions League 3rd qualifying round. He was also an unused sub in the home tie of that fixture, and was on the bench for the home leg of the Benfica tie, but never again saw first team action in 2005/06. In his 21 starts in the reserves this season the 18-year-old managed three goals, at a good rate of 0.15 per-90 minutes; on a par with John Arne Riise in the senior team in 2004/05.

Signed on a free transfer from Sevilla in July 2005, the skilful teenage full-back, who starred in his country's youth success in July 2006, would not add to those 11 minutes: a surprising £0.7m move to Deportivo La Coruna followed a year later, representing a tidy profit, but costing the Reds a very promising player. However, the good news is that the deal includes a special buy-back clause that means Barragan could return to the club in 2008, when he is 20, meaning his departure could be no more than a two-year loan, in which he can grow as a player and still return as a promising kid.

Jamie Carragher No.23						Age: 27 Height: 6'1"								Centre-Back	
Misc	Individual										Team				
YEAR COMP	GS	MINS	GOALS	ASSISTS	POINTS	GOALS (90)	ASSISTS (90)	POINTS (90)	MLG	MLG % (90)	CS	CS %	GFA	GAA	PTS
2005-06 Total	57	5153	1	6	7	0.02	0.10	0.12	3	5.24	31	53.4	1.69	0.70	2.14
2005-06 Prem	36	3240	0	4	4	0.00	0.11	0.11	0	0.00	21	58.3	1.53	0.67	2.17
2005-06 Euro	13	1163	1	1	2	0.08	0.08	0.15	1	7.74	6.6	51.0	1.47	0.54	1.99
2005-06 Cups	8	750	0	1	1	0.00	0.12	0.12	2	24.00	3	36	2.76	1.08	2.28
2004-05 Total	56	5080	0	4	4	0	0.07	0.07	4	7.09	16	28.3	1.35	0.94	1.62
2004-05 Prem	38	3420	0	3	3	0	0.08	0.08	4	10.53	7	18.4	1.37	1.08	1.53

In this age of fans demanding instant success Jamie Carragher remains a prime example of good things coming to those who wait. Under Gérard Houllier, Carragher became a regular and very consistent full-back but ask many fans back then and an up-grade could have been sought. Ask those same fans now and, with perhaps the exception of John Terry at Chelsea, they would not swap the Bootle boy for anyone in Europe, let alone England. Many people felt it would be hard for Carragher to improve on last year's amazing form. However, he once again defied the odds by posting even better numbers across the board. He managed to not only to score a goal this season — the most amazing statistical freak if ever there was one — but significantly increased his assist rate, almost doubling his total attacking production of a year ago.

His overall 'mistakes' rating was also down on a year ago — only committing three goal-costing errors this year, compared with four in the last campaign. His overall team average of 2.14 points per-game was 3rd amongst Liverpool defenders, being bettered by only Jan Kromkamp (in his small sample), and John Arne Riise.

Adding more goals would be the only logical plus from here, especially if comparing him with John Terry, but it's virtually impossible to find fault with the Liverpool vice-captain's performances over the past 24 months. He is consistency personified.

Steve Finnan No.3							Age: 29	Height: 6'0"					Right-Back	
Misc	Individual									Team				
YEAR COMP	GS	MINS	GOALS	ASSISTS	POINTS	GOALS (90)	ASSISTS (90)	POINTS (90)	MLG	MLG % (90)	CS	CS %	GFA	GAA	PTS
2005-06 Total	51	4556	0	17	17	0.00	0.34	0.34	6	11.85	30	59	1.60	0.65	2.08
2005-06 Prem	33	2931	0	9	9	0.00	0.28	0.28	4	12.28	21	64.1	1.50	0.58	2.23
2005-06 Euro	12	1045	0	1	1	0.00	0.09	0.09	2	17.22	7	60.3	1.21	0.52	1.67
2005-06 Cups	6	580	0	7	7	0.00	1.09	1.09	0	0.00	2	31	2.79	1.24	2.07
2004-05 Total	45	4015	1	4	5	0.02	0.09	0.11	1	2.24	15	33.3	1.46	0.92	1.80
2004-05 Prem	29	2546	1	4	5	0.04	0.14	0.18	0	0.00	6.1	21.6	1.48	1.06	1.65

Steve Finnan was arguably the best right-back in the Premiership in 2005/06. The massive improvements he made in his defensive game during the 2004/05 campaign were augmented the improvements in his attacking play this year, as evidenced by the increase in his assists — from a total of just one in 04/05 to 17 in 05/06. Finnan's style of attacking is not as eye-catching as someone like Ashley Cole's, who can go past people with pace, but his crossing is good and he supports the play intelligently.

Finnan's mistakes leading to opponents' goals were up, but this was mostly due to playing almost all his minutes at right-back this year (96.8%), compared with 70.8% a year ago. His Premiership team splits were excellent, recording a clean sheet in 64% of his games and accumulating the 3rd-highest points average in the team, at 2.23 per-league game. All in all the stats back up what most people agree upon: that the Irishman has improved massively since Rafa Benítez arrived, and has become an integral part of the Reds' defence.

Sami Hyypia No.4							Age: 31	Height: 6'4"					Centre-Back	
Misc	Individual									Team				
YEAR COMP	GS	MINS	GOALS	ASSISTS	POINTS	GOALS (90)	ASSISTS (90)	POINTS (90)	MLG	MLG % (90)	CS	CS %	GFA	GAA	PTS
2005-06 Total	58	5204	2	6	8	0.03	0.10	0.14	10	17.29	31	54.1	1.66	0.67	2.11
2005-06 Prem	35	3092	1	5	6	0.03	0.15	0.17	5	14.55	21	59.7	1.43	0.64	2.14
2005-06 Euro	14	1290	0	1	1	0.00	0.07	0.07	3	20.93	8	55.8	1.60	0.42	2.09
2005-06 Cups	9	822	1	0	1	0.11	0.00	0.11	2	21.90	2.8	30.7	2.63	1.20	2.01
2004-05 Total	49	4371	3	1	4	0.06	0.02	0.08	7	14.41	12	24.7	1.40	1.03	1.54
2004-05 Prem	32	2781	2	1	3	0.06	0.03	0.10	5	16.18	5	16.2	1.49	1.17	1.52

Almost certainly Gérard Houllier's best buy, and one of the best buys by any manager in the Premiership years, Sami Hyypia ended Rafa Benítez's second season as the Reds' most-used player. With no pace to lose, Hyypia's ageing limbs won't rid him of what some defenders rely on to do their job. The big Finn has always used his brain to cut out danger before it develops, rather than look to beat strikers in a foot race.

With an obvious lack of pace, many teams try to tempt Hyypia out wide and beat him down the wings. In Liverpool's 4-1 hammering by Chelsea in early October, Chelsea players continually played long diagonal balls to Didier Drogba in an attempt to pull Hyypia out of the centre, where Drogba could use his pace to beat the Finnish international. The tactic worked. On two occasions Drogba was able to get the better of Hyypia in terms of pace when setting up a pair of the Londoners' goals on the day (although in the Finn's defence, he was suffering with a stomach bug). The first, from a throw down the Liverpool left, saw Drogba flying past Hyypia, and ended with the Chelsea forward being hacked down by Djimi Traoré after a poor failed clearance. The second occurred down the Liverpool right, when the Chelsea forward span Hyypia with an uncharacteristically smart backheel, and found Damien Duff who gave the Blues back the lead.

This was not the only game where this tactic worked for the opposition. Kaunas' Arturas Rimkevicius was also able to speed past Hyypia down the team's left-hand side, and deliver a low front-post cross from which Barevicius scored the first goal of the second qualifying Champions League tie. Charlton were another team to expose the big Finn down that flank, when Luke Young scored Charlton's second goal in their 2-0 home win over Liverpool. Despite the increase in the amount of mistakes leading to goals, and a susceptibility to genuine pace if isolated in a one-on-one, Hyypia remains an important player for Benítez. In 2005/06 he racked up 5204 minutes, starting 58 of the team's 61 games. Helped by the addition of Crouch up front this season he saw a big increase in his number of goal assists, and he can always be relied upon for a few goals each year, with 26 so far in his Liverpool career at an average of almost four a season; although that average was dented with just two goals this season.

It's fair to say that with Daniel Agger and Gabriel Paletta now on the scene Hyypia has genuine competition for his place, although it may be another season or two before the young pretenders are ready to take over alongside Jamie Carragher at the heart of the Reds' defence.

Josemi No.17									Age: 25	Height: 6'0"		Right-Back/Centre-Back				
Misc		Individual											Team			
YEAR	COMP	GS	MINS	GOALS	ASSISTS	POINTS	GOALS (90)	ASSISTS (90)	POINTS (90)	MLG	MLG % (90)	CS	CS %	GFA	GAA	PTS
2005-06	Total	9	832	0	0	0	0.00	0.00	0.00	3	32.45	2.9	31.5	1.51	0.87	2.03
2005-06	Prem	3	262	0	0	0	0.00	0.00	0.00	1	34.35	0.9	31.3	0.69	1.37	1.28
2005-06	Euro	5	480	0	0	0	0.00	0.00	0.00	2	37.50	1	18.8	1.69	0.75	2.25
2005-06	Cups	1	90	0	0	0	0.00	0.00	0.00	0	0.00	1	100	3.00	0.00	3.00
2004-05	Total	19	1713	0	2	2	0	0.11	0.11	7	36.78	6	31.5	1.21	1.05	1.52
2004-05	Prem	13	1125	0	2	2	0	0.16	0.16	7	56.00	1	8	1.12	1.44	1.26

Malaga's Josemi promised much upon his arrival from the Costa Del Sol, but delivered precious little over a frustrating 18 months, where he appeared to get worse with every subsequent game. The Spanish right-back started a lot of games at the beginning of last season, having been Rafael Benítez's first signing upon his arrival from Valencia. But Josemi was prone to errors, and the lower his confidence became the more he seemed to dive recklessly into tackles. His red card at Craven Cottage in October 2004 was so telegraphed that Nostradamus foretold of it in 1555.

A liability once his early confidence had drained away, Josemi simply made too many errors (committing a mistake that led to an opponents' goal every third game). As well as mistimed tackles he failed to offer synchronicity to the offside trap, often moving up at the wrong time and allowing many a forward in behind him. A poor start to 2005/06 led to Josemi discovering what many already knew: that Benítez has no place for sentiment. The right-back was traded in the January transfer window for Jan Kromkamp, the Dutch international valued at twice the price the Reds paid Malaga 18 months earlier.

Jan Kromkamp No.2									Age: 25	Height: 6'2"	Right-Back/Right-Midfield				
Misc	Individual											Team			
YEAR	COMP	GS	MINS	GOALS	ASSISTS	POINTS	GOALS (90)	ASSISTS (90)	POINTS (90)	MLG	MLG % (90)	CS	CS %	GFA	GAA	PTS
2005-06	Total	7	765	0	1	1	0.00	0.12	0.12	1	11.76	2.6	30.6	1.88	0.82	2.38
2005-06	Prem	6	603	0	1	1	0.00	0.15	0.15	1	14.93	2.5	37.5	1.79	0.90	2.41
2005-06	Cups	1	162	0	0	0	0.00	0.00	0.00	0	0	0.1	4.9	2.22	0.56	2.26
2004-05	Total	-	-	-	-	-	-	-	-	-	-	-	-	-	-	-
2004-05	Prem	-	-	-	-	-	-	-	-	-	-	-	-	-	-	-

In Jan Kromkamp's brief appearances after his arrival in the January transfer window, there was enough evidence to suggest that Liverpool had procured a good quality right-back — if a player who looked out of his depth in midfield. While he was never going to pitch up and displace Steve Finnan overnight, he did offer genuine competition. Comparing the seasons the two reserve right-backs had for Liverpool (see Table 3) shows that the swap appeared a good move. The only statistical category in which Kromkamp had worse defensive numbers than Josemi was clean sheet percentage.

Table 3. Kromkamp vs Josemi

	GS	Mins	MLG %	CS %	GFA	GAA	PTS
Josemi	9	832	32.5	31.5	1.51	0.87	2.03
Kromkamp	7	765	11.8	30.6	1.88	0.82	2.38

Kromkamp made only one mistake following his arrival, and that was early on and in the zonal marking system, which is hard for players to adjust to anyway, let alone when arriving in mid-season. The majority of his 765 minutes — 65.9% — were actually whilst playing right-midfield. He showed he was a capable crosser of the ball, picking up his one and only assist whilst playing a right-wingback role against Newcastle — supplying a delightfully-weighted centre straight onto the head of Peter Crouch for the opening goal of the game. With promising youngsters Antonio Barragan and David Raven sold on, Kromkamp looked set to vie with Finnan for the right-back position — but a return to Holland, and PSV, was agreed on the final day of the transfer window, as the Reds sought to bring in Blackburn's Lucas Neill. With the latter able to buy out his contract — under the FIFA ruling where anyone over 28 and with one year left can pay their final season's wages to leave — it could be that the tough uncompromising Aussie eventually replaces the more genteel Dutchman.

David Raven No.31						Age: 20 Height: 6'0"						Right-Back	
Misc	Individual										Team		
YEAR COMP	GS	MINS	GOALS	ASSISTS	POINTS	GOALS (90)	ASSISTS (90)	POINTS (90)	MLG	MLG % (90)	CS	CS %	GFA	GAA	PTS
2005-06 Total	1	90	0	0	0	0.00	0.00	0.00	0	0	0	0	1.00	2.00	0.00
2005-06 Cups	1	90	0	0	0	0.00	0.00	0.00	0	0	0	0	1.00	2.00	0.00
2004-05 Total	2	233	0	0	0	0	0	0	0	0	0	0	0.39	0.77	0.38
2004-05 Prem	0	23	0	0	0	0	0	0	0	0	0	0	0.00	0.00	0.00

Former England youth captain David Raven made his Reds debut in 2004/05 with a start at Tottenham in the Carling Cup, and had a superb game, winning rave reviews. He also played in the Reds' much-publicised loss to Burnley in the FA Cup, and saw his first Premiership action soon after, playing 23 minutes at the end of the 2-0 loss Liverpool suffered to Peter Crouch and Southampton. But Raven failed to develop as expected, and in the end fell a little bit short of the quality Benítez was searching for. In July 2006 the right-back moved to League One side Carlisle on a free transfer, but clearly retains the potential to work his way back up the league ladder as he gains experience, and could well find himself back in the Premiership later in his career.

John Arne Riise No.6						Age: 24 Height: 6'1"					Left-Back/Left-Midfield			
Season	Individual										Team			
YEAR COMP	GS	MINS	GOALS	ASSISTS	POINTS	GOALS (90)	ASSISTS (90)	POINTS (90)	MLG	MLG % (90)	CS	CS %	GFA	GAA	PTS
2005-06 Total	42	3906	4	13	17	0.09	0.30	0.39	3	6.91	26	59.4	1.68	0.58	2.26
2005-06 Prem	24	2263	1	4	5	0.04	0.16	0.20	1	3.98	17	68.1	1.35	0.48	2.25
2005-06 Euro	9	972	0	3	3	0.00	0.28	0.28	0	0.00	5.7	52.4	1.48	0.46	2.07
2005-06 Cups	6	671	3	6	9	0.40	0.80	1.21	2	26.83	3	40.2	3.08	1.07	2.55
2004-05 Total	52	4656	8	12	20	0.15	0.23	0.39	2	3.87	15	29	1.41	0.89	1.69
2004-05 Prem	34	2985	6	9	15	0.18	0.27	0.45	2	6.03	5.9	18	1.42	1.03	1.60

It's fair to say that John Arne Riise has yet to win over all the cynics with regard to his ability at left-back. While he'll never be a traditional 'winger', his performances on the left of midfield are usually fairly effective, and he's certainly a goal threat from that position. You know what to expect at left-midfield, but at left-back his reputation is less clear.

This season his goalscoring exploits were diminished, and goals make headlines. Riise's goal production from a year ago was more-or-less halved, with the Norwegian netting four times at a rate of 0.09 per-90 minutes, compared with eight a year ago at 0.15 per-90. But there was a good reason for this, as Table 4 illustrates. In 2004/05 Riise played 61% of his minutes in left-midfield, whereas in 2005/06 it was a complete turnaround — 67% of his playing time was at full-back.

Table 4. Riise the left-back and Riise the left-midfielder

Riise in 2005/06

Position	Mins	Goals	Assists	Points	Goals 90	Assists 90	Points 90	GFA	GAA	CS %	PTS
LB	2617	2	7	9	0.07	0.24	0.31	1.72	0.55	61.22	2.38
LM	1736	2	6	8	0.14	0.42	0.56	1.61	0.63	55.78	2.00

Riise in 2004/05

Position	Mins	Goals	Assists	Points	Goals 90	Assists 90	Points 90	GFA	GAA	CS %	PTS
LB	1800	0	3	3	-	0.15	0.15	1.50	0.85	29.6	1.63
LM	2795	8	9	17	0.26	0.29	0.55	1.35	0.90	28.6	1.72

A year ago all eight of Riise's goals were scored when he was playing left-midfield. In addition to that he also picked up nine of his 12 assists from the more advanced left-side position. This season the numbers are reflected in the rate statistics, where Riise scored and assisted at twice the rate in left-midfield compared with when he played at left-back.

Even if his goals were down, his assists rate this season was up on 2004/05's figures (0.30 per-90 in 2005/06 compared with 0.23 per-90 a year ago), meaning that in fact his overall attacking production, even with the reduction in goals, was the same as a year ago: 0.39 attacking points-per-90 minutes. In terms of team statistics, Riise's inclusion in the side had a very positive effect. When Riise played, the team's goals-against average (0.58) and clean sheet percentage (59.42%) were the best for any defender in the team, whilst the team's points average of 2.26 per-contest was 2nd amongst defenders — only bettered by Jan Kromkamp's 2.38, from far fewer games.

Riise's Premiership figures were even better, where the team posted a goals-against average in his minutes of 0.48 per-contest, and a clean sheet percentage of over 68%. Looking at the figures in Table 4 again gives an indication as to why Riise's primary position changed in 2005/06. Even though Riise's individual statistics in 2004/05 were worse at left-back compared with left-midfield, the team statistics clearly showed the Reds played better when Riise was at the deeper position. The goals-for and goals-against averages were better, as well as the clean sheet percentage. Looking at the figures for 2005/06 shows an even greater difference now exists in how the team performs when Riise plays left-back compared with left-midfield: the goals-for average 1.72 — 1.61; the goals-against average 0.55 — 0.63; the clean sheet percentage 61% — 56%; and the points per-contest 2.38 — 2.00, all clearly better when Riise played left-back in the Liverpool line-up. Due to Riise's split in playing time his mistakes and mistake percentage can also appear misleading, with both having gone up slightly this season. But that is again due to his increased minutes at left-back, where mistakes are more likely to lead to goals. When you remove the left-midfield stats the rating tells a different story. Last year Riise committed two mistakes that led to opposition goals in 1800 minutes, whilst this year it was three in 2627 minutes in that position. Both work out to a mistakes-leading-to-goals percentage of 10% at left-back, which is indicative of extremely solid defending, and would still place him in 2nd place in the team, behind the unflappable Jamie Carragher regarding this particular statistic.

Turning 25 in September 2006, Riise is still not in his prime. His defending should further improve as he heads towards his late twenties, and picks up more positional know-how — with Benítez the right tutor. With Djimi Traoré sold and Stephen Warnock still not totally convincing at left-back, new Brazilian Fabio Aurelio presents Riise's stiffest challenge for the role in the coming seasons. It will be an interesting battle.

Djimi Traore No.21						Age: 25	Height: 6'3"						Left-Back			
Misc	Individual											Team				
YEAR COMP	GS	MINS	GOALS	ASSISTS	POINTS	GOALS (90)	ASSISTS (90)	POINTS (90)	MLG	MLG % (90)		CS	CS %	GFA	GAA	PTS
2005-06 Total	16	1396	0	0	0	0.00	0.00	0.00	7	45.13		6.7	43	1.42	0.90	1.74
2005-06 Prem	9	808	0	0	0	0.00	0.00	0.00	6	66.83		2.4	27	1.56	1.23	1.65
2005-06 Euro	5	450	0	0	0	0.00	0.00	0.00	1	20.00		3	60	0.60	0.60	1.60
2005-06 Cups	2	138	0	0	0	0.00	0.00	0.00	0	0.00		4.1	81.2	3.26	0.00	2.70
2004-05 Total	34	3115	0	1	1	0	0.03	0.03	8	23.11		12	35.7	1.27	0.95	1.65
2004-05 Prem	18	1769	0	1	1	0	0.05	0.05	5	25.44		3.4	17.1	1.32	1.27	1.41

After making fantastic strides (no pun intended) in his first season under Rafa Benítez, the 2005/06 season saw the undoing of Djimi Traoré's good work like a snagged thread unravelling a jumper. From having looked capable of finally turning into a top-class defender, the Frenchman's time at Liverpool came to a close in the summer of 2006, having apparently reverted to type.

Unlike his penultimate year at Anfield, his final season was not one he'll remember with any great pride. An injury picked up in a pre-season game against Bayer Leverkusen meant he missed the rest of training and the beginning of the season — finally making his first start against Real Betis on 13th September. Those two missed months appeared to hamper him, and he never seemed to regain a sense of being settled in the side. From being the first choice left-back a year ago Traoré slipped to third in the pecking order, behind John Arne Riise and Stephen Warnock.

Prone to lapses in concentration and ball-watching, his pace and formidable reach could not always redeem the trouble he could cause himself. A prime example of this was seen late in the year at West Ham in the Premiership. Traoré was playing centre-back and was caught looking inside at the ball whilst his man ghosted behind him, in for the penultimate pass that led to the Hammers' only goal of the night. The majority of his mistakes that led to opposition goals were of this nature, leading to a team-high figure of one mistake in 45% of all games he played this season (a whopping 68% in the Premiership).

In the end Benítez decided to cut his losses. Traoré left after seven years at Anfield, but did so with a Champions League winners' medal, amongst plenty of others. Having had a nightmarish 1st-half in Istanbul he recovered fairly well, and even made a crucial clearance on the goal-line that proved as important as any player's contribution on the night. Not bad for someone so heavily criticised. And the Reds didn't do bad either, quadrupling the original £500,000 fee paid to Laval, when Charlton stumped up £2m.

Stephen Warnock No.28						Age: 23	Height: 5'9"			Left-Back/Left-Midfield						
Misc	Individual											Team				
YEAR COMP	GS	MINS	GOALS	ASSISTS	POINTS	GOALS (90)	ASSISTS (90)	POINTS (90)	MLG	MLG % (90)		CS	CS %	GFA	GAA	PTS
2005-06 Total	23	1941	1	1	2	0.05	0.05	0.09	5	23.18		10	46.9	1.53	0.74	1.93
2005-06 Prem	15	1315	1	1	2	0.07	0.07	0.14	2	13.69		8.4	57.3	1.51	0.62	2.08
2005-06 Euro	5	380	0	0	0	0.00	0.00	0.00	1	23.68		1.7	41.1	1.66	0.71	1.94
2005-06 Cups	3	246	0	0	0	0.00	0.00	0.00	2	73.17		0	0	1.46	1.46	1.11
2004-05 Total	17	1404	0	3	3	0	0.19	0.19	0	0.00		5.2	33.6	1.15	0.77	1.70
2004-05 Prem	11	803	0	1	1	0	0.11	0.11	0	0.00		3.0	34.0	1.23	0.90	1.79

Stephen Warnock moved up to second-choice left-back in 2005/06, after starting only 10 games at the position in 2004/05 (although nine of the 10 starts were in the second half of the campaign). His early season displays actually kept Riise out of the line-up, and even earned Warnock a call up into the England squad, but his form grew patchy.

Warnock's best game this season was in fact when he played left-wingback against Newcastle at St James, and revealed what a good player he could be if feeling confident and comfortable; but it's not a formation Liverpool usually deploy. As all young full-backs must (and especially those converting from the more advanced wide positions), Warnock has had to get used to defensive positioning and the offside system. In fact all of his five mistakes that have led to opposition goals were of a positional/covering nature (CSKA away, Birmingham away in the league and Crystal Palace in the Carling Cup) or through playing the opposition onside (Chelsea's second goal at Stamford Bridge in the Premiership and the only goal in the FIFA Club World Championship final against São Paulo). He is a fierce competitor and ferocious tackler, sometimes picking up knocks and injuries due to a refusal to jump out the way of flying boots. It could be that he will now find himself at a crossroads in his career at Liverpool, with a tough fight on his hands for either left-sided position. He has the character to succeed, but does he have quite enough talent? Time will tell.

Zak Whitbread No.37										Age: 21 Height: 6'2"				Centre-Back
Misc	Individual									Team				
YEAR COMP	GS	MINS	GOALS	ASSISTS	POINTS	GOALS (90)	ASSISTS (90)	POINTS (90)	MLG	MLG % (90)	CS	CS %	GFA	GAA	PTS
2005-06 Total	2	217	0	0	0	0.00	0.00	0.00	1	41.47	1.4	58.5	2.07	0.83	1.76
2005-06 Euro	1	127	0	0	0	0.00	0.00	0.00	0	0	1.4	100	2.83	0.00	3.00
2005-06 Cups	1	90	0	0	0	0.00	0.00	0.00	1	100.00	0	0	1.00	2.00	0.00
2005-06 Total	27	2355	0	With Millwall	0.00	-	-	-	-		3.7	14	0.61	1.18	0.75
2004-05 Total	4	390	0	2	2	0	0.46	0.46	1	23.08	2	46.2	1.38	0.46	1.61
2004-05 Prem	-	-	-	-	-	-	-	-	-	-	-	-	-	-	-

In Zak Whitbread's three appearances (two starts) this season he did his best Sami Hyypia impersonation in terms of hair colour (bleached blond) and aerial skills, and even showed some promising touches on the floor, but didn't come close to emulating his elder's superb positioning skills. For the second year in a row the young American-born centre-back performed fairly well in pre– and early– season matches. The Academy graduate was duly loaned to Millwall — in what would become a permanent move in July 2006; inevitable after the arrival of two superior players of a similar age in Daniel Agger and Gabriel Paletta, and with a whole raft of promising teenage centre-backs following closely behind.

Midfielders

Xabi Alonso No.14										Age: 23 Height: 6'0"				Centre-Midfield
Misc	Individual									Team				
YEAR COMP	GS	MINS	GOALS	ASSISTS	POINTS	GOALS (90)	ASSISTS (90)	POINTS (90)	MLG	MLG % (90)	CS	CS %	GFA	GAA	PTS
2005-06 Total	47	4089	5	15	20	0.11	0.33	0.44	2	4.40	24	53.2	1.63	0.77	2.15
2005-06 Prem	29	2571	3	11	14	0.11	0.39	0.49	1	3.50	18	61.4	1.30	0.67	2.11
2005-06 Euro	11	922	0	3	3	0.00	0.29	0.29	0	0.00	4.7	46.3	1.56	0.68	2.16
2005-06 Cups	7	596	2	1	3	0.30	0.15	0.45	1	15.10	1.9	28.4	3.17	1.36	2.29
2004-05 Total	27	2470	3	12	15	0.11	0.44	0.55	0	0.00	7.3	26.6	1.46	1.02	1.51
2004-05 Prem	20	1809	2	10	12	0.10	0.50	0.60	0	0.00	3.3	16.4	1.59	1.14	1.56

Some critics feel Xabi Alonso is overshadowed by Steven Gerrard when they play in the middle together; that Gerrard's frantic style and forceful personality subdue the Spaniard. The truth is that there is absolutely nothing to back this up, and that while Liverpool have three superb midfielders with Momo Sissoko added to the equation, the central pairing of Gerrard and Alonso is as good as any in world football.

Despite Gerrard's impressive ability to find colleagues over any distance, Alonso is arguably the best passer in the team; he is certainly the player who leads the Reds' figures in that category, due to his unerring accuracy and reliability. (Gerrard, while a spectacular passer, is more hit-and-miss.) If Gerrard is the engine of the team then Alonso is the smooth power-steering. According to Opta statistics Alonso was 2nd in the Premiership for successful tackles, with 167, and tied for 4th in the league with 1820 total passes. He was the only player in the league in the top five in both categories, which just goes to highlight what a special — and balanced — player he is.

While Gerrard is seen as the better all-rounder, Alonso's stats suggest otherwise. While Alonso was steadily stealing possession from the opposition and using it wisely, Gerrard was further forward, making runs in behind defenders; his game was based more on attacking, so his tackling stats — in terms of quantity made — would have suffered as a result. He was there *to be* tackled, often in the opposition area, rather than do the tracking back. But even had he spent the season playing directly beside Alonso in a flat midfield two, his Spanish colleague's figures would have taken some beating.

When you rate the figures over 90 minutes, on average Alonso won six tackles and passed an incredible 63.4 times a game. What is even more amazing was that according to Opta, 762 of Alonso's total number of passes could be considered long-range, which put him top in the league in that category. Therefore, of his 63 total passes per-90 minutes, 26.5 of them were over a long distance. Furthermore, his accuracy on those long range passes is exceptional, rarely giving the ball away even when playing so many searching diagonal balls that need to be inch-perfect.

While Alonso impresses in a number of categories, his individual attacking numbers were a little down on a year ago. He scored at exactly the same rate as a year ago (0.11 per-90 minutes), but his assist rate dropped from 0.44 to 0.33 this season. This is perhaps best explained by the fact that other managers and players had seen him in his first season and were better prepared a year later. The addition of Momo Sissoko was key, as this not only created more room for Alonso, for whom the Malian acted as a bodyguard, but also freed Steven Gerrard to play other positions (in the hole behind Crouch, or wide right) and in so doing create more for the team.

When teams risk giving Alonso time and space he can still dominate a game with vision. His two-assist game against West Brom at the Hawthorns was evidence of this, picking out Cissé on both occasions with pinpoint accuracy from his own half. His dead ball crossing is also impressive, recording two assists on corners, and he has worked at getting the ball in with greater whip and a lower trajectory.

All five of Alonso's goals this season were scored from outside the penalty area, with one, against Luton, scored from a different post code. How often can it be said that a player is worth every penny of his transfer fee when that fee is above ten million pounds? It is rare, but then so is Alonso's talent, and so far he has indeed been worth every penny. And then some.

Steven Gerrard No.8							Age: 25 Height: 6'0"					Midfield				
Misc	Individual											Team				
YEAR	COMP	GS	MINS	GOALS	ASSISTS	POINTS	GOALS (90)	ASSISTS (90)	POINTS (90)	MLG	MLG % (90)	CS	CS %	GFA	GAA	PTS
2005-06	Total	49	4236	23	28	51	0.49	0.59	1.08	2	4.25	26	55.9	1.81	0.72	2.07
2005-06	Prem	32	2727	10	11	21	0.33	0.36	0.69	1	3.30	19	61.2	1.58	0.59	2.16
2005-06	Euro	8	724	7	5	12	0.87	0.62	1.49	0	0.00	5.3	65.8	1.86	0.62	1.83
2005-06	Cups	9	785	6	12	18	0.69	1.38	2.06	1	11.46	2.5	28.7	2.52	1.26	1.97
2004-05	Total	41	3685	13	17	30	0.32	0.42	0.73	2	4.68	10	25.1	1.27	0.98	1.55
2004-05	Prem	28	2465	7	10	17	0.26	0.36	0.62	0	0.00	4.4	16.1	1.17	1.06	1.39

What a great season for the Liverpool captain, who was fully deserving of the PFA Player of the Year award. Steven Gerrard's 23 goals placed him top amongst the team and ahead of any midfield player in the league. His 28 assists were also top in the squad, giving him 51 points for the season, and putting him over the one point per-game level, effectively meaning he was involved in a goal in some way every single game.

Gerrard had experienced an up and down time in 2004/05. Whether this was due to the foot injury he picked up against Manchester United, or the constant media hype about his possible move to Chelsea, he did not perform as consistently as he can. Gerrard did top the team's goalscoring charts last season (jointly with Milan Baros and Luis Garcia) with 13 goals, and led the team with 17 assists, but something was missing. It was picked up in his individual 'team' statistics: he was actually below the average in every single team statistic, indicating that the team actually performed less well when he was in the line-up. This backs up the suggestions made at the time — namely that for all the talk of Liverpool being a one-man team, they were not as reliant on their captain as some would have people believe.

This year the picture is completely different. He finished on or above average in every team category. He actually had the team's top goals-for average and clean sheet percentage amongst the regular midfield players, and he was definitely more valuable in the side this season. His accomplishments are even more amazing when you consider that from game to game he didn't even know what position he was going to be asked to play; consistency is so much harder when shifted from pillar to post. He has played as one of the defensive central midfield two, as a third central midfield player, right-midfield, right-wing, an attacking central midfield role and as the player in the hole/attacking midfielder off the front man. He performed very well in all roles, and as Table 5 (below) shows he out-performed last year's totals wherever he played in 2005/06. The table groups his playing time and stats into three positions: right-midfield and right-wing (RM), all central midfield positions (CM), and all attacking midfield/forward positions (AM).

Table 5. Gerrard: man of all trades?

Position	Mins	Goals	Assists	Points	Goals 90	Assists 90	Points 90	GFA	GAA	CS %	PTS
RM	1551	6	10	16	0.35	0.58	0.93	1.39	0.75	59.3	2.30
CM	1625	12	13	25	0.66	0.72	1.38	2.49	0.61	54.5	2.22
AM	1060	5	5	10	0.42	0.42	0.85	1.36	0.85	53.2	1.49

The first thing to acknowledge is that Gerrard played a lot of minutes (greater than 1000) in all three positions, so even the raw figures are comparable with such a significant sample. Both his goals and assists rates were affected when he was asked to play a position other than his more natural one in the centre of midfield. His assist rate was still very good when playing on the right of midfield, but playing there did hamper his goalscoring ability, with almost half as many goals-per-90 minutes. What he did out there, however, was provide the team with balance in the absence of a specialist for the role, and the team won more points per-game with him stationed on the wing. While Djibril Cissé scored goals at a better rate than Gerrard in that position, the team as a whole suffered when the Frenchman was stationed there; while Gerrard was prepared to go forward, he was also far more likely to cover back as well.

It was through the centre, however, where Gerrard was truly magnificent, racking up 12 goals and 13 assists to finish with an incredible attacking points total of 1.38 per-90 minutes. The individual numbers were also backed-up by the team stats when Gerrard played in each of the three positions. Liverpool averaged almost 2.5 goals-per-game when he played in central midfield, whilst in more forward positions or out wide right it was 1.3 goals per-contest. The teams' goals-against average was also significantly better at 0.61 when the Liverpool skipper played in central midfield, compared with 0.75 and 0.85 when he played right and attacking midfield respectively. The team's points total was well above average, however, for both his playing time in right and central midfield. His relatively poor statistics when playing in an advanced role behind the striker may be down to those being the toughest encounters, where Rafa Benítez wanted more solidity.

If Gerrard had played all his minutes in a central role, and the goals and assist rates he posted in the position held across his total playing time, he would have posted 31 goals and 34 assists, for a total of 65 attacking points. It is highly unlikely that his rates would have held that high, given he didn't tend to play the position in the very toughest games, but it is also fair to assume that he would have fired in a few more precious goals. With Jermaine Pennant now on the books to offer the natural wide play the team has lacked on that flank, Gerrard's appearances on the right will be a lot more limited, but not a thing of the past. It will be interesting to see if his incredible figures hold up as he spends more time in the central role.

Table 6. Goal Distance

Distance	Goals
6 yard box	1
18 yard box	10
Outside area	8
Penalty	4
Total	23

Steven Gerrard has always possessed a potent long-range shot, but this season he took it to a whole new level. Was there a better possible note on which to end the season than his out-of-this-world equaliser against West Ham in the FA Cup Final? It was the 8th goal he scored with shots from outside the area (35%).

Of those eight long-range goals, six were placed just inside the goalkeeper's right post on, or only a few inches off, the ground. The Liverpool captain scored seven game-winning goals and four game-tying goals, none more important than the one that sailed past Shaka Hislop in the 91st minute at Cardiff. At the age of 26, Gerrard is now entering the prime years of his career. In an ever-improving Liverpool side he remains the key man, but rather than having to constantly lift his team-mates and do all the work himself, he is now surrounded by enough quality to have his colleagues help him.

Dietmar Hamann No.16										Age: 31 Height: 6'3"				Centre-Midfield
Misc		Individual									Team			
YEAR	COMP	GS	MINS	GOALS	ASSISTS	POINTS	GOALS (90)	ASSISTS (90)	POINTS (90)	MLG MLG % (90)	CS	CS %	GFA	GAA PTS
2005-06 Total		23	2223	0	8	8	0.00	0.32	0.32	0 0	13	50.8	1.26	0.69 1.62
2005-06 Prem		13	1147	0	3	3	0.00	0.24	0.24	0 0	5.6	43.9	1.65	0.86 2.02
2005-06 Euro		8	836	0	4	4	0.00	0.43	0.43	0 0	5.8	62.8	0.75	0.43 1.65
2005-06 Cups		2	240	0	1	1	0.00	0.38	0.38	0 0	1.1	42.1	1.13	0.75 1.42
2004-05 Total		34	3050	1	10	11	0.03	0.30	0.32	0 0	11	31.4	1.36	0.89 1.51
2004-05 Prem		23	2026	0	7	7	0	0.31	0.31	0 0	5.0	22.4	1.33	1.07 1.37

Didi Hamann gave Liverpool Football Club seven years of exceptional service following his arrival from Newcastle in 1999. At £8m he wasn't cheap, but the Reds got full value for their money. The arrival of Momo Sissoko in 2005 hastened the departure of the German. The writing was on the wall this season, with the former No.16's minutes slashed considerably, from 3050 in 2004/05 down to 2223 in 2005/06. With Hamann about to turn 33 shortly after the start of 2006/07, Benítez opted for the young legs and strong running of the Malian, who offered a better contrast to Xabi Alonso in the heart of the midfield.

As you would expect, 'Der Kaiser' remained extremely valuable as a defensive player, as evidenced by his low team goals-against average. However, his inclusion in the team tended to result in the Reds struggling to score (although this is partly due to the German entering the fray when Rafa Benítez wanted to protect a lead).

On an individual level, Hamann's attacking figures were fairly impressive; he picked up almost as many assists this season as last, even in his reduced role as the 3rd or 4th central midfielder in the squad; even improving his rate marginally from 0.30 per-90 minutes in 2004/05 to 0.32 this year. But the low team goals-for average was a worry; the Reds registered an alarming total of nine goals below average in games in which Hamann played during the season. While he could still have offered a lot to Liverpool in Benítez's third season, and had actually played enough games this season to trigger an automatic contract extension, it was in the German's own best interests to move on, rather than remain a bit-part player. A move to Bolton Wanderers was agreed, and a contract signed, but then Hamann had a change of heart. The Reds, having let Hamann leave on a free transfer despite one year on his contract, could only watch as Bolton received a fee of approximately £500,000 from Manchester City.

Harry Kewell No.7											Age: 26	Height: 5'11		Left/Right-Midfield		
Misc	Individual												Team			
YEAR	COMP	GS	MINS	GOALS	ASSISTS	POINTS	GOALS (90)	ASSISTS (90)	POINTS (90)	MLG	MLG % (90)	CS	CS %	GFA	GAA	PTS
2005-06	Total	30	2752	3	9	12	0.10	0.29	0.39	0	0	14	44.2	1.70	0.82	1.98
2005-06	Prem	22	2010	3	7	10	0.13	0.31	0.45	0	0	11	50	1.61	0.67	2.15
2005-06	Euro	2	214	0	1	1	0.00	0.42	0.42	0	0	0.7	28.5	0.42	0.84	0.53
2005-06	Cups	6	528	0	1	1	0.00	0.17	0.17	0	0	1.7	28.4	2.56	1.36	1.91
2004-05	Total	23	2051	1	7	8	0.04	0.31	0.35	0	0	4.0	17.7	1.41	0.88	1.55
2004-05	Prem	15	1398	1	4	5	0.06	0.26	0.32	0	0	1.0	6.7	1.42	1.09	1.37

Harry Kewell's return to form was like the addition of a £10m player in mid-season, and his regular starts on the left wing helped Liverpool to their highest points total since the Premiership began. Although his individual numbers don't show it so clearly, his value to the team was significant, mainly as a headache for opposing coaches — why else would Chelsea play two full-backs down their right-hand side? But there can also be little doubt that more is required in the final third, from a player capable of scoring 10-15 goals a season if he plays enough games.

2005/06 started where the previous season ended, and ended where it started: with Kewell injured. The damaged groin finally gave way in Istanbul, and it was November before he was back in the first-team picture, albeit while patently short of match-fitness. It was notable that two of the best performances seen by the Australian in the last three years came once he had six months' playing time under his belt. In April 2006 he tortured both of Chelsea's right-backs, until he had to leave the field with an injury that would later recur to have him limp out of his third consecutive cup final; in June he was sensational for his country against Croatia in the World Cup, scoring the goal that took Australia to the knock-out stages for the first time in its history. However, Kewell would be absent from that historic game, with septic arthritis (misdiagnosed at the time as gout) — which would also curtail his involvement in Liverpool's pre-season training schedule, something he desperately needed to take part in; meaning he would miss the start to yet another season. With so many strong options for the left side of midfield, Kewell will have really stiff competition for the role in 2006/07, although his versatility means a role as the 2nd striker is always a strong option.

Luis Garcia No.10						Age: 27	Height: 5'7"				Right/Left-Midfield				
Misc		Individual										Team				
YEAR	COMP	GS	MINS	GOALS	ASSISTS	POINTS	GOALS (90)	ASSISTS (90)	POINTS (90)	MLG	MLG % (90)	CS	CS %	GFA	GAA	PTS
2005-06	Total	28	2938	11	15	26	0.34	0.46	0.80	0	0	18	54.3	1.65	0.70	2.01
2005-06	Prem	15	1580	7	9	16	0.40	0.51	0.91	0	0	11	62.3	1.65	0.80	2.07
2005-06	Euro	10	1025	3	4	7	0.26	0.35	0.61	0	0	5.3	46.2	1.40	0.53	1.92
2005-06	Cups	3	333	1	2	3	0.27	0.54	0.81	0	0	1.5	40.8	2.43	0.81	1.96
2004-05	Total	40	3556	13	8	21	0.33	0.20	0.53	0	0	13	32.4	1.39	0.96	1.64
2004-05	Prem	26	2343	8	6	14	0.31	0.23	0.54	0	0	6.1	23.3	1.42	1.08	1.54

Luis Garcia's rise to prominence saw him feature for Spain in the World Cup in Germany, having arrived at Liverpool as an uncapped Barcelona squad player. High risk, high reward sums up the skilful Spaniard. His flicks and tricks often fail to come off, and he regularly gives the ball away, but Benítez tries to make sure it's not in his own half; in the opposition half, if one of these tricks comes off it can mean hitting the jackpot. Perhaps surprisingly, in his two years at Liverpool not one needless giveaway has come back to haunt the team, as evidenced in his zero mistakes-leading-to-goals tallies both last year and this, although it's impossible to tell how many more goals *might* have been scored had possession been retained when he instead over-elaborated. What's almost certain is that he created and scored enough goals to prove his value to the team.

Garcia's movement is supreme. He's so busy, buzzing around and taking up inviting positions. The comparison with Raul at the World Cup was interesting. While Garcia started the competition in place of the Real Madrid idol, Raul's poacher's strike in the second game won him back his place. Beyond that fine finish, Raul did next-to-nothing. Spain played far better with Garcia in the side, and he was popping up in great positions all over the final third.

For Liverpool, Garcia's overall goals rate was the same this year as a season ago, bagging 11 goals at a rate of 0.34 per-90 minutes, but most impressively, his assist rate more than doubled from 0.20 per-90 a year ago to 0.46 per-90 in 2005/06. His individual 'team' stats were all around the averages, except his clean sheet percentage which was actually above average, which comes as a surprise. Equally surprising to his critics would be that he was at his most effective in the Premiership this season, and not Europe, as would be expected.

Table 7. Versatile Garcia

Position	Mins	Goals	Assists	Points	Goals 90	Assists 90	Points 90	GFA	GAA	CS %	PTS
AM	636	2	5	7	0.28	0.71	0.99	2.26	0.42	44.7	2.21
RM	1736	8	9	17	0.41	0.47	0.88	1.76	0.62	51.3	1.96
LM	566	1	1	2	0.16	0.16	0.32	0.62	1.27	74.0	1.90

Luis Garcia's attacking versatility is another strong suit. However, as Table 7 shows, it is as an attacking central player where Garcia is most effective. Although he only played 22% of his minutes in this position it was by far his most effective role, and from the numbers a very advantageous one for the team, too. His scoring rate from the right was more prolific (0.41 per-90 minutes compared with 0.28), but his assist rate almost doubled in the more central forward position to 0.71 assists-per-90 minutes. He was essentially directly involved in a goal for every 90 minutes of playing time when stationed just off the main striker. The team scored half a goal more per-game when Garcia was in the 'hole' as opposed to on the right flank, and gave away 0.2 goals-per-game less. The team was able to turn those gains into a quarter of a point more per-contest.

In his two years at Liverpool Garcia has managed to score 24 goals (at a rate of 0.33 per-90 minutes), which is an exceptional total for someone who is not an out-and-out striker. He may miss some easy chances, but he also scores vital goals. This year alone he scored the winner against Chelsea in the FA Cup Semi-final, the winner against Arsenal at home in the league, the winner against Real Betis in Spain, the winner against Everton at home and the winner at Sunderland away. In addition to that he also had key equalisers against Arsenal away, Bolton away, and Birmingham away. That means that eight of his 11 goals were either eventual game winners or equalising goals at the time they were scored. A year ago he also had five game-winning goals, giving him an amazing 10 winners in total over the last two years. And that serves as a fitting testament to his talent.

Darren Potter No.34								Age: 20 Height: 6'1"			Right-Midfield			
Misc	Individual										Team				
YEAR	COMP	GS	MINS	GOALS	ASSISTS	POINTS	GOALS (90)	ASSISTS (90)	POINTS (90)	MLG	MLG % (90)	CS	CS %	GFA	GAA	PTS
2005-06	Total	5	400	0	0	0	0.00	0.00	0.00	0	0	2.2	50.5	2.48	0.90	1.98
2005-06	Euro	4	310	0	0	0	0.00	0.00	0.00	0	0	2.2	65.2	2.90	0.58	2.56
2005-06	Cups	1	90	0	0	0	0.00	0.00	0.00	0	0	0	0	1.00	2.00	0.00
2005-06	Total	9	923	0	With Southampton		0.00	-	-	-	-	3.6	35.5	0.98	0.78	1.49
2004-05	Total	5	546	0	2	2	0	0.33	0.33	0	0	2.1	34.2	1.15	0.66	1.23
2004-05	Prem	0	54	0	0	0	0	0	0	0	0	0	0	0	0	0.06

The Republic of Ireland under-21 international made five starts this season, the same as a year ago, when Rafa Benítez gave Darren Potter his first-team debut in the Reds' 2-0 Champions League qualifier win away to Graz AK. Originally a central midfielder, Potter has played the vast majority of his first-team minutes as a right winger and performed adequately if unspectacularly. Not a flashy player, Potter has shown a good passing game and the ability to cross from the flank, picking up two assists in his 546 minutes a year ago. Loaned out to Southampton in the January transfer window he managed to rack up almost 1000 minutes for the south coast side. In August 2006 he joined Wolves on a year's loan.

Mohamed Sissoko No.22								Age: 20 Height: 6'2"			Centre-Midfield			
Misc	Individual										Team				
YEAR	COMP	GS	MINS	GOALS	ASSISTS	POINTS	GOALS (90)	ASSISTS (90)	POINTS (90)	MLG	MLG % (90)	CS	CS %	GFA	GAA	PTS
2005-06	Total	37	3416	0	4	4	0.00	0.11	0.11	0	0	20	53.7	1.55	0.63	2.17
2005-06	Prem	21	1954	0	1	1	0.00	0.05	0.05	0	0	13	57.4	1.34	0.60	2.20
2005-06	Euro	8	756	0	0	0	0.00	0.00	0.00	0	0	4.9	58.5	1.31	0.24	1.98
2005-06	Cups	8	706	0	3	3	0.00	0.38	0.38	0	0	3	38.2	2.42	1.15	2.28
2004-05	Total	-	-	-	-	-	-	-	-	-	-	-	-	-	-	-
2004-05	Prem	-	-	-	-	-	-	-	-	-	-	-	-	-	-	-

Any Red could be excused a shudder at the thought of Momo Sissoko ending up across Stanley Park in 2005. That was a distinct possibility, with Everton making the first move, before Benítez stepped in like Franz Beckenbauer at his prime to ease David Moyes off the ball.

Sissoko is raw in many areas but his tackling, non-stop running and all-round midfield battling are first-class, with the potential to become world-class. He never stops running — easily covering the greatest distance of any player in the team. Opta have him second in the team in tackles in the Premiership, a category in which he led the whole league (and by a large margin) until he was injured against Benfica. However, his average tackles per-90 minutes is almost two more than Alonso's, at eight successful tackles a contest.

Sissoko has already shown he is a quick learner. After his sending-off at Sunderland in November — for going to ground to tackle — he very rarely left his feet again all season. His passing is sometimes a little short, and is an area for definite improvement, but his ability to surge forward with the ball is a handy way of getting it into advanced areas, even if his passing can be awry.

Checking his individual 'team' stats for the season shows just how valuable he has become — posting a better goals-against average, clean sheet percentage and points-won-per-contest than the team average. In fact the team's goals-against average (0.63) and the points-won-per-contest (2.17) when he was in the line-up were the best figure amongst all Liverpool's regular midfielders. Still only 21, his first season has left him with a lot to live up to. But if he continues to learn quickly, he'll be something to behold.

Boudewijn Zenden No.30											Age: 28 Height: 5'10					Left-Midfield
Misc	Individual											Team				
YEAR	COMP	GS	MINS	GOALS	ASSISTS	POINTS	GOALS (90)	ASSISTS (90)	POINTS (90)	MLG	MLG % (90)	CS	CS %	GFA	GAA	PTS
2005-06 Total		11	1095	2	5	7	0.16	0.41	0.58	0	0	8.1	66.2	2.05	0.25	2.39
2005-06 Prem		5	451	2	1	3	0.40	0.20	0.60	0	0	4.3	84.9	1.80	0.00	2.30
2005-06 Euro		8	644	0	4	4	0.00	0.56	0.56	0	0	3.8	53.1	2.24	0.42	2.46
2004-05 Total		49	4126	8	With Middlesbrough	0.17										
2004-05 Prem		36	3062	5		0.15										

It was a shame that Bolo Zenden's season was cut short after only 11 starts, as his numbers suggest he was having a very good opening to his Liverpool career. His individual and team statistics are impressive, but slightly inflated by early qualifying games in Europe. His Premiership rates are off the charts for the five games he started, picking up his two goals and one of his five assists on the year.

What is even more amazing is that Liverpool started poorly in the Premiership, and were only just beginning the long run of clean sheets when he got injured. Yet in his 451 league minutes on the pitch Liverpool never conceded a single goal, whilst scoring nine of their own. The team averaged a clean sheet in almost 85% of the games Zenden played in, and 2.30 points per-contest. Zenden's goal rate this year was almost exactly the same as a year ago when playing so impressively for Middlesbrough, and although he probably wouldn't have played as many minutes with Liverpool it still robbed the team of another 3–4 goals on the year.

Only time will tell how successfully Zenden can come back from the knee surgery that finished his season in Liverpool's 24th contest, but the signs were good in August 2006. As he approaches his 30th birthday he'll offer the team his extensive experience, picked up at some of Europe's premier clubs (*and* Middlesbrough), with Rafa Benítez hinting that Didi Hamann's departure could see the Dutchman playing in his favoured attacking central midfield role.

Forwards

Djibril Cissé No.9							Age: 24	Height: 6'1"	Striker/Right-Midfield							
Misc		Individual										Team				
YEAR	COMP	GS	MINS	GOALS	ASSISTS	POINTS	GOALS (90)	ASSISTS (90)	POINTS (90)	MLG	MLG % (90)	CS	CS %	GFA	GAA	PTS
2005-06	Total	29	2871	19	11	30	0.60	0.34	0.94	0	0	17	52.6	1.82	0.78	2.23
2005-06	Prem	19	1718	9	7	16	0.47	0.37	0.84	0	0	12	61.5	1.41	0.63	2.24
2005-06	Euro	6	729	8	2	10	0.99	0.25	1.23	0	0	3.8	47.1	2.10	0.62	2.13
2005-06	Cups	5	424	2	2	4	0.42	0.42	0.85	0	0	1.2	26.2	2.97	1.70	2.36
2004-05	Total	14	1363	5	3	8	0.33	0.20	0.53	0	0	6.0	39.5	1.45	0.66	1.76
2004-05	Prem	10	931	4	2	6	0.39	0.19	0.58	0	0	2.8	26.9	1.93	0.87	1.87

Djibril Cissé provided one long talking point throughout the season. There was much to admire, but he set about his own personal crusade to prove that every action has an equal and opposite reaction — as such, there were significant amounts to cause vexation. In a season that saw the French striker play on both wings and through the middle he frustrated management and fans alike, but finished the season as the most prolific forward in the team.

Surprisingly, Cissé assisted at about the same rate as Fernando Morientes, but it was his scoring rate that impressed. In his 29 starts Cissé scored 19 goals, at a rate of 0.60 per-90 minutes — easily top for the team. With his improved assist rate his overall attacking production was 0.94 attacking points-per-90 minutes, good enough for second in the team behind Steven Gerrard. The statistics the team put up in Cissé's appearances were also eye-opening, as his team goals-for average (1.82) and points per-contest (2.23) were both top amongst forwards in the squad, and top overall amongst players who made over 15 starts. His two defensive team stats, however, were both a shade under the team averages, revealing that the Frenchman's inclusion was at the expense of defensive stability. So no surprise there.

Looking at Cissé's splits in his player table reveals how the forward's form varied considerably from competition to competition, and brings into the focus the player's inconsistent form. One game Cissé could be scintillating (West Ham away), and then in others he'd be woeful, missing easy chances and looking like his mind is elsewhere. He was even inconsistent *during* games, as evidenced by his FA Cup final performance — scoring and looking dominant in the first half and then disappearing in the second, while looking disinterested during periods of the game.

His overall goals-per-90 minutes rate was top for the team, but his Premiership rate was far lower at 0.47 per-90 minutes (where he scored nine goals, dropping him to second behind Fowler's 0.58). Cissé's European form was excellent, however, firing in eight goals in 729 minutes, which equates to approximately a goal a game. Analysing Cissé's 19 goals in more detail (See Table 5) reveals that a good percentage were actually very important, and not just goals that came when the game was already effectively over — *garbage goals*, to borrow the ice hockey terminology. However, he did score a big percentage in the final ten minutes.

Table 8. Djibril Cissé goal by goal

Opponent	Goal time	Score after goal	Final score	Goal type
TNS (A)	26	1-0	3-0	Game winner
Kaunas (A)	27	1-1	3-1	Game tier
Kaunas (H)	86	2-0	2-0	Garbage goal
CSKA Sofia (A)	25	1-0	3-1	First goal
CSKA Moscow (N)	82	1-1	3-1	Game tier
CSKA Moscow (N)	102	2-1	3-1	Game winner
Birmingham (A)	85 (pen)	2-2	2-2	Game tier
Blackburn (H)	75	1-0	1-0	Game winner
Anderlecht (A)	20	1-0	1-0	Game winner
Anderlecht (H)	89	3-0	3-0	Garbage goal
Portsmouth (H)	39	2-0	3-0	-
Everton (A)	47	3-1	3-1	-
Newcastle (A)	52 (pen)	3-1	3-1	-
Birmingham (A)	89	7-0	7-0	Garbage goal
West Brom (A)	38	2-0	2-0	-
West Ham (A)	19	1-0	2-1	First goal
West Ham (A)	54	2-1	2-1	Game winner
Portsmouth (A)	89	3-1	3-1	-
West Ham (N)	32	1-2	3-3	First goal

Of Cissé's 19 goals this season five were game winners, tying him with Luis Garcia in 2nd place; three were very important game-tying goals; and only three were of the garbage variety. What is interesting is that in the 17 games in which Cissé scored Liverpool won 15 times, and drew twice. The team never lost and had a winning percentage of 88%. Another interesting point to note from Table 8 was the number of away or neutral grounds at which Cissé scored. Of Cissé's 19 goals 15 were scored away from home or at a neutral stadium. An explanation for this is perhaps that Cissé's speed was more of a factor away from home, but what it also did was provide more frustration at Anfield. Cissé also seemed to draw the short straw when it came to the rotation system up front, with Morientes and Crouch getting most of the minutes through the middle, and then later Fowler proved another popular option for the manager. Cissé scored his first 10 goals whilst playing in a central striker role — the last of which he scored as a second-half substitute against Anderlecht on November 1st. The problem was that in the Premiership Cissé just didn't look his best in a central position; most of these goals were in Europe. His inability to stay onside was a problem, while his confidence in front of goal just wasn't present when starting as a striker, perhaps due to the increased expectation on him scoring. Playing on the flank enabled him to run from deeper positions, and thus presented less chance of falling foul of the linesman.

In fact, when you compare his minutes as a striker with those when he played in either wide midfield positions (see Table 9) you can see some interesting numbers.

Table 9. Cissé on wing vs Cissé as striker

Position	Mins	Goals	Assists	Points	Goals 90	Assists 90	Points 90	GFA	GAA	CS %	PTS
Wing	1031	7	4	11	0.61	0.35	0.96	1.92	0.79	51.8	2.08
Striker	1840	12	7	19	0.59	0.34	0.93	1.76	0.78	53.1	2.31

Djibril Cissé played 36% of all his minutes on either wing, whilst the remainder of his minutes were played more centrally, either as the lone man up front or with a partner in tandem. As Table 9 shows, Cissé was actually a more prolific scorer, and had a fractionally higher assist rate per-90 minutes, when playing wide midfield. His attacking production from the wing was slightly greater than that seen through the middle, and was just under one point per-90 minutes (0.96) — meaning he was directly involved in a goal for virtually every 90 minutes of playing time.

His stats reveal the same distinction in terms of the team's goals-for average. The Reds scored 1.92 goals-per-game when Cissé was on either wing, and 1.76 goals-per-game when he played through the middle. When you break down his playing time and goals in the two positions in Premiership play the numbers become even more startling. Cissé played almost a 50-50 split between positions in league playing time (821 minutes on the wing, 897 minutes as a striker) but scored six of his nine Premiership goals from wide midfield. His goals-per-90 minutes rate of 0.3 when up front was below average for the position, but his 0.66 midfield goals rate would actually place him above Frank Lampard — and into first place in the charts for goalscoring rate for midfielders in the entire league; typical of the paradoxical nature of his time at Liverpool.

Despite this, the negatives outweighed the positives in the mind of the one person who mattered most: Rafael Benítez. As Cissé represented a significant investment for the club in 2004, the chance to recoup a large amount of the fee was too good to resist, and it was possible the Reds could recoup as much as £10m from France, where his reputation remains high; after all, his record there is second-to-none in recent years. Both Gérard Houllier's Lyon and Marseilles, the team Cissé supported as a boy, made genuine enquiries, but yet again Houllier was denied the chance to work with the striker. In May 2006 history repeated itself, with Cissé suffering his second horrific leg fracture in little over 18 months. Marseilles, however, were still happy to take the player off Liverpool's wage bill, with the expectation of a permanent deal to follow.

All the same, it clearly hampered Benítez's summer spending plans. Whether a good fee can still be sought in 2007 remains to be seen, depending on whether the player makes a good recovery, in terms of both fitness and form.

Either way, it marks the end of a mixed experiment. Had Cissé cost Liverpool nothing, by coming through the youth system, his time at Anfield might have been looked upon more favourably. In no way a total failure, given he scored and created goals on the way to winning both the Champions League and the FA Cup (with key contributions in both finals), as well as the fact that his overall goals-rate was not at all shoddy, he also clearly failed to live up to his steep price tag.

Peter Crouch No.15											Age: 24 Height: 6'7"				Centre-Forward	
Misc	Individual												Team			
YEAR	COMP	GS	MINS	GOALS	ASSISTS	POINTS	GOALS (90)	ASSISTS (90)	POINTS (90)	MLG	MLG % (90)	CS	CS %	GFA	GAA	PTS
2005-06 Total	42	3298	13	18	31	0.35	0.49	0.85	1	2.73	20	53.8	1.75	0.87	1.98
2005-06 Prem	27	2140	8	10	18	0.34	0.42	0.76	1	4.21	13	54.7	1.72	0.84	1.99
2005-06 Euro	8	592	0	3	3	0.00	0.46	0.46	0	0.00	4.1	62.3	1.06	0.61	1.73
2005-06 Cups	7	566	5	5	10	0.80	0.80	1.59	0	0.00	2.6	41.3	2.54	1.27	2.21
2004-05 Total	24	2351	16	With Southampton		0.61									
2004-05 Prem	18	1813	12			0.60									

Like Djibril Cissé, Peter Crouch split opinion amongst many fans, although a good majority of Reds warmed to Crouch fairly quickly given his workrate and commitment. He is the classic example of a player who should be judged on what he brings to the team, rather than derided for things he cannot do. You wouldn't expect a guide dog to outrun a greyhound at the Walthamstow, track, while a greyhound wouldn't be much use to the blind. (That said, Crouch did need some assistance in finding the goal in his initial months at the club.)

For the tallest striker in the league, his heading was seen as the weakest aspect to his game. According to Opta, Crouch was number one in the Premiership in headed attempts on goal, but only scored three headers himself in the league (five of his 13 were headers in total, while two of his six England goals to date have been with his head). As a team Liverpool were adjudged by Opta to have led the league in headed attempts, with 134, but only scored six — the worst headed goal percentage in the league. It has to be said that Fernando Morientes, whose reputation was built on bullet headers, let the team down more in this respect than Crouch, who scored five times as many headers this season.

Despite not being the best technical header of a ball, he is still a danger in the air, causing the opposition to panic at how to deal with him and often forcing them to double-mark him, leaving others spare. (A classic example of this was in one of his early England games, against Argentina. He came on as a sub with ten minutes to go, and suddenly Michael Owen headed an equaliser followed quickly by the winner, both caused by the Argentines focusing on the tall substitute). With no great bodyweight to throw behind a cross Crouch can end up winning lots in the air but sending soft headers towards goal; other times he tries too hard to summon some power, and the timing goes awry. When he stuck to well-timed accurate headers, without trying too hard, he scored goals and set up others, with headers that sailed into the corner of the net, and assured cushioned assists.

What is apparent is that when the cross carries more power Crouch has the accuracy to score by simply redirecting the ball; his lack of strong neck muscles becomes irrelevant. High, looping crosses often don't provide him with the pace on the ball needed to trouble top flight goalkeepers; those lofted crosses help him win the ball in the air in the first place, due to his height, but make it hard for him to score — unless he has found space at the back post, and the ball cuts out the goalkeeper.

But if the cross is whipped in Crouch can apply a deft header to redirect it home with enough pace to be a problem. Rafa Benítez's addition of three noted crossers — Fabio Aurelio, Jermaine Pennant and Mark Gonzalez — will surely supply a better quality of ball into the box, so it will be interesting to see how Crouch's goals rate is affected. (As a side note, in the first two weeks of the 'new' season, Crouch scored three headers for club and country, taking him to eleven headed goals in nine months.)

It's become a cliché, but nothing can be written about Crouch without referencing his 'fantastic touch for a big man'. This is backed up with evidence of his superb link play, as he picked up 18 assists in his first season at Anfield, at just under 0.5 per-90 minutes on the pitch. This was in direct contrast to his goal production, which was very streaky. He scored his first seven goals in eight straight games around Christmas, once the proverbial monkey was lifted from his back, and then had little luck until four goals in three straight games in March. These included his first goals within the six-yard box, with more to follow: either he was foraging deeper into the box, or his team-mates were now able to supply the right delivery into the most dangerous areas; or possibly a mix of both.

Crouch's team statistics were also a mixed bag, as his figures placed him well above average in one category, average in another, and then below average in the remaining two. When Crouch played, the team had the second-highest goals-for average (1.75) for any forward in the team, with only Cissé's higher (1.82), and the third-highest average overall of players who started more than 15 games. Crouch also had a clean sheet percentage slightly above average, but his goals-against and points-per-contest were lower than the team mean. Crouch was substituted a total of 31 times in his 42 starts in 2005/06 (74%), at an average time in the game of 71.5 minutes. Although it might be easy for someone so tall to stand around up front and present a target to hit, he does a lot of running for the team, and perhaps runs out of steam later in games.

His team goals-against average might also give another clue. There is very little doubt that Crouch offers extra height and heading ability when Liverpool defend set pieces, but his other defensive skills are a little raw. He does run hard but without pace, so is not a great hustler or harrier, and is often being pulled up for fouls by the referee when attempting tackles. His team goals-against average of 0.87 per-game was equivalent to Josemi's, and only a little better than the 0.90

average put up by the Reds in games in which Djimi Traoré played, which was the worst of any regular player in the team who made 15 starts or more. In Crouch's defence, he was utilised in nearly all of the toughest fixtures, and in the thankless task of lone striker, so that won't have helped that particular average.

Rather than be used as an impact sub, as many expected, Crouch clearly started lots of games. However, it was as a late sub, against his old team Aston Villa, where he showed how quickly he could change a game; he still couldn't score, but won a penalty and had a big hand in the second goal. But more often than not he was starting games. It was often in the closing 20 minutes, when Benítez wanted to 'shut up shop', that the No.15 gave way to a player who could bolster the midfield. Fernando Morientes and Robbie Fowler, who both had team goals-against averages of 0.52 per game, would drop into deeper areas than Crouch, to link play but also to help break up the opposition's possession. In fact, of Crouch's 31 substitutions, 18 of them involved either Morientes (10), Fowler (three), or an extra defender or midfielder (five) coming on in his place. In those circumstances, it's easy to see why better defensive numbers would be put up in Crouch's absence.

While it's fast becoming another cliché that Peter Crouch 'is not a 25-goals-a-season man', it's clear that he can still score goals at an impressive rate. Ten goals in thirteen games for England, with only seven being starts, gives him a far better goals-per-game and goals-per-minute ratio than both Michael Owen and Wayne Rooney; that is unlikely to last, but it's hard to wonder how he could have done any better. By September 2006 he had achieved something for England that not even Jimmy Greaves, Gary Lineker, Alan Shearer or Michael Owen could match, in becoming the first man to score ten goals in a calendar year, with this feat achieved with three further international fixtures in 2006, and without the aid of penalties. It all goes towards showing what he is capable of, as a goalscorer.

Crouch's disappointing scoring rate in his first season with Liverpool, due largely to the terrible start, was almost exactly half the figure he posted with Southampton in 2004/05. In the Saints' relegation season, Crouch fired 12 goals in 1813 minutes, for a rate of 0.595 — which actually beats the 'top 10' rates put up by Robbie Fowler and Craig Bellamy in 2005/06. Indeed, once his dry start to his time at Anfield was out of the way, Crouch was much closer to matching this rate; showing what he can achieve if in the right frame of mind.

Robbie Fowler No.11						Age: 30	Height: 5'11			Centre-Forward				
Misc	Individual		.							Team				
YEAR COMP	GS	MINS	GOALS	ASSISTS	POINTS	GOALS (90)	ASSISTS (90)	POINTS (90)	MLG	MLG % (90)	CS	CS %	GFA	GAA	PTS
2005-06 Total	10	859	5	2	7	0.52	0.21	0.73	0	0	4.9	51.1	1.26	0.52	2.26
2005-06 Prem	9	773	5	2	7	0.58	0.23	0.82	0	0	4.9	56.8	1.40	0.47	2.51
2005-06 Euro	1	86	0	0		0.00	0.00	0.00	0	0	0	0	0	1.05	0
2005-06 Total	11	1010	9	With Both Teams		0.80									
2005-06 Prem	9	834	6			0.65									
2005-06 Total	1	151	4	With Man City		2.38									
2005-06 Prem	0	61	1			1.48									
2004-05 Total	29	2590	11	With Man City		0.38									
2004-05 Prem	28	2500	10			0.36									

Just like old times? In many ways the first four months couldn't have gone any better for Robbie Fowler after his return to Liverpool. Although he started just ten games, he did enough to ensure it wouldn't be his last action in the famous red shirt, and duly earned a one-year contract which, as with Dennis Bergkamp for many years at Arsenal, could turn into a perennial extension.

If the goals didn't flow quite as freely as a decade earlier, Fowler still managed to score above the 0.5 goals-per-90 minutes level that marks out 'real' goalscorers — and even approached the 0.6 goals-per-game level in the Premiership after rejoining the club. He finished second in the team in that category, and actually led at one stage of the season, until Cissé started scoring in the final weeks of the season to overtake him. Add to his Liverpool numbers the four goals Fowler scored at Man City, and he suddenly jumps into Thierry Henry's realm of 0.8 goals-per-game — but without the Frenchman's regular penalty strikes (just one of Fowler's in 2005/06 was from the spot, in City's FA Cup against Scunthorpe).

Fowler's five goals for the Reds this season came from just nine attempts on target, and 18 in total; the conversion rate is quite stunning, at 1.8 shots on target for every goal. To put this into context, Cissé needed four shots on target for every league goal, Crouch 5.3 and Morientes an alarming 7.2.

Fowler's combined Premiership rate of 0.65 goals-per-90 minutes actually placed him 5th in the entire league in that category. His team statistics were also impressive, having the best team goals-against average (tied with Morientes) and points-per-contest of any forward at Liverpool.

The goals-for average is skewed downwards, however, as Fowler rejoined just as the Reds were entering a goal drought. The collective striking confidence was disconcertingly low, and Fowler's fitness was not such that he was in a position to immediately remedy the situation. Bad luck — with two harshly disallowed goals and one correctly ruled-out effort (which would have sent his figures positively stellar) — didn't help matters, as he struggled to get off the mark, although the linesman at Blackburn later atoned for the errors of his colleagues with the most generous offside decision of the player's career. (Rumours have it that the linesman's guide dog was advising his master to raise his flag but the official missed the signal.)

Even so, it didn't alter the fact that had Fowler got quickly off the mark, as his finishing warranted, more goals would almost certainly have followed; something that proved to be the case from mid-March onwards, by which time the season was unfortunately in its death throes. The end to 2005/06 came too soon for Fowler, but only after proving that there's life in the old dog yet. (As an additional note, Fowler scored the Reds' first league goal of the 'new' season, at Bramall Lane; as with Peter Crouch, who scored in the Community Shield, he would not have a long wait to get off the mark in 2006/07.)

Anthony Le Tallec No.13						Age: 20	Height: 6'1"		Centre-Forward/M'field						
Misc		Individual										Team				
YEAR	COMP	GS	MINS	GOALS	ASSISTS	POINTS	GOALS (90)	ASSISTS (90)	POINTS (90)	MLG	MLG % (90)	CS	CS %	GFA	GAA	PTS
2005-06	Total	2	148	0	2	2	0.00	1.22	1.22	0	0	1.6	100	2.43	0.00	3.00
2005-06	Euro	2	148	0	2	2	0.00	1.22	1.22	0	0	1.6	100	2.43	0.00	3.00
2005-06	Total	15	1522	5	With Sunderland		0.30	-	-	-	-	3.7	21.7	1.01	1.83	0.74
2004-05	Total	3	310	0	1	1	0	0.29	0.29	0	0	0.4	11.6	1.16	1.16	1.15
2004-05	Prem	0	218	0	0	0	0	0	0	0	0	0.3	13.8	0.41	0.83	0.41

Following Rafa Benítez's arrival Anthony Le Tallec did not get to play a great deal in the Liverpool first team, but performed well enough when given the opportunity in pre-season games and Champions League qualifiers. However, a chance for further appearances in the red shirt now looks remote. In August 2006 the striker was loaned to FC Sochaux-Montbéliard for the 'new' season, with the return to his homeland likely to end in a permanent deal. It is the fourth season-long loan Le Tallec has been sent on, following a year with Le Havre after signing for the Reds, an ill-fated move to St Etienne which was cut short, and a year in the north-east with Sunderland. For a player who still promises so much, time remains on his side. He is still only 21, despite having seemed to have been around forever. It may not be until he reaches his mid-to-late 20s that Le Tallec's thinking brand of football comes to the fore; strikers without pace, and who rely on thought, tend to have to pick up experience to out-fox their opponents. It took Teddy Sheringham, whose style Le Tallec most closely mirrors, until his mid-20s to make waves at the top level of English football; 16 years later the former England man is still going strong.

Le Tallec's first (and best) game for Liverpool in 2004/05 was a fine showing against Juventus in the Champions League, assisting on Luis Garcia's wonder strike to give Liverpool a 2-0 lead. This year he again put in a good first performance, assisting on the first two of Steven Gerrard's three goals in the opening game of the season against TNS at Anfield, in mid-July. He was subsequently loaned out to Sunderland for the whole season, which would certainly be an education into the tougher aspects of the English game. For someone who likes time on the ball, simply getting a touch proved challenging in one of the worst teams to grace the top flight of English football in recent years.

Le Tallec's preferred position is to play in the 'hole' between attack and midfield, similar to the role often played by Luis Garcia in the Liverpool team. In no way an athlete, the young Frenchman is a good passer and creator of chances, as seen in his assist numbers over the last two years, even in reduced minutes. Meanwhile, Le Tallec's goal rate with Sunderland (five goals at 0.30 per-90 minutes) is only a fraction below that put up by Luis Garcia in the Liverpool team over the last two years, and was well above midfielders such as Zenden and Kewell, and even above Fernando Morientes' combined rate over the last two years.

Neil Mellor No.33											Age: 22 Height: 6'0"						Centre-Forward	
Misc	Individual												Team					
YEAR	COMP	GS	MINS	GOALS	ASSISTS	POINTS	GOALS (90)	ASSISTS (90)	POINTS (90)	MLG	MLG % (90)		CS	CS %	GFA	GAA	PTS
2005-06	Total	5	364	1	With Wigan		0.25	-	-	-	-		0	0	0.99	0.99	1.15
2004-05	Total	11	854	5	1	6	0.53	0.11	0.63	0	0		3.1	32.2	1.48	0.63	1.96
2004-05	Prem	6	478	2	0	2	0.38	0	0.38	0	0		0.8	14.2	1.69	0.94	2.05

Neil Mellor must have thought he had finally 'arrived' in the winter of 2004, when his stunning goal beat Arsenal, followed by a fine finish against Newcastle and the monumentally-important poacher's strike against Olympiakos. However, surgery on both knees quickly followed, to end his involvement in last season while his rehabilitation lasted well into this. Upon his recovery he made one reserve appearance for the Reds, scoring a goal, and was then loaned out to Wigan in the January transfer window. He made a fantastic debut for the Premiership new boys, scoring the last-minute winner in a 3-2 victory at Middlesbrough, but only managed to start five games, again due to injury. A superb six-yard box predator, Mellor certainly knows how to score goals, and Preston should be the beneficiaries: signing the player on a three-year deal in August 2006.

Fernando Morientes No.19											Age: 29 Height: 6'0"						Centre-Forward	
Misc	Individual												Team					
YEAR	COMP	GS	MINS	GOALS	ASSISTS	POINTS	GOALS (90)	ASSISTS (90)	POINTS (90)	MLG	MLG % (90)		CS	CS %	GFA	GAA	PTS
2005-06	Total	33	2947	9	11	20	0.27	0.34	0.61	0	0		17	52.8	1.56	0.52	2.13
2005-06	Prem	20	1823	5	9	14	0.25	0.44	0.69	0	0		13	65.0	1.53	0.44	2.47
2005-06	Euro	9	729	3	1	4	0.37	0.12	0.49	0	0		3.1	33.9	1.23	0.49	1.65
2005-06	Cups	4	395	1	1	2	0.23	0.23	0.46	0	0		1.1	24.3	2.28	0.91	1.47
2004-05	Total	14	1179	3	4	7	0.23	0.31	0.53	0	0		2.1	16.3	1.15	0.92	1.28
2004-05	Prem	12	1015	3	3	6	0.27	0.27	0.53	0	0		1.1	10.0	1.15	1.06	1.22

With the exception of his time in a Spanish shirt, Fernando Morientes had never been an out-and-out goalscorer before arriving at Liverpool in January 2005 (as Table 10, below, indicates). Only once in the last nine years has he gone over a goals-per-90-minutes rate of 0.6, the rate of a very good striker.

In 2003/04 Morientes was loaned out by Real Madrid to Monaco for the season, and enjoyed a fine year, scoring 19 goals in total. His goal rate per-90 minutes, however, was still 'only' 0.56. This is a good goal rate for a striker, but not a phenomenal one, and that season, rather than be the making of Morientes, proved a difficult one to live up to.

Table 10. Morientes' goalscoring rates over the last nine years

Season	Team	Minutes	Goals	Goals per 90
2005/06	Liverpool	2947	9	0.27
2004/05	Liverpool	1179	3	0.23
2004/05	Real Madrid	456	2	0.39
2003/04	Monaco	3056	19	0.56
2002/03	Real Madrid	704	5	0.64
2001/02	Real Madrid	3588	21	0.53
2000/01	Real Madrid	2418	10	0.37
1999/00	Real Madrid	3588	19	0.48
1998/99	Real Madrid	2964	19	0.58
1997/98	Real Madrid	3354	16	0.43

* figures exclude appearances in French cup in 2003/04 and Spanish cup in all Real Madrid years

Of the 19 goals Morientes scored in 2003/04, 10 were in the French league, at a rate of 0.44 per-90 minutes, while nine were scored in the Champions League at a rate of 0.79 goals-per-90. The 0.44 rate in the league was more true to Morientes' past form, whilst his 0.79 goals-per-90 minutes rate in the Champions League was uncharacteristically prolific for the Spanish forward. In leading his Monaco team-mates into the final of the competition, where they would eventually lose to Jose Mourinho's Porto 3-0, Morientes won the Golden Boot for the most goals in the tournament, and it looked like he'd finally escaped the shadow of Raul to become a genuine star player in his own right. Real Madrid duly recalled 'El Moro', but only to have him sit on the (gold-plated marble?) subs' bench at the Bernabeu. With Ronaldo, Raul and newly acquired Michael Owen in the squad Morientes played an amazing total of 456 substitute minutes. In this period any confidence or improved form from the previous year's Champions League was lost. By the time he arrived at Anfield he was rusty and lacking sharpness, and he never seemed to recover from a slow start. He managed just three goals in his 1179 minutes in 2004/05, for a rate per-90-minutes of only 0.23. But a lot more was expected when the forward returned to full fitness to begin 2005/06, when he would surely show his undoubted class, even if he might not hit a sackful of goals.

Alas, he never came close to consistently finding his best form, and too often looked well off the frantic pace of the Premiership. He struggled to nine goals in 2005/06 in a total of 2947 minutes, at a rate of 0.27 per-90. His Premiership rate of 0.25 goals per-90 was 62nd in the league, with 15 midfielders actually having a better rate than the Liverpool forward.

His heading skills posed another concern. Known throughout Europe as an expert header of the ball, especially after scoring the majority of his nine goals in the 03/04 Champions League in the air, even that skill seemed to desert him. Opta had Morientes in the top five of headed efforts in the Premiership this season, yet he did not score a single goal with his head in the league, and only managed one all year in all competitions, scoring against CSKA Sofia from a Gerrard free-kick cross. This from a man who once scored four headers in a single Spanish league game.

Just as the world's best golfers can find their timing abandon them, as they experience their long or short game fall apart for no apparent reason, Morientes found his aerial coordination inexplicably evaporate. He still adopted technically-perfect stances, but often went up too early; other times he glanced the ball too finely or too heavily. When the contact was good more often than not he sent thumping headers straight at the keeper.

His assist rates were decent, and his team stats show what a fantastic defensive forward he is, as the Reds posted their lowest goals-against average (0.52 per-game) when he was in the line-up, compared with any other Liverpool regular. Incredibly, the Reds won an average of 2.47 Premiership points during his minutes on the pitch, suggesting his inclusion helped Benítez's team gel. But it just wasn't enough to take his time at Anfield into a third season. Morientes had looked unhappy in his second season, and it was in the interest of both player and manager to cut their losses. In early June Morientes was sold to Valencia for £3.5m, ending his disappointing 18-month spell with the Reds.

| Florent Sinama-Pongolle No.24 | | | | | | | Age: 20 | Height: 5'7" | | | Striker/Right-M'field | | | | |
| Misc | | Individual | | | | | | | | | Team | | | | |
YEAR	COMP	GS	MINS	GOALS	ASSISTS	POINTS	GOALS (90)	ASSISTS (90)	POINTS (90)	MLG	MLG % (90)	CS	CS %	GFA	GAA	PTS
2005-06	Total	4	538	3	0	3	0.50	0.00	0.50	0	0	1.8	30.5	1.51	0.84	1.67
2005-06	Prem	3	273	0	0	0	0.00	0.00	0.00	0	0	1.3	42.9	0.00	0.99	1.21
2005-06	Euro	1	167	1	0	1	0.54	0.00	0.54	0	0	0.2	12.6	2.69	0.54	2.33
2005-06	Cups	0	98	2	0	2	1.84	0.00	1.84	0	0	0.3	26.5	3.67	0.92	1.81
2005-06	Total	8	708	1	With Blackburn		0.13	-	-	-	-	4.7	59.3	1.65	0.51	2.08
2004-05	Total	11	1146	4	2	6	0.31	0.16	0.47	0	0	4.5	35.6	1.10	0.63	1.59
2004-05	Prem	6	662	2	1	3	0.27	0.14	0.41	0	0	2.1	29.2	1.09	0.82	1.46

Florent Sinama-Pongolle — still a youngster — could yet be on the cusp of turning into a special talent. Too much was expected too soon after he and Anthony Le Tallec wowed Gérard Houllier with their trophy-winning exploits in the French under 17 World Championship in September 2001. Sinama-Pongolle won the Golden Boot for being the tournament's top goalscorer, netting nine times, and the Golden Ball for being best player.

There are signs of life in his numbers with Liverpool that suggest he could yet have a big future in the Premiership, and even international football one day; he has certainly looked no worse than Luis Saha did at the same age. While Nicolas Anelka was an awesome 18-year-old at the very top level of the game, someone like Saha can provide the young Liverpool striker with inspiration. It was the late-developer Saha, and not Anelka, who went to the World Cup in 2006.

Sinama-Pongolle netted four goals a year ago at a rate of 0.31, and was just starting to show some very impressive form when a serious knee injury curtained his season, and as with Neil Mellor, ate into the beginning of 2005/06. When 'Flo' did make his first start of the season he made an immediate impact, scoring a fantastic lobbed goal against Real Betis in Sevilla. Just as he had the previous year against Olympiakos, he played the role of supersub again in 2005/06 — scoring twice in Liverpool's dramatic turnaround at Luton in the FA Cup 3rd round. His goal rate this year with Liverpool was a very healthy 0.5 per-90 minutes, and his speed up front was definitely missed when Liverpool's goalscoring fortunes dipped in February, just after being loaned out for the remainder of the season to Blackburn. He managed another goal as the Ewood Park outfit battled for a European place, to give him a total of five for the year, and he linked particularly well with Craig Bellamy; a partnership that might possibly be reprised at Anfield in the future, albeit in emergencies.

Further evidence of the Frenchman's goalscoring ability can be seen in his reserve team figures, where he netted three times in only 320 minutes for an impressive rate of 0.84 goals per-90-minutes. Time is still on Sinama-

Pongolle's side, and he still has a very bright future in the game, although the odds are that it will be away from Liverpool on a permanent basis. As with his cousin, Anthony Le Tallec, it might take a couple of years before he finally finds the form he is capable of producing on a consistent basis. A year's loan to newly promoted *La Liga* side Recreativo de Huelva, which was agreed in late August, should provide him with regular playing time on the big stage, and a chance to further develop his game.

Chapter Seven
2006/07 and Beyond

We have prodded, poked, scratched, sniffed and dissected the 2005/06 season in great detail. So what can it tell us about the future? Are Liverpool really on the cusp of something big? Or have Rafa's Reds hit the ceiling of their potential?

The right age for success?

It's not going to guarantee the Premiership title, but one of the positive aspects of the squad Rafa Benítez has assembled, in addition to its obvious quality and depth, is its average age. It has the look of a squad full of hunger, with the right blend of age-groups and the varying attributes you get from players at different stages of their career.

The peak years of a footballer's career were always seen as from 27/28 to 31/32, with the perfect balance between legs still willing, lungs still strong and a mind more experienced and thoughtful. Perhaps as the game gets faster and more intense, especially in England, the average for peak years has lowered slightly, to between 26 and 30. There will always be those individuals who reach their best at a younger age, and those who peak later, but the average won't have altered that much. For every near-pre-pubescent prodigy there's an evergreen elder statesman at the other end of the spectrum.

These days a lot of people seem to think players are washed up by the age of 28. That is sometimes the case, due to injuries and a loss of appetite for the game, and there will continue to be players like George Best, whose best years were their first years. Quick young strikers often seem less effervescent in the second half of their careers, although their positional sense should be better. They may dazzle less, but they can still get the job done by conserving their energy and thinking quickly. Goalkeepers, on the other hand, tend to mature later; most Premiership keepers are in their 30s.

All this brings us to the average age of this Liverpool squad going into the new campaign. The blend looks right; it's not top-heavy with players on the wane, nor is it replete with kids who need to be relied upon long before they are ready to perform consistently at the top level. Assembling a squad of players at the right age is pointless if they are all of limited ability, but getting the right ratio of experience to youthful exuberance is crucial if they instead happen to be the right players. It's about having the right players at the right time. It's extremely rare for a team to win major honours with an average age lower than 26. It's also unheard of for a team to win major honours with an average age in excess of 31; teams like Juventus and AC Milan, both of whom have seemed like a collections of OAPs at times in recent years, still have an average age of 28/29, due to the youngsters who also get games.

If it's important to get the right balance to a team in terms of its varying talents and personalities, it's also true that a balance in age is important. You need your runners with their stamina, and you need your older, calmer heads, to dictate proceedings. Much was made of the Manchester United side of 1996, when Alan Hansen infamously said 'You win nothing with kids', but all those youngsters played alongside experienced pros like Cantona, Bruce, Pallister, Keane and Schmeichel. It was not a young side, merely a side containing youngsters. There's a big difference. In the early years of Gérard Houllier's reign the average age of his Liverpool side was as low as 24. This was fully understandable, given he was at the start of a building process, and theoretically the team could mature together over the coming years.

The middle of Houllier's reign saw the remarkable Treble followed by a 2nd-placed finish, and this coincided with the added experience of players like Nicky Barmby, Christian Ziege, Markus Babbel, Jari Litmanen and most notably, Gary McAllister. Robbie Fowler, aged 26 at the end of 2000/01, contributed significantly to the cup successes in particular. The balance in terms of experience and youthful exuberance seemed perfect, and we were all optimistic. But none of these players would still be at the club by the summer of 2002. Much is made of the quality of the signings made that summer, with Salif Diao, Bruno Cheyrou and El Hadji Diouf seen as abject failures, but perhaps as relevant was their age. Experience was replaced with inexperience.

By the end of Houllier's reign the average age was back down to near where it had started, and the team was slipping out of the Champions League places, falling back to the level of when he took over. Was this coincidental? And did the age of that squad present clues as to its limitations? The average age of what Houllier arguably saw as his strongest ten outfield players going into the 2003/04 season was 25, which is fairly young. Most notably, the rest of the squad in 2003 was made up almost entirely of players well below that age, such as Anthony Le Tallec, John Arne Riise, Djimi Traoré, Florent Sinama-Pongolle, Milan Baros and Chris Kirkland. Quite staggeringly, the age of the squad as a whole was actually below 24. With the aid of hindsight, that seems far too young to challenge for the title. While top-quality younger players are essential for the future of any club, and must always be sought, there comes a point in a manager's reign — once he has settled in and stabilised a club — when he has to deliver in the present; paying attention to the future remains essential, but not to the detriment of the current campaign.

Rafa Benítez is trying to assure a bright future for the club with a whole raft of great young kids, but most of these have been procured with one eye on 'tomorrow', and any unexpectedly rapid progress they make in the meantime is a bonus. Should Paul Anderson feature in 2006/07 it will not be as a player the Reds desperately rely upon, but as an added extra. The age range of players bought by Benítez runs the gamut, from teenagers to 30-somethings.

Pepe Reina, Mark Gonzalez, Xabi Alonso and Momo Sissoko were all bought aged between 20-22 and capable of immediately shining for the first team; indeed, Reina is a bit of an exception to the rule, as an incredibly experienced young keeper, while Alonso is also an unusually mature player for his age. Luis Garcia, Fabio Aurelio, Peter Crouch, Craig Bellamy, Dirk Kuyt and Jan Kromkamp all arrived in their mid-20s, when approaching their peak years. At the other end of the spectrum, Bolo Zenden, Robbie Fowler, and Fernando Morientes were signed during what are seen as a player's peak years. Only Mauricio Pellegrino, aged 108*, was signed by Benítez when over the age of 31 at the time. (*quite possibly untrue.)

The average age of those who make up the 'main' 20 players currently at the club is 26. It's hard to say what the average age of the Reds' strongest XI would be, as Benítez's sides are never the easiest to predict; unlike some managers he doesn't seem to settle upon a regular eleven, but chops and changes to meet the requirements of each match, while injuries obviously affect his thinking. But based on a rough XI of Reina, Finnan, Hyypia, Carragher, Riise, Kewell, Gerrard, Sissoko, Alonso, Crouch and Bellamy, the average again works out at 26. Replacing either of the strikers with Kuyt makes no real difference.

Crucially, the other nine players also have an average of 26. When Fowler, Zenden, Garcia, Gonzalez and Aurelio are taken into consideration — as the five likely to feature most, and who might even play more regularly than some of the aforementioned starting XI — the average age of what might well be the 'first 16' edges up towards 27, which is a near-perfect squad age. So let's be clear: this is not an ageing squad assembled in the desperate attempt of one last hurrah, nor a team of kids who won't be ready to challenge Chelsea before Mourinho draws his pension. With the age-range looking so good, the manager can only hope that his players live up to their billing.

Addressing the gaps

As we enter Benítez's third year at the helm, do the statistics we've presented pinpoint any clear weaknesses from 2005/06, and what hitherto missing ingredients do the new signings add?

When we analysed the team statistics from the 2005/06 season we saw that the team was improving in almost every area needed for the Benítez design. The time of possession, the shots fired at goal, and the low amount of goals conceded were all improved to match the level of a top side. But the overall picture was still some way short of perfection.

With the addition of Momo Sissoko the back four had even better protection, and the team conceded only two long range goals — and one of those was a fluke cross shot. The zonal marking system on set pieces was fully implemented and drilled, resulting in the team rarely conceding at all from set plays: improvements that led to the team posting 33 clean sheets, one short of the club record.

All these improvements were on the defensive side of the ball; while the attacking side of the game saw better figures than a year earlier, it still left plenty of room for improvement. The corners won, shots on target and goals went up, but so did the opponents' goalkeepers' saves — and by a larger amount than the goals increased. The increase in shots did not increase the goalscoring by as much as it should have: Liverpool were very inconsistent at converting their chances (see Table 1). The range of different values for the number of shots the team had on goal to the number of goals the team scored just goes to show the inconsistent nature of Liverpool's finishing. In all competitions it doesn't look too bad; the Reds scored one goal for every 3.9 shots-on-goal, which is okay. However, in the Premiership the ratio went up to five, which was actually *higher* than the team's 2004/05 Premiership ratio of 4.6 shots-on-goal per goal. Liverpool scored a total of five more goals in the Premiership this season, but that total took an extra 42 shots on target.

As discussed earlier, a team's true weakness comes out in the games against the top teams. In the games against the Premiership's top five finishers Liverpool managed a total of 6.0 shots per-game, just below their overall season rate of 6.6, and easily second in the category behind Chelsea. However, the Reds only scored four goals in these contests, for an average of 0.5 goals-per-game, and a shots-on-goal to goal ratio of 12 shots for every goal scored. This was by far the worst ratio in such games, with Chelsea averaging a goal every 3.7 shots-on-goal, Man United one every 5.7 shots-on-goal, and both Arsenal and Tottenham being around the 8.5 shots-on-goal per goal mark.

Table 1. Shots-on-goal to goals ratios for Liverpool and the Premiership top five teams in games against each other in 2005/06

Competition	SOG	GFA	Shots to goals ratio
Overall	6.6	1.68	3.9
Premiership	7.5	1.5	5
Premiership Home	9.3	1.68	5.5
Premiership Away	5.6	1.32	4.2
Premiership Top 5	6	0.5	12
Premiership Top 5 Home	7.3	0.75	9.7
Premiership Top 5 Away	4.8	0.25	19.2
Europe	4.6	0.75	6.1
FA Cup	5.8	3.33	1.7
Chelsea versus Top 5	7.4	2	3.7
Man United versus Top 5	5	0.88	5.7
Arsenal versus Top 5	4.4	0.5	8.8
Tottenham versus Top 5	5.3	0.63	8.4

Further evidence of the team's problems up front can be seen in the number of games in which the team failed to score, and the number of goals scored from inside the six-yard box. The team's failure to score rate did improve in 2005/06, only drawing blanks in 15 games this season, compared with 20 in 2004/05. In the Premiership this total also fell from 13 in 2004/05 to nine in 2005/06. As discussed in the Team Statistic chapter, an improvement here could significantly increase the league points in 2006/07. In terms of goals scored from inside the six-yard box, the Reds had managed only five from that distance in their first 50 games of the year. The team eventually finished with 17 goals close-range efforts, down from 19 close-range efforts the year before (when the team scored 22 fewer goals in total). The addition of Fowler really helped here, but also Crouch appeared to be getting deeper into the box in the later stages of the season.

The player statistics indicated a lack of depth and scoring from wide midfielders in the team — the left wing in particular — and that the scoring from defence was almost non-existent, especially in the Premiership. When the attacking production of the team is broken down by playing position it indicates some interesting problems within the team (see Table 3). The Reds managed a total of just five goals from defensive positions on the year: three from centre-backs and only two from full-backs. In terms of points-per-90 minutes the most productive defensive position was right back, with 17 assists but no goals. The left-back position was almost as unproductive as the centre-backs, only posting stats of two goals and eight assists due to Riise sometimes playing in left-midfield. The replacements for Riise just didn't bring anything to the attacking production of the team whatsoever.

Liverpool are stacked in the centre of midfield. No obvious changes nor additions were needed here, especially once Jermaine Pennant arrived to allow Gerrard to spend more time in the centre in 2006/07. Rafa Benítez could even afford to let Didi Hamann leave, something that would have been fairly unthinkable 24 months earlier.

Table 2. Attacking production of different positions in the Liverpool team in 2005/06

Position	Goals	Assists	Points	Goals (90)	Assist (90)	Points (90)
GK	0	4	4	0.00	0.06	0.06
CB (2)	3	12	15	0.02	0.10	0.12
RB	0	17	17	0.00	0.27	0.27
LB	2	8	10	0.03	0.13	0.16
RM	19	25	44	0.30	0.40	0.70
LM	11	21	32	0.18	0.34	0.51
CM (2)	17	40	57	0.14	0.32	0.45
F (2)	49	50	99	0.39	0.40	0.79

Analysing the attacking production from wide midfielders this season brings up some interesting facts. The right side of midfield was in fact far more productive than the left, even though there was such a hole in personnel for the position. Players playing on the right-hand side of midfield scored eight more goals and collected four more assists than those playing on the left. The right hand side was made-up of stand-ins, including Steven Gerrard and Djibril Cissé, whilst the left was manned by Harry Kewell most of the year. Bolo Zenden's injury really did change the strength of the left side, with only John Arne Riise and Stephen Warnock left for cover. Luis Garcia played the most on the right side, and although it wasn't their natural position Kromkamp, Cissé and Gerrard provided cover.

Even with the impressive stats for the right side of midfield it remained a position in need of a specialist player, but with cover in Garcia and Gerrard there's little chance of the Reds being weak on that flank. The problem with the two aforementioned players in the role is that both like to drift infield, to get involved in the play and look to score goals; the shape of the team can be affected, and the strikers will surely benefit from Pennant, who is prepared to go outside and get crosses in, and will add a new dimension even if he doesn't start every game. On the left greater depth was definitely needed, and that was instantly addressed by the work permit finally awarded to Mark Gonzalez, and Bolo Zenden's return from injury after missing two-thirds of 2005/06. The mind really does boggle as to what could have happened had Gonzalez joined as planned and Benfica's Simao come on board.

Summer signings, and those who got away

Defenders

Daniel Alves, Sevilla		Age: 23		Right-Back	
Misc		Individual			
YEAR	COMP	GS	MINS	GOALS	GOALS (90)
2005-06	Total	48	4224	3	0.06
2005-06	La Liga	35	3079	3	0.09
2004-05	Total	31	2962	2	0.06

The main link of the summer was Sevilla's Daniel Alves, with Rafa Benítez seeing him as the solution to the right-sided problem. Alves, who can play in defence or midfield, was extremely keen to play for the Reds but as with

Simao and Benfica, his club priced him out of a move. With Sevilla looking for more than £12m, Benítez eventually switched his sights to Jermaine Pennant, whom he procured for half that price.

Alves had a very good season for Sevilla, and was part of the team that thumped Middlesbrough in the Uefa Cup final; even providing the assist on the first goal of the game with a quite stunning cross from a deep position that swerved viciously past the bemused Boro defenders. He is a very quick and talented player who covers a lot of ground with aggressive running, making him a real all-rounder. Able to play full-back with assurance, at 5' 8" he is perhaps too short to be an unreserved success in such a role in English football. It's easy to see why Benítez was interested in him for the right midfield role, but not only did Jermaine Pennant provide better value for money, the English winger would have no trouble settling into the pace of the Premiership.

Fabio Aurelio No.12						Age: 26	Height: 5'10"			Left-Back/Left-Midfield			
Misc	Individual									Team			
YEAR	COMP	GS	MINS	GOALS	ASSISTS	POINTS	GOALS (90)	ASSISTS (90)	POINTS (90)	MLG	MLG % (90)	CS	CS %	GFA	GAA	PTS
2005-06 La Liga	11	1080	2	3	5	0.17	0.25	0.42	-	-	4.5	37.7	1.50	0.83	1.48
2004-05 La Liga	16	1352	0	With Valencia		0									

Had Daniel Alves arrived at Anfield he would have been only the second Brazilian to sign for the club; the first, Fabio Aurelio, arrived on a free transfer in July 2006, from Rafa Benítez's old club, Valencia. The left-back was only really a bit-part player and frequent substitute at the Mestalla following Benítez's departure in 2004, but the Spanish manager was well aware of what the player could offer the Reds. An assured attacking full-back with a great cross, he is also a real free-kick expert, something the Reds have lacked in recent seasons. (Riise, Hamann, Gerrard and Alonso have all shared the duties, but Gerrard's drives from indirect kicks aside, none has scored more than one free-kick goal per season; Riise has still only registered two in five full seasons.) Aurelio posted an impressive goals-per-90 minute rate for a defender in 2005/06, at 0.17; a far more impressive rate than any of the Liverpool full-backs.

Benítez even went so far as to say that Aurelio was a better passer than Xabi Alonso; high praise indeed. Having worked with both he was certainly able to make that distinction. The Brazilian is also not afraid of a tackle, and is more sturdy and brave than the national stereotype. For a free transfer it may be a case of adding more options, rather than Aurelio becoming a first team regular, but on the surface it looks another canny bit of business by Benítez.

Wide Midfielders

Mark Gonzalez No.11						Age: 22	Height: 5'9"				Left-Midfield	
Misc		Individual							Team			
YEAR	COMP	GS	MINS	GOALS	ASSISTS	POINTS	GOALS (90)	ASSISTS (90)	POINTS (90)	MLG	MLG % (90)	CS	CS %	GFA	GAA	PTS
2005-06 Total		13	995	4	3	7	0.36	0.27	0.63	0	0	3.7	33.3	1.27	1.27	1.33
2005-06 La Liga		13	995	4	3	7	0.36	0.27	0.63	0	0	3.7	33.3	1.27	1.27	1.33
2004-05 La Liga		15	1386	5	With Albacete		0.32									

In June 2006 Mark Gonzalez finally gained clearance to play in the Premiership, a year after Liverpool first applied for a work permit. In the interim he had been loaned to Real Sociedad, where he earned rave reviews in the Spanish press and received begging letters from fans to stay — which, of course, was never an option. A change in FIFA world football rankings in July 2006 came a year too late for the Reds with regard to the Chilean speedster. Having needed to be in the top 70 teams over a two year average, Chile spent their time fractionally outside the cut-off point. The new system, implemented by Sepp Blatter straight after the World Cup, instantly catapulted Chile into the mid-40s, which was a far more accurate reflection of their ability. By then Gonzalez had proven to his case to the DoE with an excellent few months in Spain, and been cleared to represent the Reds.

'Speedy' Gonzalez will offer blistering pace on the left, to balance with Jermaine Pennant on the right. Benítez could certainly use him putting up similar goals-per-90 minutes rates in keeping with both his Real Sociedad and Albacete numbers. In Spanish football, if he played 2000 minutes he'd score eight goals; such a rate would get him well into double figures over the course of a full season, providing he can quickly find his feet in English football.

The 'new' season couldn't have started any better for him, with a goal after just three minutes of his debut, having come on as a sub against Maccabi Haifa; it proved to be the crucial strike which took Liverpool into the Champions League proper. Having kept Sociedad in the Spanish top division with priceless match-winning goals, he started life at Anfield where he'd just left off.

Simão, Benfica			Age:26	Left/Right-Midfield	
Misc		Individual			
YEAR	COMP	GS	MINS	GOALS	GOALS (90)
2005-06	SuperLiga	25	2186	9	0.37
2004-05	SuperLiga	34	2956	15	0.46

The attempt to sign Simao Sabrosa represented one of the great sagas of 2005; the Reds agreed a fee of £10m, only for Benfica to add £3m to the price at the very last minute. So what did Liverpool miss out on?

Simao's mobility and goalscoring from wide midfield could certainly have been utilised in 2005/06, although both Gerrard and Cissé scored well from the right wing, which is where the Portuguese international would have played. Having said that, Simao is arguably more effective cutting in on his right foot from the left wing. In five years, since returning to his homeland after an ill-fated spell with Barcelona as a youngster, he has racked up 65 goals in the Portuguese top division — a good, if not great league — which goes to show his talent. He scored nine league goals this year, and added two in the Champions League (both on English soil, against Manchester United and, of course, Liverpool), for an overall goals-per-90 minutes rate of 0.35. In 2002/03 Simao scored 18 league goals, at a rate of 0.57 goals-per-90 minutes; top strikers would be proud of such stats, and it goes to show the player's prolific rate from wide positions. It's impossible to say what might have been, but the reason behind the Reds' interest is clear to see.

Stelios, Bolton		Age:31		Right-Midfield	
Misc		Individual			
YEAR	COMP	GS	MINS	GOALS	GOALS (90)
2005-06	Total	41	3517	12	0.31
2005-06	Prem	29	2545	9	0.32
2004-05	Total	31	2638	8	0.27

Stelios Giannakopoulous was another right-sided midfielder who came close to joining the Reds in 2005. Just like Simao, the Bolton man posted a one-in-three goals rate this season, although the Greek international did so in English football, which makes comparisons with Liverpool players easier. Stelios has scored a total of 20 goals over the last two seasons, at a rate of 0.29 per-90 minutes. Having turned 32 in the summer of 2006, he would only have presented a short-term solution to the problem position.

Jermaine Pennant No.16						Age: 23 Height: 5'9"					Right-Midfield				
Misc	Individual										Team				
YEAR	COMP	GS	MINS	GOALS	ASSISTS	POINTS	GOALS (90)	ASSISTS (90)	POINTS (90)	MLG	MLG % (90)	CS	CS %	GFA	GAA	PTS
2005-06	Total	45	4035	3	18	21	0.07	0.40	0.47	0	0	11.4	25.5	0.35	1.34	1.08
2005-06	Prem	35	3142	2	11	13	0.06	0.32	0.37	0	0	7.5	21.5	0.72	1.29	0.85
2005-06	Cups	10	893	1	7	8	0.10	0.71	0.81	0	0	3.9	39.5	1.31	1.51	1.79
2004-05	Total	12	1016	0	with Birmingham		0									

After what seemed like a thousand possibilities for the right-hand midfield slot, which stopped just short of asking Terry McDermott to come out of retirement, Rafa Benítez finally plumped for Birmingham's Jermaine Pennant, a player he had been tracking since his arrival in English football. A very gifted, fleet-footed winger, Pennant's difficulties have been off the field rather than on it. His problems at Arsenal — for whom he signed in 1999, aged just 15 — were numerous, but the main ones were the quality of his rivals for a place in the team, and his own tender age. Robert Pires was far too good at that stage, both in terms of individual talent and how he linked with Thierry Henry and Patrick Vieira, while Freddie Ljungberg had a phenomenal goalscoring record from wide positions. No teenager was going to break up that wide pairing, while Arsenal were purring as a side, and in no need of any tinkering. Needs must; Liverpool needed a right winger in 2006, and back then, Arsenal clearly didn't.

Pennant, meanwhile, was too young and too impatient. Perhaps signing for a big club for £2m at the age of 15 sped up his expectations, but he wanted action before he'd proved he was ready. When omitted from the Arsenal first-team picture, rather than train harder to prove Arsene Wenger wrong he showed his immaturity, and admitted to giving up. The ability was never in doubt: clearly seen when he was loaned to Leeds for the season in 2003/04, and then again at Birmingham, as well as on his full Premiership debut for Arsenal, when he scored a hat-trick. But a succession of driving offences ended with a prison sentence, and his career appeared to be heading for the dump before he'd made it far into his twenties. With Arsenal willing to cut their losses on the wayward star, Pennant headed to the midlands, to rebuild his career.

At Birmingham he performed notably in a struggling side, putting in by far and away the highest amount of crosses of any Premiership player in 2005/06, but for strikers who could not take advantage of them; Emile Heskey can be a very effective striker at times, but reliability in front of goal is not his biggest asset. It's been a while coming, but Pennant is now at a level where he can get regular games at a top club, even if he cannot expect to play every week; no one at Liverpool has that right, and another point to watch out for is his reaction to being out of the side. At 23 he is at a good age, particularly as he has a fair bit of experience under his belt — he's not a raw 23-year-old — not to mention an understanding of what it's like at a big club (even if that came with some harsh lessons). He can add more goals to his game, but that will be easier in a team dominating matches. At Leeds and Birmingham his main role was just getting the ball from a defensive area into the opposition half, and to try and put in crosses — which he did with impressive results, averaging 14 crosses per-game, and finding a team-mate 25% of the time — which may not sound a lot, but is a very high ratio.

Pennant has been relegated twice in the last three seasons, but as with Peter Crouch he showed his ability and character in a struggling side. He's now at an age where he's ready to go up a gear or two in a better side, one which plays to his strengths and where he receives more possession, and receives that possession in more dangerous areas. Like Craig Bellamy and Mark Gonzalez, Pennant offers genuine pace with the ball under tight control — not the 'wild' running that Djibril Cissé provided, where the Frenchman would launch the ball forward in pursuit of it. Pennant will clearly suit the tactics and pass-and-move style better than Cissé, but he could also do with getting close to the amount of goals the Frenchman plundered. If he can't do that, then a high number of assists will be equally helpful.

Forwards
It has been up front where Rafa Benítez has had to perform the most reconstruction at Anfield. First Michael Owen left for Real Madrid in August 2004, with Emile Heskey having already been sold that summer by Gérard Houllier; El Hadji Diouf joined the exodus, with a move to Bolton. Milan

Baros had a spell as Liverpool's first choice striker, but despite some good performances — and contributing to the Champions League success — he was too much of a maverick on the pitch. Djibril Cissé, who was signed by Houllier but arrived after the manager had been sacked, failed to convince Benítez of his worth, and lasted just two seasons, one of which was decimated by injury; even so, he still played 79 times for the club, and scored 24 goals in 43 starts. Benítez's own signing, Fernando Morientes, spent 18 months at Anfield without sparking into full life, scoring less than a goal per month, and was also culled in 2006. Meanwhile Neil Mellor, Anthony Le Tallec and Florent Sinama-Pongolle all played in some important games for the Reds, but were then loaned out for long periods.

By the end of 2005/06 Peter Crouch and Robbie Fowler, two players Benítez bought to the club, were the only strikers certain to be at Anfield in 2006/07. Some new strikers would duly arrive — Dirk Kuyt and Craig Bellamy — and others were pursued.

Jermain Defoe, Tottenham		Age:23			Striker
Misc		Individual			
YEAR	COMP	GS	MINS	GOALS	GOALS (90)
2005-06	Total	24	2325	9	0.35
2005-06	Prem	23	2215	9	0.37
2004-05	Total	35	2801	22	0.71

In January 2006 there was strong talk of a Liverpool/Tottenham swap deal, with Djibril Cissé heading to White Hart Lane and Jermaine Defoe coming in the other direction. But nothing transpired. The rumours resurfaced several months later, but Spurs were apparently looking for £14m for a player they were essentially using as a reserve at the time.

Even though Defoe had an off year, scoring nine goals at rate per-90 of 0.35, he was not playing regularly and unable to get into any kind of rhythm. An excellent finisher who is razor sharp in and around the box, he didn't seem to quite fit in with Martin Jol's tactical plan at Spurs; that didn't make him a bad player in any sense. In 2004/05 Defoe knocked in 22 goals at a rate of 0.71 (top five rate territory), with 13 coming in the Premiership, at a rate of 0.55, which placed him 8th in the league.

Darren Bent, Charlton		Age:22			Striker
Misc		Individual			
YEAR	COMP	GS	MINS	GOALS	GOALS (90)
2005-06	Total	43	3842	22	0.52
2005-06	Prem	36	3167	18	0.51
2004-05	Total	50	4389	20	0.41

A great buy for Charlton at £2.5m, but is Darren Bent worth bigger clubs pursuing now his value has exceeded £10m? His 18 goals in the Premiership placed him 3rd overall, but his goals rate dropped him all the way out of the top 10, to 13th place, just a shade above where Djibril Cissé finished. Bent got off to a fast start, scoring his first nine goals on the year in his first 11 appearances for a rate per-90 minutes of 0.87. He then scored 13 more over the rest of the season, but at the more pedestrian rate of 0.4 per-90 minutes. Looking at who Bent scored against reveals he racked up eight goals against poor teams: three against relegated Sunderland, two against relegated Birmingham, and one each against Brentford, Sheffield Wednesday and Hartlepool. Still, they all count.

Against the top five Premiership teams he scored a penalty against Liverpool, a gifted goal from a failed Robert Huth back-header against Chelsea in the Carling Cup, and a brace against Tottenham. Bent averaged 18 goals a season in his previous three seasons in the Championship with Ipswich, playing a lot of games for someone so young. Between the ages of 19 and 22 Bent made a total of 156 starts, which is close to burnout territory for a young player, although he looks very strong physically. In the summer of 2006 he signed a new four-year deal with Charlton, so isn't likely to be heading anywhere too soon.

Michael Owen, Newcastle			Age:26		Striker	
Misc		Individual				
YEAR	COMP	GS	MINS	GOALS	GOALS (90)	
2005-06	Total	10	884	7	0.71	
2005-06	Prem	10	884	7	0.71	
2004-05	Total	20	1862	14	0.68	

All talk of a possible return to Anfield ended when Michael Owen suffered a serious knee injury for England at the World Cup. Newcastle were able to hang onto their record signing for a second season at least, but yet again they were employing a man on crutches. Having paid £17m, the Geordies may get just 10 games out of Owen in his first two seasons with them.

Owen has always been a bit of a streaky goalscorer, grabbing his goals in bunches, but always delivers the goods over the course of a season, and often in the big matches. From 1996-2004 with Liverpool he scored 119 Premiership goals at an average of 17 per-season. He hit 19 goals three times, with a low of 11 in injury-ravaged 1999-2000. He scores at a 'top-five strikers' rate per-90 minutes in the 0.6 – 0.7 range. The former Liverpool man even netted seven Premiership goals this season in only 884 minutes for Newcastle.

Even in 2004/05, in a diminished role with Real Madrid, the little England man fired in 14 goals at a rate of 0.68 per-90 minutes played. At the age of 26 he has seen more injuries than the entire Rambo trilogy, but it hasn't stopped him getting over 200 goals for club and country.

Dirk Kuyt No.18							Age: 25 Height: 6'1"				Striker/Centre-Forward			
Misc		Individual									Team				
YEAR	COMP	GS	MINS	GOALS	ASSISTS	POINTS	GOALS (90)	ASSISTS (90)	POINTS (90)	MLG	MLG % (90)	CS	CS %	GFA	GAA	PTS
2005-06	Total	37	3336	25	-	-	0.67	-	-	-	-	11	29.7	2.19	1.08	1.91
2005-06	Ere'sde	33	2972	22	-	-	0.67	-	-	-	-	11	33.3	2.42	1.15	2.12
2004-05	Total	41	3572	32	With Feyenoord		0.81									

Dirk Kuyt scored more often in Holland than an Englishman on a stag weekend in Amsterdam. After an admiration dating back to his Valencia days, Rafa Benítez finally got his man in August 2006, paying £10.2m for the

Dutch international who usurped Ruud van Nistelrooy in the national team. In recent years only a couple of players have comparable records in the Dutch league. But is Kuyt the next van Nistelrooy or the next Mateja Kezman?

Of course, he is neither. He is a separate individual, with no connections to the other two beyond scoring lots of goals in the *Eredivisie*. Bad strikers do not score 25-35 goals-a-season in Dutch football, but the question is whether or not such prolific scoring can be translated to another league, where goals are harder to come by. Ruud van Nistelrooy proved capable of doing so; Mateja Kezman did not, although he was not given many starts in the blue of Chelsea.

Table 3: Dirk Kuyt's Dutch football stats

Team	Season	League		Dutch Cup		Europe		Playoffs		Total	
		Games	Goals	Games	Goals	Games	Goals	Games	Goals	Games	Goals
Feyenoord	2005/06	33	22	1	0	2	1	2	2	38	25
Feyenoord	2004/05	34	29	3	4	7	3	0	0	44	36
Feyenoord	2003/04	34	20	2	1	4	1	0	0	40	22
Total		101	71	6	5	13	5	2	2	122	83
FC Utrecht	2002/03	34	20	4	2	2	1	0	0	40	23
FC Utrecht	2001/02	34	7	3	3	4	1	0	0	41	11
FC Utrecht	2000/01	32	13	5	3	0	0	0	0	37	16
FC Utrecht	1999/00	32	6	4	4	0	0	0	0	36	10
FC Utrecht	1998/99	28	5	2	1	0	0	0	0	30	6
Total		160	51	18	13	6	2	0	0	184	66
Dutch Career		261	122	24	18	19	7	2	2	306	149

Kuyt's record suggests he is a hugely reliable finisher. He was a goalscoring winger at FC Utrecht, getting into double figures from the flanks in three successive seasons, until the new manager, Foeke Booy, moved him to centre-forward at the start of 2002/03. It paid instant dividends: Kuyt scored 20 league goals that season. His versatility is clear to see with his ability to play wide — the position he has occupied most frequently for his country.

In the last two seasons he notched up a total of 57 goals in league and European games, at a rate of 0.74 per-90 minutes. Van Nistelrooy leads to an interesting comparison. In his two full seasons at PSV van Nistelrooy racked up an average of 30 goals-a-season; in his four injury-free seasons with Manchester United in the Premiership (thus excluding 2004/05) he averaged 22 goals each year — a 25% reduction in goals coming from the *Eredivisie* to the Premiership. Van Nistelrooy also scored 55 goals in 68 cup games at United, a quite staggering record. Meanwhile, Kuyt scored an average of 24 goals-per-season in his three years with Feyenoord; if he saw a similar reduction in his league statistics when heading from the top flight in Holland to the top flight in England he could still find himself close to 20 league goals a season.

Kuyt is so sharp and lively in and around the box, and a real poacher of goals. He has a number of assets that suggest English football will suit him; indeed, the Feyenoord fans saw him as an 'English' striker. His strength has seen him compared with Alan Shearer. Kuyt's work-rate is prodigious, which is always near the top of Benítez's check-list of requirements. His fitness levels have been staggering: between March 2001 and April 2006 he played 179 consecutive matches, and missed only five games out of the last 238 his Dutch teams played;

all the more incredible given it's in a position where kicks and knocks are always picked up. At Liverpool he will have to get used to Benítez's rotation policy, and better rivals for the striking berth; but also midfielders far superior to any he's ever had the luxury of linking with in club football — so the supply should be better, too. Providing he can find his scoring rhythm when in and out of the side he should prove yet another canny bit of business by Benítez, whose expensive signings have rarely missed the mark.

Craig Bellamy No.17							Age: 27 Height: 5'9"				Striker/Centre-Forward			
Misc		Individual									Team				
YEAR	COMP	GS	MINS	GOALS	ASSISTS	POINTS	GOALS (90)	ASSISTS (90)	POINTS (90)	MLG	MLG % (90)	CS	CS %	GFA	GAA	PTS
2005-06 Total		26	2411	17	8	25	0.63	0.30	0.93	0	0	10.9	40.8	1.61	1.23	1.68
2005-06 Prem		22	2014	13	5	18	0.58	0.22	0.80	0	0	9.5	42.5	1.34	1.30	1.50
2005-06 Cups		4	397	4	3	7	0.91	0.68	1.59	0	0	1.4	32.0	2.95	0.91	2.55
2004-05 Total		43	3736	20	With Newcastle & Celtic		0.48									

Craig Bellamy is one of those players opposing fans love to hate. But judging by the comments made by the Newcastle and Blackburn faithful in recent times, he's a player fans love to have in their team; he gives it his all, including no shortage of 'verbals', and riles the opposition; kind of like Robbie Savage — only with talent. Rafa Benítez was fully aware of the baggage that comes with Bellamy — it's almost the full matching set — but this was a player in his mid-20s who desperately wanted to represent the club. It was always going to be a gamble, given past misdemeanours, but a calculated gamble.

Players mature. Mentally and emotionally, and in terms of talent. Frank Lampard was not pulling up trees at 24; nor, to be honest, was Jamie Carragher. Peter Crouch was barely even on the radar. Bellamy has always been an exciting player, but he has finally become a very potent one. A very good footballer has turned top-class. It happened to Lampard and Carragher at a similar age — 26. Bellamy is not necessarily quite at their level yet, but he's about to play in the best team he'll ever have experienced, and under the most talented manager. His level should go up another notch, especially as he enters what are seen as the peak years for a footballer.

Liverpool became Craig Bellamy's fourth club in two years, and the sixth of his short career. After a troubled end to his time at Newcastle, and a New Year's break in Glasgow with Celtic in 2004/05, everything came together at Blackburn for the Welsh forward in 2005/06. His 13 league goals in only 22 starts produced a goals-per-90 minutes rate of 0.58, which placed him 8th in the league, just behind his new Liverpool team-mate Robbie Fowler; but as with Michael Owen, another quick and small striker, Bellamy has experienced persistent hamstring problems and missed a fair few games over the years. The Welshman's career statistics show that up until now he's been a one-in-three striker, scoring over 100 goals in 300 games, and nine in 30 starts for his country. But he's also becoming more prolific, the older he gets. His league record over the years is slightly better than his overall record, with 85 strikes in 225 starts.

The key to signing Bellamy was the £6m release clause in his contract. With strikers like Bent and Defoe being rated in excess of £10m, it's fair to say the Welshman arrived at Anfield as an absolute bargain. It's testament to the shrewd dealings of Benítez that Liverpool are now the only team with two top ten strikers in goals-per-90 minutes (based on the 2005/06 season), and it cost them £3m per player. Crucially, both were desperate to be at the club. On top of this, the Reds now have Dirk Kuyt, whose scoring rate would have put him the top five in English football.

But Bellamy is not an out-and-out goalscorer. He is an incredibly quick and mobile front runner who can also work the channels, going past defenders to set up chances for a partner who'll happily remain more central. On paper, Bellamy's partnerships with either Peter Crouch or Kirk Kuyt look ideal — in the way he and Alan Shearer dovetailed so effectively at Newcastle — although these things can sometimes take time to cement. Despite the understandable reservations, Craig Bellamy remains an exciting signing for Liverpool Football Club.

Appendix
Line-ups, scorelines, goals and assists

Key:
A1 = final pass to goalscorer
A2 = penultimate pass to goalscorer
M = mistake leading to opposition goal

JULY 2005

July 13, 2005 – UEFA Champions League Qualifier

Liverpool **3 - 0** **T.N.S.**
Steven Gerrard 8'
(A1 Morientes, A2 Le Tallec)
Steven Gerrard 21'
(A1 Le Tallec, A2 Hyypia)
Steven Gerrard 89'
(A1 Riise)

Liverpool
25 Jose Reina, 23 Jamie Carragher, 3 Steve Finnan, 4 Sami Hyypia, 14 Xabi Alonso, 8 Steven Gerrard, 34 Darren Potter, 6 John Arne Riise, 28 Stephen Warnock, 13 Anthony Le Tallec, 19 Fernando Morientes **Substitutions** B Zenden for S Warnock (64), D Cissé for D Potter (76)
T.N.S.
1 Gérard Doherty, 4 Phillip Baker, 5 Steve Evans, 6 Tommy Holmes, 18 Michael Jackson, 2 Martin Naylor, 3 Christopher King, 7 Scott Ruscoe, 17 Nicky Ward, 9 Michael Wild, 15 Jamie Wood **Substitutions** S Beck for M Wild (59), J Lawless for T Holmes (72), J Leah for N Ward (82)

July 19, 2005 – UEFA Champions League Qualifier

T.N.S. **0 - 3** **Liverpool**
Djibril Cissé 26'
(A1 Riise, A2 Alonso)
Steven Gerrard 85'
(A1 Hamann)
Steven Gerrard 86'
(A1 Garcia)

Agg 0 - 6

T.N.S.
1 Gérard Doherty, 4 Phillip Baker, 5 Steve Evans, 6 Tommy Holmes, 2 Martin Naylor, 10 Steven Beck, 14 Hogan, 3 Christopher King, 7 Scott Ruscoe, 12 John Toner, 15 Jamie Wood **Substitutions** Lloyd-Williams for J Wood (58), N Ward for S Beck (68), M Jackson for S Evans (78)
Liverpool
25 Jose Reina, 23 Jamie Carragher, 3 Steve Finnan, 4 Sami Hyypia, 14 Xabi Alonso, 16 Dietmar Hamann, 34 Darren Potter, 6 John Arne Riise, 30 Boudewijn Zenden, 9 Djibril Cissé, 13 Anthony Le Tallec **Substitutions** Z Whitbread for J Carragher (53), S Luis Garcia for A Le Tallec (58), S Gerrard for X Alonso (67)

FBK Kaunas	1 - 3	**Liverpool**

FBK Kaunas
Giedrius Barevicius 21'
(*M1 Hyypia, positional/over played*)

Liverpool
Djibril Cissé 27'
(*A1 Crouch, A2 Zenden*)
Jamie Carragher 30'
(*A1 Gerrard*)
Steven Gerrard pen 54'
(*unassisted*)

FBK Kaunas
12 Eduardas Kurskis, 18 Mindaugas Baguzis, 5 Tomas Kancelskis, 6 Nukri Manchkhava, 3 Irmantas Zelmikas, 7 Giedrius Barevicius, 4 Mindaugas Pacevicius, 25 Tomas Tamosauskas, 13 Arkadiusz Klimek, 19 Eimantas Poderis, 11 Arturas Rimkevicius **Substitutions** V Petrenko for M Pacevicius (45), T Papeckys for G Barevicius (71), N Maciulis for T Tamosauskas (87)
Liverpool
25 Jose Reina, 23 Jamie Carragher, 4 Sami Hyypia, 17 Josemi, 14 Xabi Alonso, 8 Steven Gerrard, 34 Darren Potter, 6 John Arne Riise, 30 Boudewijn Zenden, 9 Djibril Cissé, 15 Peter Crouch **Substitutions** M Sissoko for S Gerrard (60), S Luis Garcia for D Potter (63), F Morientes for P Crouch (74)

Monthly Summary
Team Form

July	G	W	D	L	F	A	GD	GFA	GAA	PPG	Pts	Rank	League Position
Total	3	3	0	0	9	1	8	3.00	0.33	3.00	9	-	-
Premiership	-	-	-	-	-	-	-	-	-	-	-	-	-

A good start by the Reds in the defence of their European title, albeit against very limited opposition. Professional displays avoided any embarrassment these ties can cause. A trio of three-goal flourishes in the month, two away from home, with only one goal conceded.

Player Form Summary

Player	Games	Goals	Assists	Points	Mistakes leading to goals
Steven Gerrard	3	6	1	7	-
Djibril Cissé	3	2	0	2	-
John Arne Riise	3	0	2	2	-
Anthony Le Tallec	2	0	2	2	-
Jamie Carragher	3	1	0	1	-
Sami Hyypia	3	0	1	1	1

Sparkling early season form from the Liverpool skipper, with a hat-trick, a brace and a penalty conversion in the three games. Add to that an assist on Carragher's belief-defying goal against Kaunas and you have seven attacking points in only three matches. A good opening month from Djibril Cissé too, with two goals in the two starts he made. Only the one goal conceded in July, with Sami Hyypia being credited with a mistake: reacting slowly to the throw-in down the left flank to Arturas Rimkevicius, resulting in the Kaunas goal.

August 2005

Aug. 2, 2005 – UEFA Champions League Qualifier

Liverpool 2 - 0 **FBK Kaunas**
Steven Gerrard 77'
(A1 Zenden)
Djibril Cissé 86'
(A1 Garcia, A2 Zenden)

Agg: 5 – 1

Liverpool
20 Scott Carson, 3 Steve Finnan, 4 Sami Hyypia, 37 Zak Whitbread, 16 Dietmar Hamann, 10 Luis Garcia, 22 Mohamed Sissoko, 28 Stephen Warnock, 30 Boudewijn Zenden, 15 Peter Crouch, 19 Fernando Morientes **Substitutions** D Cissé for F Morientes (45), D Potter for P Crouch (55), S Gerrard for D Hamann (75)
FBK Kaunas
1 Sarunas Kilijonas, 18 Mindaugas Baguzis, 5 Tomas Kancelskis, 23 Dainius Kunevicius, 6 Nukri Manchkhava, 3 Irmantas Zelmikas, 20 Givi Kvaratskhelia, 30 Vadim Petrenko, 31 Edin Pehlic, 19 Eimantas Poderis, 11 Arturas Rimkevicius **Substitutions** A Klimek for V Petrenko (45), G Barevicius for E Pehlic (66), N Maciulis for E Poderis (87)

Aug. 10, 2005 – UEFA Champions League Qualifier

CSKA Sofia 1 - 3 **Liverpool**
Velizar Dimitrov 45' Djibril Cissé 25'
(M1 Finnan, slow close down. *(A1 Gerrard, A2 Garcia)*
M2 Warnock, covering) Fernando Morientes 31'
(A1 Gerrard)
Fernando Morientes 58'
(A1 Gerrard, A2 Cissé)

CSKA Sofia
31 Evgeni Hmaruk, 29 Ibrahima Gueye, 33 Slavko Matic, 27 Tiago Silva, 30 Yordan Todorov, 2 Radoslav Zabavnik, 23 Emil Gargorov, 18 Murad Hidiued, 7 Hristo Yanev, 8 Velizar Dimitrov, 11 Guillame Zadi **Substitutions** P Dimitrov for H Yanev (34), S Sakaliev for V Dimitrov (59), E Yordanov for G Zadi (80)

Liverpool
25 Jose Reina, 23 Jamie Carragher, 3 Steve Finnan, 4 Sami Hyypia, 14 Xabi Alonso, 8 Steven Gerrard, 10 Luis Garcia, 6 John Arne Riise, 28 Stephen Warnock, 9 Djibril Cissé, 19 Fernando Morientes **Substitutions** D Hamann for X Alonso (64), M Sissoko for S Gerrard (70), A Barragan for F Morientes (79)

Aug 13, 2005 – English Premiership

Middlesbrough 0 - 0 **Liverpool**

Middlesbrough
1 Mark Schwarzer, 4 Ugo Ehiogu, 3 Franck Queudrue, 2 Michael Reiziger, 6 Gareth Southgate, 7 George Boateng, 19 Stewart Downing, 14 Gaizka Mendieta, 15 Ray Parlour, 9 Jimmy Floyd Hasselbaink, 20 Aiyegbeni Yakubu **Substitutions** S Nemeth for G Mendieta (65), M Viduka for J Hasselbaink (67), M Bates for A Yakubu (75)
Liverpool
25 Jose Reina, 23 Jamie Carragher, 3 Steve Finnan 4, Sami Hyypia, 28 Stephen Warnock, 14 Xabi Alonso, 8 Steven Gerrard, 10 Luis Garcia, 22 Mohamed Sissoko, 30 Boudewijn Zenden, 19 Fernando Morientes, **Substitutions** D Cissé for S Luis Garcia (57), M Baros for F Morientes (67).

<u>Aug. 20, 2005 – English Premiership</u>

Liverpool   I – o   **Sunderland**
Xabi Alonso 23'
(unassisted)

Liverpool
25 Jose Reina, 23 Jamie Carragher, 3 Steve Finnan, 4 Sami Hyypia, 14 Xabi Alonso, 8 Steven Gerrard, 22 Mohamed Sissoko, 28 Stephen Warnock, 30 Boudewijn Zenden, 9 Djibril Cissé, 19 Fernando Morientes **Substitutions** Luis Garcia for S Gerrard (55), J Riise for B Zenden (63), M Baros for D Cissé (75)
Sunderland
1 Kelvin Davis, 5 Gary Breen, 12 Nyron Nosworthy, 22 Alan Stubbs, 33 Julio Arca,
18 Andy Gray, 17 Liam Lawrence, 14 Tommy Miller, 4 Carl Robinson, 8 Dean Whitehead, 11 Andrew Welsh **Substitutions** C Brown for A Gray (66), S Elliott for L Lawrence (66), M Woods for C Robinson (81)

<u>Aug. 23, 2005 – UEFA Champions League Qualifier</u>

Liverpool   o – I   **CSKA Sofia**
                                                         Valentin Iliev 16'
                                                         (M1 Team, no 2nd level marking.
                                                         M2 Josemi, slow to react/cover)
Agg: 3 – 2

Liverpool
20 Scott Carson, 3 Steve Finnan, 4 Sami Hyypia, 17 Josemi, 16 Dietmar Hamann, 34 Darren Potter, 6 John Arne Riise, 22 Mohamed Sissoko, 28 Stephen Warnock, 9 Djibril Cissé, 19 Fernando Morientes **Substitutions** Luis Garcia for D Potter (45), B Zenden for S Warnock (64), F Sinama Pongolle for D Cissé (83)
CSKA Sofia
1 Dejan Maksic, 29 Ibrahima Gueye, 14 Valentin Iliev, 27 Tiago Silva, 30 Yordan Todorov, 2 Radoslav Zabavnik, 23 Emil Gargorov, 18 Murad Hidiued, 20 Iordan Yurukov, 8 Velizar Dimitrov, 11 Guillame Zadi **Substitutions** S Sakaliev for I Yurukov (72), P Dimitrov for G Zadi (84)

<u>Aug. 26, 2005 – UEFA Super Cup Final</u>

Liverpool   3 – I   **CSKA Moscow (aet)**
Djibril Cissé 82'   da Silva Daniel Carvalho (28)
(A1 Garcia, A2 Reina)   *(M1 Josemi, Positional*
Djibril Cissé 102'   *M2 Riise, Awareness)*
(A1 Hamann)
Luis Garcia 109'
(A1 Cissé, A2 Hamann)

Liverpool
25 Jose Reina, 23 Jamie Carragher, 3 Steve Finnan, 4 Sami Hyypia, 17 Josemi, 14 Xabi Alonso, 16 Dietmar Hamann, 10 Luis Garcia, 6 John Arne Riise, 30 Boudewijn Zenden, 19 Fernando Morientes **Substitutions** F Sinama Pongolle for S Finnan (55), M Sissoko for X Alonso (71), D Cissé for J Riise (79)
CSKA Moscow
35 Igor Akinfeev, 6 Alexei Berezutsky, 24 Vasili Berezutsky, 4 Sergei Ignashevich, 15 Chidi Odiah, 22 Eugeni Aldonin, 7 da Silva Daniel Carvalho, 17 Milos Krasic, 25 Elver Rahimic, 18 Yuri Zhirkov, 11 Silva Vagner Love **Substitutions** D Semberas for Y Zhirkov (66), A Dudu for M Krasic (85), R Gusev for C Odiah (90)

Monthly summary

Team Form

August	G	W	D	L	F	A	GD	GFA	GAA	PPG	Pts	Rank	League Position
Total	6	4	1	1	9	3	6	1.50	0.50	2.17	13	-	-
Premiership	2	1	1	0	1	0	1	0.50	0.00	2.00	4	9	7th

The start of the Premiership campaign began with two clean sheets but only one goal, and saw Liverpool finish the month in 7th place. More success was had in the four non-Premiership matches within the month, with three wins and one loss. The loss came at the hands of CSKA Sofia by a single goal to nil, but it did not prevent Liverpool from reaching the group stages of the Champions League thanks to a 3-1 win away from home. The Reds secured their first silverware of the season as well, beating CSKA Moscow in Monaco in another thrilling comeback to claim the European Super Cup for the second time in the last five years.

Player Form Summary

Player	Games	Goals	Assists	Points	Mistakes leading to goals
Djibril Cissé	6	4	2	6	-
Steven Gerrard	6	1	3	4	-
Luis Garcia	6	1	3	4	-
Fernando Morientes	6	2	0	2	-
Bolo Zenden	5	0	2	2	-
Josemi	2	0	0	0	2

Great form from Cissé in August but only in the non-Premiership games. A goal against Kaunas, a goal and an assist against Sofia away then a great display against CSKA Moscow coming on as a late substitute and contributing two goals and an assist. Steven Gerrard continued his fine early season form with a late goal against Kaunas at Anfield and a 3 assist game in the away tie in Sofia. Luis Garcia got into the act scoring his first goal of the season in the Super cup final with Morientes (two) and Alonso's curling free-kick against Sunderland accounting for the other goals in the month. Josemi continued from where he left off last season (two mistakes leading to goals in two games) committing an all-too-common error against CSKA Moscow of stepping up at the wrong time, getting himself out of position, allowing the ball to be played in behind where he just vacated, leading to an all too easy goal for the opposition.

September 2005

Sept. 10, 2005 – English Premiership

Tottenham   0 - 0   **Liverpool**

Tottenham
1 Paul Robinson, 30 Anthony Gardner, 26 Ledley King, 16 Young-Pyo Lee, 7 Paul Stalteri, 23 Michael Carrick, 5 Edgar Davids, 28 Jermaine Jenas, 25 Aaron Lennon, 18 Jermain Defoe, 9 Grzegorz Rasiak **Substitutions** M Brown for A Lennon (82), R Keane for G Rasiak (82)
Liverpool
25 Jose Reina, 23 Jamie Carragher, 3 Steve Finnan, 4 Sami Hyypia, 8 Steven Gerrard, 16 Dietmar Hamann, 10 Luis Garcia, 6 John Arne Riise, 28 Stephen Warnock, 9 Djibril Cissé, 15 Peter Crouch **Substitutions** M Sissoko for D Hamann (45), X Alonso for S Warnock (69), D Traoré for P Crouch (77)

Sep. 13, 2005 – UEFA Champions League Group Stage

Real Betis	1 - 2	**Liverpool**
Garcia Arzu 51'		Florent Sinama Pongolle 2'
(M1 Hyypia, positional)		*(A1 Crouch, A2 Carragher)*
		Luis Garcia 14'
		(A1 Zenden, A2 Crouch)

Real Betis
13 Antonio Doblas, 16 Oscar Lopez, 4 Juanito, 27 Juan Andreu Melli, 5 David Rivas, 7 Fernando Varela, 8 Garcia Arzu, 20 Marcos Assuncao, 9 Fernando, 17 Sanchez Joaquin, 12 Ricardo Oliveira **Substitutions** Dani for Fernando (36), M Xisco for Juanito (45), J Capi for G Arzu (72)
Liverpool
25 Jose Reina, 23 Jamie Carragher, 4 Sami Hyypia, 17 Josemi, 21 Djimi Traoré, 14 Xabi Alonso, 10 Luis Garcia, 22 Mohamed Sissoko, 30 Boudewijn Zenden, 15 Peter Crouch, 24 Florent Sinama Pongolle **Substitutions** D Cissé for P Crouch (59), J Riise for B Zenden (66), S Gerrard for F Sinama Pongolle (74)

Sep. 18, 2005 – English Premiership

Liverpool	0 - 0	**Man Utd**

Liverpool
25 Jose Reina, 23 Jamie Carragher, 3 Steve Finnan, 4 Sami Hyypia, 14 Xabi Alonso, 8 Steven Gerrard, 10 Luis Garcia, 6 John Arne Riise, 28 Stephen Warnock, 15 Peter Crouch, 24 Florent Sinama Pongolle **Substitutions** M Sissoko for F Sinama Pongolle (71), D Cissé for P Crouch (79), D Traoré for S Warnock (84)
Man Utd
19 Edwin Van der Sar, 5 Rio Ferdinand, 22 John O'Shea, 27 Mikael Silvestre, 16 Roy Keane, 23 Kieran Richardson, 7Cristiano Ronaldo, 18 Paul Scholes, 8 Wayne Rooney, 14 Alan Smith, 10 Ruud van Nistelrooy **Substitutions** D Fletcher for W Rooney (88), R Giggs for R Keane (88), Park for C Ronaldo (90)

Sep. 24, 2005 – English Premiership

Birmingham	2 - 2	**Liverpool**
Stephen Warnock og 72'		Luis Garcia 68'
(M1 Reina, failed punch		*(A1 Gerrard, A2 Crouch)*
M2 Warnock, clearance)		
Walter Pandiani 75'		Djibril Cissé pen 85'
(M1 Reina, save M2 Hyypia, clearance) *(unassisted)*		

Birmingham
1 Maik Taylor, 3 Jamie Clapham, 4 Kenny Cunningham, 29 Mario Melchiot, 5 Matthew Upson, 21 Julian Gray, 22 Damien Johnson, 15 Neil Kilkenny, 7 Jermaine Pennant, 9 Mikael Forssell, 16 Emile Heskey **Substitutions** W Pandiani for M Forssell (73), O Tebily for E Heskey (90)
Liverpool
25 Jose Reina, 23 Jamie Carragher, 4 Sami Hyypia, 17 Josemi, 14 Xabi Alonso, 8 Steven Gerrard, 16 Dietmar Hamann, 28 Stephen Warnock, 30 Boudewijn Zenden, 15 Peter Crouch, 24 Florent Sinama Pongolle **Substitutions** Luis Garcia for F Sinama Pongolle (60), D Cissé for B Zenden (68), J Riise for D Hamann (79)

Sep. 28, 2005 – UEFA Champions League Group Stage

Liverpool	0 - 0	**Chelsea**

Liverpool
25 Jose Reina, 23 Jamie Carragher, 3 Steve Finnan, 4 Sami Hyypia, 21 Djimi Traoré, 14 Xabi Alonso, 8 Steven Gerrard, 16 Dietmar Hamann, 10 Luis Garcia, 9 Djibril Cissé, 15 Peter Crouch **Substitutions** F Sinama Pongolle for D Cissé (78)
Chelsea
1 Petr Cech, 13 William Gallas, 20 Renato Paulo Ferreira, 6 Alberto Ricardo Carvalho, 26 John Terry, 11 Damien Duff, 5 Michael Essien, 8 Frank Lampard, 4 Claude Makelele, 16 Arjen Robben, 15 Didier Drogba **Substitutions** S Wright-Phillips for A Robben (65), H Crespo for D Duff (75), R Huth for D Drogba (90)

Monthly Summary

Team Form

September	G	W	D	L	F	A	GD	GFA	GAA	PPG	Pts	Rank	League Position
Total	5	1	4	0	4	3	1	0.80	0.60	1.40	7	-	-
Premiership	3	0	3	0	2	2	0	0.67	0.67	1.00	3	13	13th

Draws were the flavour of the month, with four in total, and just one win in the five games. Two more clean sheets in the three Premiership games this month; the remaining game being a 2-2 draw with Birmingham at St Andrews, all of which left Liverpool in 13th place at the end of the month. In the Champions League group phase Liverpool started well, with a 2-1 win over Real Betis in Betis and a 0-0 draw against Chelsea at Anfield.

Player Form Summary

Player	Games	Goals	Assists	Points	Mistakes leading to goals
Peter Crouch	5	0	3	3	-
Luis Garcia	5	2	0	2	-
Djibril Cissé	5	1	0	1	-
Sinama-Pongolle	4	1	0	1	-
Sami Hyypia	5	0	0	0	2
Jose Reina	5	0	0	0	2

No goals Peter Crouch in September, but he still made a contribution. Crouch had a fine game at Betis, being directly involved in both goals: picking up two of his three assists from the month. Luis Garcia continued his early season form with another two goals (one away at Betis and one away at Birmingham). Djibril Cissé, meanwhile, continued to get on the score sheet, confidently despatching the equalising penalty at St Andrews. Jose Reina's near-perfect start came to an end with a two-mistake game against Birmingham, being directly or indirectly responsible for both goals: the first when coming a long way for a cross and flapping at it, only for the return ball to fly in off Warnock's head; the second after dropping an Emile Heskey header in the box for Birmingham to pounce on the loose ball and take the lead.

October

Oct. 2, 2005 – English Premiership

Liverpool	1 - 4	**Chelsea**
Steven Gerrard 36'		Frank Lampard pen 27'
(A1 Carragher, A2 Riise)		*(M1 Traoré, foul/missed clearance)*
		Damien Duff 43'
		(M1 Hyypia, missed tackle)
		Jole Cole 63'
		(M1 Finnan, positional)
		Njitap Geremi 82'
		(M1 Finnan, positional)

Liverpool
25 Jose Reina, 23 Jamie Carragher, 3 Steve Finnan, 4 Sami Hyypia, 21 Djimi Traoré, 14 Xabi Alonso, 8 Steven Gerrard, 16 Dietmar Hamann, 10 Luis Garcia, 6 John Arne Riise, 15 Peter Crouch **Substitutions** M Sissoko for D Hamann (68), F Sinama Pongolle for S Hyypia (71), D Cissé for D Traoré (81)
Chelsea
1 Petr Cech, 3 Asier Del Horno, 13 William Gallas, 6 Alberto Ricardo Carvalho, 26 John Terry, 10 Joe Cole, 11 Damien Duff, 5 Michael Essien, 8 Frank Lampard, 4 Claude Makelele, 15 Didier Drogba **Substitutions** A Robben for J Cole (67), N Geremi for D Duff (76), R Huth for A Del Horno (83)

Oct. 15, 2005 – English Premiership

Liverpool   **1 - 0**   **Blackburn**
Djibril Cissé 75'
(A1 Alonso)

Liverpool
25 Jose Reina, 23 Jamie Carragher, 3 Steve Finnan, 17 Josemi, 21 Djimi Traoré, 14 Xabi Alonso, 22 Mohamed Sissoko, 28 Stephen Warnock, 30 Boudewijn Zenden, 9 Djibril Cissé, 15 Peter Crouch, **Substitutions** Luis Garcia for G Josemi (60), F Morientes for P Crouch (66), J Riise for S Warnock (74)
Blackburn
1 Brad Friedel, 33 Michael Gray, 3 Zurab Khizanishvili, 2 Lucas Neill, 6 Ryan Nelsen, 29 David Bentley, 12 Morten Gamst Pedersen, 8 Robbie Savage, 16 Kerimoglu Tugay, 10 Paul Dickov, 9 Shefki Kuqi **Substitutions** Todd for P Dickov (35), B Emerton for M Pedersen (67), A Mokoena for K Tugay (67)

Oct. 19, 2005 – UEFA Champions League Group Stage

Anderlecht   **0 - 1**   **Liverpool**
                                              Djibril Cissé 20'
                                              (A1 Hamann)

Anderlecht
13 Silvio Proto, 3 Olivier Descacht, 30 Hannu Tihinen, 37 Anthony Vanden Borre, 14 Bart Goor, 31 De Man, 4 Yves Vanderhaeghe, 17 Christian Wilhelmsson, 21 Par Johan Zetterberg, 8 Nenad Jestrovic, 9 Mbo Mpenza **Substitutions** L Traoré for H Tihinen (50), W Bassegio for Y Vanderhaeghe (61), S Akin for O Descacht (75)
Liverpool
25 Jose Reina, 23 Jamie Carragher, 4 Sami Hyypia, 17 Josemi, 21 Djimi Traoré, 14 Xabi Alonso, 16 Dietmar Hamann, 10 Luis Garcia, 6 John Arne Riise, 22 Mohamed Sissoko, 9 Djibril Cissé **Substitution** H Kewell for D Cissé (75), B Zenden for M Sissoko (82), S Warnock for J Riise (88)

Oct. 22, 2005 – English Premiership

Fulham   **2 - 0**   **Liverpool**
Collins John 30'
(M1 Josemi, positional/hold line M2 Traoré, covering/hold line)
Luis Boa Morte 90'
(M1 Traoré, missed tackle M2 Hyypia, positional)

Fulham
1 Mark Crossley, 3 Carlos Bocanegra, 24 Alain Goma, 33 Niclas Jensen, 2 Moritz Volz1, 4 Papa Bouba Diop, 18 Ahmad Elrich, 8 Claus Jensen, 4 Steed Malbranque, 11 Luis Boa Morte, 15 Collins John **Substitutions** T Warner for M Crossley (63), L Rosenior for N Jensen (69), B McBride for A Elrich (76)
Liverpool
25 Jose Reina, 23 Jamie Carragher, 4 Sami Hyypia, 17 Josemi, 21 Djimi Traoré, 14 Xabi Alonso, 7 Harry Kewell, 6 John Arne Riise, 22 Mohamed Sissoko, 9 Djibril Cissé, 19 Fernando Morientes **Substitutions** Luis Garcia for D Traoré (59), P Crouch for H Kewell (75)

Oct. 25, 2005 – English Carling Cup

Crystal Palace   **2 - 1**   **Liverpool**
Dougie Freedman 37'   Steven Gerrard (40)
(M1 Whitbread, marking/covering)   *(A1 Hamann, A2 Crouch)*
Marco Reich 66'
(M1 Team, marking
M2 Warnock, marking/covering)

Crystal Palace
28 Julian Speroni, 21 Emmerson Boyce, 25 Fitz Hall, 5 Mark Hudson, 18 Gary Borrowdale, 17 Michael Hughes, 22 Marco Reich, 19 Tom Soares, 14 Ben Watson, 9 Dougie Freedman, 11 Clinton Morrison **Substitutions** W Andrews for C Morrison (74), T Black for D Freedman (77), S Togwell for M Reich (84)
Liverpool
20 Scott Carson, 4 Sami Hyypia, 31 David Raven, 37 Zak Whitbread, 8 Steven Gerrard, 16 Dietmar Hamann, 7 Harry Kewell, 34 Darren Potter, 28 Stephen Warnock, 15 Peter Crouch, 19 Fernando Morientes **Substitutions** F Sinama Pongolle for F Morientes (62), Luis Garcia for H Kewell (65), D Traoré for S Warnock (76)

Liverpool   **2 - 0**   **West Ham**
Xabi Alonso 18'
(A1 Garcia)
Boudewijn Zenden 82'
(A1 Riise, A2 Garcia)

Liverpool
25 Jose Reina, 23 Jamie Carragher, 3 Steve Finnan, 4 Sami Hyypia, 14 Xabi Alonso, 8 Steven Gerrard, 10 Sanz Luis Garcia, 6 John Arne Riise, 22 Mohamed Sissoko, 9 Djibril Cissé, 19 Fernando Morientes **Substitutions** B Zenden for D Cissé (73), P Crouch for F Morientes (90)
West Ham
34 Shaka Hislop, 5 Anton Ferdinand, 4 Daniel Gabbidon, 3 Paul Konchesky, 17 Hayden Mullins, 2 Tomas Repka, 15 Yossi Benayoun, 11 Matthew Etherington, 20 Nigel Reo-Coker, 21 David Bellion, 10 Marlon Harewood **Substitutions** J Aliadiere for D Bellion (60), T Sheringham for M Etherington (67), J Collins for T Repka (81)

Monthly Summary

Team Form

October	G	W	D	L	F	A	GD	GFA	GAA	PPG	Pts	Rank	League Position
Total	6	3	0	3	6	8	-2	1.00	1.33	1.50	9	-	-
Premiership	4	2	0	2	4	6	-2	1.00	1.50	1.50	6	9	12th

October was an all-or-nothing month, with three wins and three defeats in total (two wins and two defeats in the Premiership). The Reds started the month with the horrible 4-1 home defeat to Chelsea, suffering another set back at Fulham (0-2) and crashing out of the Carling Cup at the first hurdle (1-2 at Crystal Palace). The form has little effect on the Reds' league placing, moving up one spot to 12th.

Player Form Summary

Player	Games	Goals	Assists	Points	Mistakes leading to goals
Steven Gerrard	3	2	0	2	-
Djibril Cissé	5	2	0	2	-
Xabi Alonso	5	1	1	2	-
Didi Hamann	3	0	2	2	-
Luis Garcia	6	0	2	2	-
Djimi Traore	5	0	0	0	3

No single player stood out this month, although Steven Gerrard did pick up two goals in the three games he played. Djibril Cissé continued his good start, netting twice this month, one from a free-kick strike against Blackburn and the other a superb volley away at Anderlecht. Xabi Alonso got his second goal of the season, against West Ham, whilst Bolo Zenden scored his first for the club in the same game. Djimi Traoré had an awful month, registering three errors that led to opposition goals in four starts, most notably the mad rush of blood to bring down Didier Drogba and turn the Premiership home tie with Chelsea on its head.

November

Nov. 1, 2005 – UEFA Champions League Group Stage

Liverpool	**3 - 0**	**Anderlecht**

Fernando Morientes 34'
(A1 Gerrard, A2 Alonso)
Luis Garcia 61'
(A1 Finnan, A2 Alonso)
Djibril Cissé 89'
(A1 Kewell, A2 Riise)

Liverpool
25 Jose Reina, 23 Jamie Carragher, 3 Steve Finnan, 4 Sami Hyypia, 14 Xabi Alonso, 8 Steven Gerrard, 10 Luis Garcia, 6 John Arne Riise, 22 Mohamed Sissoko, 15 Peter Crouch, 19 Fernando Morientes **Substitutions** B Zenden for F Morientes (52), D Cissé for P Crouch (72), H Kewell for S Gerrard (79)
Anderlecht
13 Silvio Proto, 5 Roland Juhasz, 30 Hannu Tihinen, 6 Michal Zewlakow, 14 Bart Goor, 31 De Man, 4 Yves Vanderhaeghe, 17 Christian Wilhelmsson, 21 Par Johan Zetterberg, 24 Serhat Akin, 9 Mbo Mpenza **Substitutions** G Pujol for Y Vanderhaeghe (70), N Jestrovic for S Akin (70), W Bassegio for M Mpenza (82)

Nov. 5, 2005 – English Premiership

Aston Villa	**0 - 2**	**Liverpool**

Steven Gerrard pen 85'
(unassisted)
Xabi Alonso 89'
(A1 Crouch, A2 Zenden)

Aston Villa
1 Thomas Sorensen, 6 Gareth Barry, 2 Mark Delaney, 4 Olof Mellberg, 19 Liam Ridgewell, 24 Eirik Bakke, 12 Steven Davis, 8 Gavin McCann, 11 James Milner, 10 Milan Baros, 20 Kevin Phillips **Substitutions** J Angel for K Phillips (61), L Hendrie for E Bakke (82)
Liverpool
25 Jose Reina, 23 Jamie Carragher, 3 Steve Finnan, 4 Sami Hyypia, 14 Xabi Alonso, 8 Steven Gerrard, 10 Luis Garcia, 6 John Arne Riise, 22 Mohamed Sissoko, 9 Djibril Cissé, 19 Fernando Morientes **Substitutions** B Zenden for Luis Garcia (57), P Crouch for F Morientes (68), H Kewell for D Cissé (76)

Nov. 19, 2005 – English Premiership

Liverpool	**3 - 0**	**Portsmouth**

Boudewijn Zenden 23'
(A1 Crouch)
Djibril Cissé 39'
(A1 Hamann, A2 Hyypia)
Fernando Morientes 80'
(A1 Hyypia, A2 Crouch)

Liverpool
25 Jose Reina, 23 Jamie Carragher, 3 Steve Finnan, 4 Sami Hyypia, 8 Steven Gerrard, 16 Dietmar Hamann, 10 Luis Garcia, 28 Stephen Warnock, 30 Boudewijn Zenden, 9 Djibril Cissé, 15 Peter Crouch **Substitutions** F Morientes for Luis Garcia (22), X Alonso for D Cissé (69), G Josemi for S Gerrard (83)
Portsmouth
15 Jamie Ashdown, 16 Andy Griffin, 5 Andrew O'Brien, 6 Brian Priske, 14 Matthew Taylor, 7 Gregory Vignal, 22 Richard Hughes, 26 Gary O'Neil, 11 Laurent Robert, 4 John Viafara, 32 Lomana Tresor LuaLua **Substitutions** Z Vukic for L Robert (64), C Mbesuma for L LuaLua (70), G Skopelitis for R Hughes (74)

Nov. 23, 2005 – UEFA Champions League Group Stage

Liverpool   0 - 0   Real Betis

Liverpool
25 Jose Reina, 23 Jamie Carragher, 3 Steve Finnan, 4 Sami Hyypia, 8 Steven Gerrard, 16 Dietmar Hamann, 6 John Arne Riise, 22 Mohamed Sissoko, 30 Boudewijn Zenden, 15 Peter Crouch, 19 Fernando Morientes **Substitutions** D Cissé for F Morientes (67), H Kewell for P Crouch (84), D Potter for S Gerrard (90)
Real Betis
13 Antonio Doblas, 19 Óscar López, 4 Juanito, 27 Juan Andreu Melli, 5 David Rivas, 8 Garcia Arzu, 20 Marcos Assuncao, 9 Fernando, 17 Sanchez Joaquin, 18 Alberto Rivera, 21 Munoz Xisco **Substitutions** J Capi for M Assuncao (70), B Israel for Fernando (78)

Nov. 26, 2005 – English Premiership

Man City   0 - 1   Liverpool
John Arne Riise 61'
(A1 Gerrard, A2 Hamann)

Man City
1 David James, 5 Sylvain Distin, 22 Richard Dunne, 18 Danny Mills, 8 Joey Barton, 40 Lee Croft, 38 Stephen Ireland, 41 Stephen Jordan, 14 Kiki Musampa, 9 Andy Cole, 11 Darius Vassell **Substitutions** T Sinclair for K Musampa (68), S Jihai for S Jordan (75), B Wright-Phillips for D Mills (83)
Liverpool
25 Jose Reina, 23 Jamie Carragher, 3 Steve Finnan, 4 Sami Hyypia, 8 Steven Gerrard, 16 Dietmar Hamann, 6 John Arne Riise, 22 Mohamed Sissoko, 28 Stephen Warnock, 9 Djibril Cissé, 15 Peter Crouch **Substitutions** H Kewell for D Cissé (51), Luis Garcia for J Riise (77), F Morientes for P Crouch (81)

Nov. 30, 2005 – English Premiership

Sunderland 0 - 2 Liverpool
Luis Garcia 30'
(A1 Alonso, A2 Finnan)
Steven Gerrard 45'
(A1 Alonso, A2 Finnan)

Sunderland
13 Ben Alnwick, 5 Gary Breen, 6 Steven Caldwell, 32 Justin Hoyte, 31 Christian Bassila, 15 Danny Collins, 7 Liam Lawrence, 14 Tommy Miller, 8 Dean Whitehead, 20 Chris Brown, 9 Jonathan Stead **Substitutions** A Welsh for T Miller (57), N Nosworthy for J Hoyte (77), A Gray for L Lawrence (86)
Liverpool
25 Jose Reina, 23 Jamie Carragher, 3 Steve Finnan, 4 Sami Hyypia, 14 Xabi Alonso, 8 Steven Gerrard, 10 Luis Garcia, 6 John Arne Riise, 22 Mohamed Sissoko, 15 Peter Crouch, 19 Fernando Morientes **Substitutions** H Kewell for F Morientes (60), D Traoré for P Crouch (79), S Warnock for J Riise (90)

Monthly Summary

Team Form

November	G	W	D	L	F	A	GD	GFA	GAA	PPG	Pts	Rank	League Position
Total	6	5	1	0	11	0	11	1.83	0.00	2.67	16	-	-
Premiership	4	4	0	0	8	0	8	2.00	0.00	3.00	12	1	4th

Five wins and one draw; six clean sheets and 11 goals scored; four wins from four games in the Premiership: November finally saw the Reds hitting their stride. Add to those the 2-0 win against West Ham at the end of October, and you have five from five, with 10 goals scored and none conceded. The form saw Liverpool fly up the table, from a lowly 12th at the end of October to 4th at the end of November. The 12 points in the four Premiership games in the month were the most by any club, and equalled the top single-month points tally with Chelsea (August) and Wigan (October).

Player Form Summary

Player	Games	Goals	Assists	Points	Mistakes leading to goals
Xabi Alonso	4	1	4	5	-
Steven Gerrard	6	2	2	4	-
Steve Finnan	6	0	3	3	-
Peter Crouch	6	0	3	3	-
Fernendo Morientes	6	2	0	2	-
Djibril Cissé	5	2	0	2	-
Luis Garcia	5	2	0	2	-

Xabi Alonso shone in November, despite picking up an injury in the win over Portsmouth and missing the next two games. A two-assist game to begin the month against Anderlecht, a goal against Aston Villa, and another two-assist game to finish off the month away at Sunderland accounted for his five points. Steve Finnan's improved crossing and all around forward play bore fruit this month with three assists (two in the Sunderland game, when he found Alonso with passes) and Peter Crouch again picking up three attacking points; all were assists, as he was still searching for his first goal of the season.

December

Dec. 3, 2005 – English Premiership

Liverpool 3 - 0 Wigan
Peter Crouch 19'
(A1 Garcia, A2 Finnan)
Peter Crouch 42'
(A1 Finnan, A2 Reina)
Luis Garcia 70'
(A1 Morientes, A2 Gerrard)

Liverpool
25 Jose Reina, 23 Jamie Carragher, 3 Steve Finnan, 4 Sami Hyypia, 14 Xabi Alonso, 8 Steven Gerrard, 7 Harry Kewell, 10 Luis Garcia, 28 Stephen Warnock, 15 Peter Crouch, 19 Fernando Morientes **Substitutions** J Riise for H Kewell (62), D Hamann for X Alonso (67), D Cissé for P Crouch (73)
Wigan
12 Michael Pollitt, 26 Leighton Baines, 2 Pascal Chimbonda, 16 Arjan De Zeeuw, 6 Stephane Henchoz, 21 Jimmy Bullard, 17 Damien Francis, 11 Graham Kavanagh, 7 Henri Camara, 10 Lee McCulloch, 30 Jason Roberts **Substitutions** M Jackson for A De Zeeuw (35), D Connolly for D Francis (66), J Skoko for G Kavanagh (78)

Dec. 6, 2005 – UEFA Champions League Group Stage

Chelsea   0 - 0   **Liverpool**

Chelsea
1 Petr Cech, 13 William Gallas, 20 Renato Paulo Ferreira, 6 Alberto Ricardo Carvalho, 26 John Terry, 11 Damien Duff, 5 Michael Essien, 8 Frank Lampard, 16 Arjen Robben, 15 Didier Drogba, 22 Eidur Gudjohnsen **Substitutions** A Del Horno for R Paulo Ferreira (45), C Cole for A Robben (73), S Wright-Phillips for D Duff (74)
Liverpool
25 Jose Reina, 23 Jamie Carragher, 3 Steve Finnan, 4 Sami Hyypia, 21 Djimi Traoré, 8 Steven Gerrard, 16 Dietmar Hamann, 10 Luis Garcia, 6 John Arne Riise, 22 Mohamed Sissoko, 15 Peter Crouch **Substitutions** H Kewell for J Riise (61), F Morientes for P Crouch (68), F Sinama Pongolle for S Luis Garcia (81)

Dec. 10, 2005 – English Premiership

Liverpool   2 - 0   **Middlesbrough**
Fernando Morientes 72'
(A1 Garcia, A2 Gerrard)
Fernando Morientes 77'
(A1 Carragher, A2 Gerrard)

Liverpool
25 Jose Reina, 23 Jamie Carragher, 3 Steve Finnan, 4 Sami Hyypia, 14 Xabi Alonso, 8 Steven Gerrard, 7 Harry Kewell, 6 John Arne Riise, 22 Mohamed Sissoko, 15 Peter Crouch, 19 Fernando Morientes **Substitutions** Luis Garcia for P Crouch (67), D Cissé for H Kewell (82), G Josemi for F Morientes (87)
Middlesbrough
1 Mark Schwarzer, 26 Matthew Bates, 3 Franck Queudrue, 5 Chris Riggott, 6 Gareth Southgate, 7 George Boateng, 17 Guidoni Junior Doriva, 25 James Morrison, 10 Fabio Rochemback, 39 Mark Viduka, 20 Aiyegbeni Yakubu **Substitutions** J Hasselbaink for J Morrison (75), U Ehiogu for A Yakubu (86)

Dec. 15, 2005 – FIFA Club World Championship

Saprissa   0 - 3   **Liverpool**
Peter Crouch 3'
(A1 Cissé, A2 Riise)
Steven Gerrard 32'
(A1 Riise, A2 Crouch)
Peter Crouch 58'
(A1 Riise, A2 Gerrard)

Saprissa
1 J Porras, 16 G Badilla, 23 T Bennett, 3 V Cordero, 5 J Drummond, 4 R Gonzalez, 19 R Azofeifa, 2 C Bolanos, 8 Walter Centeno, 11 R Gomez, 12 Alvaro Saborio **Substitutions** A Solis for T Bennett (46), G Drummond for R Gomez (76), A Aleman for A Saborio (83)
Liverpool
25 Jose Reina, 23 Jamie Carragher, 4 Sami Hyypia, 17 Josemi, 21 Djimi Traoré, 14 Xabi Alonso, 8 Steven Gerrard, 6 John Arne Riise, 22 Mohamed Sissoko, 9 Djibril Cissé, 15 Peter Crouch **Substitutions** F Sinama Pongolle for S Gerrard (64), Luis Garcia for S Hyypia (72), D Hamann for X Alonso (79)

Dec. 18, 2005 – FIFA Club World Championship

São Paulo 1 - 0 Liverpool
Carlos Mineiro 27'
(M1 Hyypia, positional
M2 Warnock, positional/hold line)

São Paulo
C Rogerio, C Edcarlos, R Fabio Santos, Cicinho, Jenilson Junior, D Lugano, G Danilo, A Josue, C Mineiro, Aloisio, Marcio Amoroso **Substitutions** L Grafite for Aloisio (75)
Liverpool
25 Jose Reina, 23 Jamie Carragher, 3 Steve Finnan, 4 Sami Hyypia, 14 Xabi Alonso, 8 Steven Gerrard, 7 Harry Kewell, 10 Luis Garcia, 22 Mohamed Sissoko, 28 Stephen Warnock, 19 Fernando Morientes **Substitutions** J Riise for S Warnock (79), F Sinama Pongolle for M Sissoko (79), P Crouch for F Morientes (85)

Dec. 26, 2005 – English Premiership

Liverpool 2 - 0 Newcastle
Steven Gerrard 14'
(A1 Crouch, A2 Garcia)
Peter Crouch 43'
(A1 Kewell, A2 Morientes)

Liverpool
25 Jose Reina, 23 Jamie Carragher, 3 Steve Finnan, 4 Sami Hyypia, 14 Xabi Alonso, 8 Steven Gerrard, 7 Harry Kewell, 10 Luis Garcia, 6 John Arne Riise, 15 Peter Crouch, 19 Fernando Morientes **Substitutions** F Sinama Pongolle for H Kewell (67), D Cissé for P Crouch (72), Josemi for S Finnan (78)
Newcastle
1 Shay Given, 33 Celestine Babayaro, 6 Jean-Alain Boumsong, 26 Peter Ramage, 27 Steven Taylor, 11 Lee Bowyer, 15 Amady Faye, 14 Charles N'Zogbia, 20 Albert Luque, 10 Michael Owen, 9 Alan Shearer **Substitutions** T Bramble for S Taylor (28), N Solano for C N'Zogbia (45), S Ameobi for A Luque (86)

<u>Dec. 28, 2005</u> – English Premiership

| **Everton** | **1 - 3** | **Liverpool** |

James Beattie 42'
(M1 Finnan, positional)

Peter Crouch 11'
(A1 Gerrard, A2 Cissé)
Steven Gerrard 18'
(A1 Finnan, A2 Hyypia)
Djibril Cissé 47'
(A1 Kewell, A2 Warnock)

Everton
25 Nigel Martyn, 22 Tony Hibbert, 18 Phil Neville, 19 Jorge Nuno Valente, 5 David Weir, 4 Joseph Yobo, 6 Mikel Arteta, 17 Tim Cahill, 10 Simon Davies, 14 Kevin Kilbane, 8 James Beattie **Substitutions** J McFadden for S Davies (57)
Liverpool
25 Jose Reina, 23 Jamie Carragher, 3 Steve Finnan, 4 Sami Hyypia, 14 Xabi Alonso, 8 Steven Gerrard, 7 Harry Kewell, 22 Mohamed Sissoko, 28 Stephen Warnock, 9 Djibril Cissé, 15 Peter Crouch **Substitutions** F Morientes for P Crouch (77), J Riise for H Kewell (80), Luis Garcia for S Gerrard (85)

<u>Dec. 31, 2005</u> – English Premiership

| **Liverpool** | **1 - 0** | **West Brom** |

Peter Crouch 52'
(A1 Kewell, A2 Riise)

Liverpool
25 Jose Reina, 23 Jamie Carragher, 3 Steve Finnan, 4 Sami Hyypia, 14 Xabi Alonso, 8 Steven Gerrard, 7 Harry Kewell, 10 Luis Garcia, 6 John Arne Riise, 9 Djibril Cissé, 15 Peter Crouch **Substitutions** F Sinama Pongolle for H Kewell (67), M Sissoko for P Crouch (81), D Traoré for D Cissé (89)
West Brom
29 Tomasz Kuszczak14 Martin Albrechtsen, 6 Neil Clement19 Curtis Davies, 3 Paul Robinson, 24 Ronnie Wallwork, 16 Steve Watson, 17 Darren Carter, 12 Richard Chaplow, 21 Kevin Campbell, 9 Geoff Horsfield **Substitutions** J Greening for R Chaplow (65), D Kamara for R Wallwork (76), N Ellington for K Campbell (80)

Monthly Summary

Team Form

December	G	W	D	L	F	A	GD	GFA	GAA	PPG	Pts	Rank	League Position
Total	8	6	1	1	14	2	12	1.75	0.25	2.38	19	-	-
Premiership	5	5	0	0	11	1	10	2.20	0.20	3.00	15	3	3rd

Another outstanding month saw the Reds moving up to 3rd in the table. Even though the Liverpool won five out of five in the Premiership (with only one goal conceded) it was only the 3rd-highest points total for the month. Chelsea were able to win six out of six, and Manchester United picked up 17 points, albeit from 7 games. The Reds were able to win six games in total, plus one draw, coming against Chelsea in the Champions League, and one defeat, coming in the FIFA Club World Championship Final.

Player Form Summary

Player	Games	Goals	Assists	Points	Mistakes leading to goals
Peter Crouch	8	7	2	9	-
Steven Gerrard	8	3	5	8	-
Fernendo Morientes	6	2	2	4	-
Luis Garcia	8	1	3	4	-
John Arne Riise	8	0	4	4	-
Harry Kewell	7	0	3	3	-
Djibril Cissé	6	1	2	3	-
Steve Finnan	7	0	3	3	1

Christmas came early for Peter Crouch, with seven goals and two assists for a total of nine points in December: a brace against Wigan, another two with an assist against Deportivo Saprissa, a goal and an assist against Newcastle, and goals against Everton and West Brom to finish the month. Steven Gerrard also had a good month, with eight points in eight games comprising three goals and five assists. Again his consistency must be commended, picking up at least one point in seven of the eight games. Morientes had a good month with two goals and two assists in four games, the goals coming in his brace against Middlesbrough. Luis Garcia and John Arne Riise both picked up four point months, with Harry Kewell, Djibril Cissé and, for the second month in a row, Steve Finnan picking up a total of three points.

January

Jan. 2, 2006 – English Premiership

Bolton	2 - 2	**Liverpool**
Radhi Jaidi 10'		Steven Gerrard pen 67'
(M1 Reina, dropped cross)		*(unassisted)*
El-Hadji Diouf 71'		Luis Garcia 82'
(M1 Troare, positional/		*(A1 Alonso, A2 Crouch)*
Holding line)		

Bolton
22 Jussi Jaaskelainen, 15 Radhi Jaidi, 5 Bruno N'Gotty, 25 Abdoulaye Faye, 11 Ricardo Gardner, 7 Stelios Giannakopoulos, 4 Kevin Nolan, 24 Joey O'Brien, 6 Gary Speed, 14 Kevin Davies, 21 El-Hadji Diouf **Substitutions** T Ben Haim for E Diouf (83), K Fadiga for G Speed (90)
Liverpool
25 Jose Reina, 23 Jamie Carragher, 3 Steve Finnan, 4 Sami Hyypia, 21 Djimi Traoré, 8 Steven Gerrard, 16 Dietmar Hamann, 7 Harry Kewell, 22 Mohamed Sissoko, 15 Peter Crouch, 24 Florent Sinama Pongolle **Substitutions** Luis Garcia for F Sinama Pongolle (62), X Alonso for D Hamann (64), D Cissé for M Sissoko (83)

Jan. 7, 2006 – English FA Cup

Luton	3 - 5	**Liverpool**
Steve Howard 31'		Steven Gerrard 16'
(M1 Riise, positional)		*(A1 Cissé, A2 Crouch)*
Steve Robinson 43'		Florent Sinama Pongolle 62'
(M1 Carragher, positional/turned)		*(A1 Gerrard, A2 Finnan)*
K Nicholls pen 53' Xabi Alonso 69'		
(M1 Hyypia, missed clearance)		*(A1 Crouch, A2 Carragher)*
Florent Sinama Pongolle 74'		
(A1 Finnan, A2 Gerrard)		
		Xabi Alonso 90'
		(A1 Riise, A2 Gerrard)

Luton
1 Marlon Beresford, 4 Chris Coyne, 2 Kevin Foley, 26 Markus Heikkinen, 6 Paul Underwood, 18 Ahmet Brkovic, 7 Carlos Edwards, 8 Kevin Nicholls, 11 Steve Robinson, 19 Steve Howard, 9 Rowan Vine **Substitutions** L Barnett for M Heikkinen (74), W Feeney for C Edwards (81), E Showunmi for A Brkovic (81)
Liverpool
20 Scott Carson, 23 Jamie Carragher, 3 Steve Finnan, 4 Sami Hyypia, 14 Xabi Alonso, 8 Steven Gerrard, 7 Harry Kewell, 6 John Arne Riise, 22 Mohamed Sissoko, 9 Djibril Cissé, 15 Peter Crouch **Substitutions** F Sinama Pongolle for M Sissoko (57), J Kromkamp for P Crouch (79), S Warnock for D Cissé (89)

Jan. 14, 2006 – English Premiership

Liverpool   **1 - 0**   **Tottenham**
Harry Kewell 59'
(*A1 Finnan, A2 Morientes*)

Liverpool
25 Jose Reina, 23 Jamie Carragher, 3 Steve Finnan, 4 Sami Hyypia, 14 Xabi Alonso, 8 Steven Gerrard, 7 Harry Kewell, 6 John Arne Riise, 22 Mohamed Sissoko, 15 Peter Crouch, 19 Fernando Morientes **Substitutions** D Cissé for P Crouch (66), S Warnock for F Morientes (83), J Kromkamp for M Sissoko (90)
Tottenham
1 Paul Robinson, 20 Michael Dawson, 26 Ledley King, 16 Young-Pyo Lee, 7 Paul Stalteri, 23 Michael Carrick, 5 Edgar Davids, 28 Jermaine Jenas, 6 Teemu Tainio, 10 Robbie Keane, 15 Ahmed Mido **Substitutions** J Defoe for T Tainio (67), A Lennon for E Davids (78)

Jan. 22, 2006 – English Premiership

Man Utd   **1 - 0**   **Liverpool**
Rio Ferdinand 90'
(*M1 Team, marking*
M2 Kromkamp, marking/covering)

Man Utd
19 Edwin Van der Sar, 6 Wes Brown, 3 Patrice Evra, 5 Rio Ferdinand, 2 Gary Neville, 22 John O'Shea, 24 Darren Fletcher, 11 Ryan Giggs, 23 Kieran Richardson, 8 Wayne Rooney, 10 Ruud van Nistelrooy **Substitutions** L Saha for J O'Shea (45)
Liverpool
25 Jose Reina, 23 Jamie Carragher, 3 Steve Finnan, 4 Sami Hyypia, 14 Xabi Alonso, 8 Steven Gerrard, 7 Harry Kewell, 6 John Arne Riise, 22 Mohamed Sissoko, 9 Djibril Cissé, 15 Peter Crouch **Substitutions** F Morientes for P Crouch (59), F Sinama Pongolle for D Cissé (75), J Kromkamp for M Sissoko (89)

Jan. 29, 2006 – English FA Cup

Portsmouth   **1 - 2**   **Liverpool**
Sean Davis 54'   Steven Gerrard pen 37'
(*no mistake*)   (*unassisted*)
                              John Arne Riise 41'
                              (*A1 Morientes, A2 Sissoko*)

Portsmouth
33 Dean Kiely, 5 Andrew O'Brien, 2 Linvoy Primus, 3 Dejan Stefanovic, 14 Matthew Taylor, 7 Gregory Vignal, 28 Sean Davis, 22 Richard Hughes, 26 Gary O'Neil, 30 Miguel Pedro Mendes, 17 Vincent Pericard **Substitutions** S Todorov for G Vignal (45), A Karadas for V Pericard (66), B Priske for L Primus (88)
Liverpool
25 Jose Reina, 23 Jamie Carragher, 4 Sami Hyypia, 14 Xabi Alonso, 8 Steven Gerrard, 2 Jan Kromkamp, 6 John Arne Riise, 22 Mohamed Sissoko, 28 Stephen Warnock, 9 Djibril Cissé, 19 Fernando Morientes **Substitutions** P Crouch for F Morientes (72), S Finnan for S Gerrard (80), H Kewell for D Cissé (83)

Monthly Summary

Team Form

January	G	W	D	L	F	A	GD	GFA	GAA	PPG	Pts	Rank	League Position
Total	5	3	1	1	10	7	3	2.00	1.40	2.00	10	-	-
Premiership	3	1	1	1	3	3	0	1.00	1.00	1.33	4	9	3rd

The run of ten straight Premiership wins was dented at the beginning of the month, with an away draw at Bolton. After a win against Tottenham in the next match, the 12-game unbeaten run was ended by Manchester United at Old Trafford. The four

Premiership points picked up by the Reds in the month only ranked 9th in the league, but were enough for the Reds to hang onto the 3rd spot in the table. The two remaining games were both away wins in the FA cup, 5-3 at Luton and 2-1 at Portsmouth.

Player Form Summary

Player	Games	Goals	Assists	Points	Mistakes leading to goals
Steven Gerrard	5	3	3	6	-
Peter Crouch	5	0	3	3	-
Xabi Alonso	5	2	1	3	-
John Arne Riise	4	1	1	2	1
Steve Finnan	5	0	2	2	-
Fernendo Morientes	3	0	2	2	-
Sinama-Pongolle	3	2	0	2	-
Jamie Carragher	5	0	1	1	1

Another profitable month from Steven Gerrard, with six points in five games, courtesy of the first goal against Luton followed by three assists in the same game, and two penalty conversions in January, one against Bolton in the league and against Portsmouth in the FA Cup. The goalscoring for Peter Crouch dried up again, but his involvement in goals did not, picking up another three assists (one against Bolton and two in the Luton game). Xabi Alonso had a strong month courtesy of the Luton game, as did Sinama-Pongolle, with both scoring two goals in the dramatic 5-3 win. Jamie Carragher picked up an assist in that game, as well as picking up his first costly mistake, when Robinson was able to shake him off to fire Luton into the lead in the FA Cup tie.

February 2006

<u>Feb. 1, 2006 – English Premiership</u>

Liverpool   1 - 1   **Birmingham**
Steven Gerrard 62'   Xabi Alonso og 88'
(A1 Morientes, A2 Garcia)   *(M1 Alonso, clearance)*

Liverpool
25 Jose Reina, 5 Daniel Agger, 3 Steve Finnan, 4 Sami Hyypia, 8 Steven Gerrard, 16 Dietmar Hamann, 7 Harry Kewell, 10 Luis Garcia, 6 John Arne Riise, 15 Peter Crouch, 19 Fernando Morientes **Substitutions** R Fowler for P Crouch (63), X Alonso for S Gerrard (72)
Birmingham
1 Maik Taylor, 8 Martin Latka, 29 Mario Melchiot, 5 Matthew Upson, 10 David Dunn, 21 Julian Gray, 22 Damien Johnson, 15 Neil Kilkenny, 7 Jermaine Pennant, 16 Emile Heskey, 40 Chris Sutton **Substitutions** S Lazaridis for D Dunn (34), O Tebily for N Kilkenny (64), A Bruce for S Lazaridis (90)

<u>Feb. 5, 2006 – English Premiership</u>

Chelsea   2 - 0   **Liverpool**
William Gallas 35'
(M1 Team, marking
M2 Riise, positional/pulled out)
Hernan Crespo 68'
(M1 Warnock, positional/hold line)

Chelsea
1 Petr Cech, 3 Asier Del Horno, 13 William Gallas, 6 Alberto Ricardo Carvalho, 26 John Terry, 10 Joe Cole, 5 Michael Essien, 8 Frank Lampard, 4 Claude Makelele, 9 Hernan Crespo, 16 Arjen Robben **Substitutions** D Duff for J Cole (74), E Gudjohnsen for D Duff (79), L Diarra for C Makelele (84)
Liverpool
25 Jose Reina, 23 Jamie Carragher, 3 Steve Finnan, 4 Sami Hyypia, 14 Xabi Alonso, 8 Steven Gerrard, 7 Harry Kewell, 6 John Arne Riise, 22 Mohamed Sissoko, 28 Stephen Warnock, 15 Peter Crouch **Substitutions** Luis Garcia for J Riise (61), D Cisse for M Sissoko (74), J Dudek for Luis Garcia (83)

Feb. 8, 2006 – English Premiership

Charlton   **2 - 0**   **Liverpool**

Darren Bent pen 42'
(M1 Dudek, slow reactions/foul)
Luke Young 45'
(M1 Hyypia, positional/angle to the ball
M2 Traoré, urgency/covering
M3 Dudek, save)

Charlton
36 Thomas Myhre, 3 Hermann Hreidarsson, 5 Chris Perry, 23 Jonathan Spector, 2 Luke Young, 20 Bryan Hughes, 7 Radostin Kishishev, 25 Alexei Smertin, 6 Marcus Bent, 10 Darren Bent, 14 Jerome Thomas **Substitutions** D Ambrose for J Thomas (79), T El Karkouri for A Smertin (83)
Liverpool
1 Jerzy Dudek, 23 Jamie Carragher, 3 Steve Finnan, 4 Sami Hyypia, 21 Djimi Traoré, 14 Xabi Alonso, 7 Harry Kewell, 22 Mohamed Sissoko, 9 Djibril Cissé, 15 Peter Crouch, 19 Fernando Morientes **Substitutions** R Fowler for P Crouch (60), J Riise for S Hyypia (70), J Kromkamp for D Cissé (78)

Feb. 11, 2006 – English Premiership

Wigan   **0 - 1**   **Liverpool**

                       Sami Hyypia 30'
                       (A1 Carragher,
                       A2 Finnan)

Wigan
12 Michael Pollitt, 16 Arjan De Zeeuw, 6 Stephane Henchoz, 4 Matt Jackson, 18 Paul Scharner, 23 Reto Ziegler, 21 Jimmy Bullard, 8 Andreas Johansson, 11 Graham Kavanagh, 27 David Thompson, 20 Gary Teale **Substitutions** L Baines for A Johansson (84)
Liverpool
1 Jerzy Dudek, 23 Jamie Carragher, 3 Steve Finnan, 4 Sami Hyypia, 14 Xabi Alonso, 8 Steven Gerrard, 16 Dietmar Hamann, 7 Harry Kewell, 6 John Arne Riise, 11 Robbie Fowler, 19 Fernando Morientes **Substitutions** J Kromkamp for R Fowler (66), D Cissé for F Morientes (70)

Feb. 14, 2006 – English Premiership

Liverpool   **1 - 0**   **Arsenal**

Luis Garcia 87'
(A1 Hamann)

Liverpool
1 Jerzy Dudek, 23 Jamie Carragher, 3 Steve Finnan, 4 Sami Hyypia, 14 Xabi Alonso, 8 Steven Gerrard, 7 Harry Kewell, 6 John Arne Riise, 22 Mohamed Sissoko, 11 Robbie Fowler, 19 Fernando Morientes **Substitutions** D Hamann for X Alonso (72), D Cissé for R Fowler (80), Luis Garcia for M Sissoko (84)
Arsenal
1 Jens Lehmann, 27 Emmanuel Eboue, 20 Philippe Senderos, 2 Kolo Toure, 19 Gilberto Silva, 15 Francesc Fabregas, 16 Mathieu Flamini, 8 Fredrik Ljungberg, 7 Robert Pires, 25 Emmanuel Adebayor, 14 Thierry Henry **Substitutions** A Hleb for R Pires (79)

Feb. 18, 2006 – English FA Cup

Liverpool   **1 - 0**   **Man Utd**

Peter Crouch 19'
(A1 Finnan, A2 Gerrard)

Liverpool
25 Jose Reina, 23 Jamie Carragher, 3 Steve Finnan, 4 Sami Hyypia, 8 Steven Gerrard, 16 Dietmar Hamann, 7 Harry Kewell, 6 John Arne Riise, 22 Mohamed Sissoko, 15 Peter Crouch, 19 Fernando Morientes **Substitutions** Luis Garcia for F Morientes (62), J Kromkamp for H Kewell (82), D Cissé for P Crouch (88)
Man Utd
19 Edwin Van der Sar, 6 Wes Brown, 2 Gary Neville, 27 Mikael Silvestre, 15 Nemanja Vidic, 24 Darren Fletcher, 11 Ryan Giggs, 23 Kieran Richardson, 7 Cristiano Ronaldo, 8 Wayne Rooney, 10 Ruud van Nistelrooy **Substitutions** L Saha for M Silvestre (45), A Smith for D Fletcher (76), J Park for A Smith (90)

Benfica   **1 - 0**   **Liverpool**

Luisao 84'

(M1 Hyypia, positional/marking/reaction)

Benfica
31 Moretto de Souza, 13 Eduardo Alcides, 3 Anderson Cléber Beraldo, 5 Leo, 4 Luisão, 16 Gilberto Galdino Beto, 14 Manuel Fernandes, 6 Armando Petit, 34 Laurent Robert, 20 Simao, 21 Nuno Gomes **Substitutions** G Karagounis for G Beto (58), Nélson for L Robert (77), R Rocha for Leo (87)

Liverpool
25 Jose Reina, 23 Jamie Carragher, 3 Steve Finnan, 4 Sami Hyypia, 14 Xabi Alonso, 7 Harry Kewell, 10 Luis Garcia, 6 John Arne Riise, 22 Mohamed Sissoko, 11 Robbie Fowler, 19 Fernando Morientes **Substitutions** D Hamann for M Sissoko (35), D Cissé for R Fowler (66), S Gerrard for F Morientes (78)

Feb. 26, 2006 – English Premiership

Liverpool   **1 - 0**   **Man City**

Harry Kewell 40'

(A1 Gerrard, A2 Hyypia)

Liverpool
25 Jose Reina, 5 Daniel Agger, 3 Steve Finnan, 4 Sami Hyypia, 14 Xabi Alonso, 8 Steven Gerrard, 7 Harry Kewell, 2 Jan Kromkamp, 6 John Arne Riise, 15 Peter Crouch, 19 Fernando Morientes **Substitutions** D Hamann for X Alonso (31), Luis Garcia for P Crouch (75), D Traoré for H Kewell (85)

Man City
1 David James, 5 Sylvain Distin, 22 Richard Dunne, 18 Danny Mills, 8 Joey Barton, 41 Stephen Jordan, 14 Kiki Musampa, 19 Albert Riera, 28 Trevor Sinclair, 20 Georgios Samaras, 10 Antoine Sibierski **Substitutions** B Wright-Phillips for A Sibierski (45), S Ireland for T Sinclair (67), L Croft for A Riera (78)

Monthly Summary

Team Form

February	G	W	D	L	F	A	GD	GFA	GAA	PPG	Pts	Rank	League Position
Total	8	4	1	3	5	6	-1	0.63	0.75	1.63	13	-	-
Premiership	6	3	1	2	4	5	-1	0.67	0.83	1.67	10	1	3rd

February was a busy month for the Reds. It was also a very odd one from a statistical point of view. Liverpool produced four wins, one draw, and three defeats in the eight games, but with a goals-for average of only 0.63 per-game. The goals-against average was still a very respectable 0.75, with four 1-0 wins (three at home). Three of the four 1-0 victories were in the Premiership; the Reds' 10 points in the month actually was the best for any team, but at only 1.67 points per-game it was with the greater number of games played by Liverpool that accounted for the success. In non-Premiership games the Reds suffered the 1-0 away defeat to Benfica, but won through to the next round of the FA Cup with a 1-0 victory over Manchester United at Anfield.

Player Form Summary

Player	Games	Goals	Assists	Points	Mistakes leading to goals
Steven Gerrard	7	1	2	3	-
Luis Garcia	5	1	1	2	-
Sami Hyypia	8	1	1	2	2
Steve Finnan	8	0	2	2	-
Peter Crouch	5	1	0	1	-
Harry Kewell	8	1	0	1	-

Sami Hyypia stands out here, with a very mixed month. The Finish centre-back was on the scoresheet with the winner against Wigan, and assisted in Harry Kewell's decisive strike against Man City at Anfield. But he was also at fault for two of the goals Liverpool conceded during February, being slow to react to Benfica's winner from a free-kick cross and getting caught and turned down the Charlton left flank for the cross that led to the second goal in the 2-0 defeat away at The Valley.

March

March 4, 2006 – English Premiership

Liverpool   0 - 0   **Charlton**

Liverpool
25 Jose Reina, 23 Jamie Carragher, 4 Sami Hyypia, 21 Djimi Traoré, 8 Steven Gerrard, 16 Dietmar Hamann, 7 Harry Kewell, 2 Jan Kromkamp, 9 Djibril Cissé, 15 Peter Crouch, 11 Robbie Fowler **Substitutions** J Riise for S Hyypia (45), X Alonso for D Hamann (73), F Morientes for P Crouch (80)
Charlton
36 Thomas Myhre, 3 Hermann Hreidarsson, 5 Chris Perry, 23 Jonathan Spector, 2 Luke Young, 18 Darren Ambrose, 8 Matthew Holland, 20 Bryan Hughes, 7 Radostin Kishishev, 6 Marcus Bent, 10 Darren Bent **Substitutions** J Bothroyd for M Bent (53), J Euell for R Kishishev (77), C Powell for D Ambrose (87)

March 8, 2006 – UEFA Champions League Knock-out Stage

Liverpool 0 - 2 Benfica
Simao 36'
(M1 Traoré, positional
M2 Carragher, clearance)
Fabrizio Miccoli 89'
(M1 Team, positional
M2 Finnan, positional/marking)
Agg: 0-3

Liverpool
25 Jose Reina, 23 Jamie Carragher, 3 Steve Finnan, 21 Djimi Traoré, 14 Xabi Alonso, 8 Steven Gerrard, 7 Harry Kewell, 10 Luis Garcia, 28 Stephen Warnock, 15 Peter Crouch, 19 Fernando Morientes **Substitutions** D Cissé for H Kewell (64), R Fowler for F Morientes (70), D Hamann for S Warnock (70)
Benfica
31 Moretto de Souza, 13 Eduardo Alcides, 3 Anderson Cléber Beraldo, 5 Leo, 4 Luisão, 16 Gilberto Galdino Beto, 14 Manuel Fernandes, 11 Marcio Geovanni, 34 Laurent Robert, 20 Simao, 21 Nuno Gomes **Substitutions** G Karagounis for M Geovanni (60), R Rocha for L Robert (70), F Miccoli for N Gomes (77)

March 12, 2006 – English Premiership

Arsenal   2 - 1   **Liverpool**
Thierry Henry 21'   Luis Garcia 76'
(M1 Finnan, positional/reaction)   *(A1 Gerrard, A2 Alonso)*
Thierry Henry 83'
(M1 Gerrard, pass)

Arsenal
1 Jens Lehmann, 27 Emmanuel Eboue, 20 Philippe Senderos, 28 Kolo Toure, 19 Gilberto Silva, 15 Francesc Fabregas, 16 Mathieu Flamini, 13 Aleksander Hleb, 8 Fredrik Ljungberg, 25 Emmanuel Adebayor, 14 Thierry Henry **Substitutions** R Pires for F Ljungberg (15), D Bergkamp for E Adebayor (67)
Liverpool
25 Jose Reina, 23 Jamie Carragher, 3 Steve Finnan, 4 Sami Hyypia, 2 Jan Kromkamp, 14 Xabi Alonso, 8 Steven Gerrard, 16 Dietmar Hamann, 10 Luis Garcia, 28 Stephen Warnock, 15 Peter Crouch **Substitutions** H Kewell for J Kromkamp (45), R Fowler for D Hamann (73)

March 15, 2006 – English Premiership

Liverpool   5 - 1   **Fulham**
Robbie Fowler 16'   Collins John 25'
(A1 Garcia, A2 Kewell)   *(M1 Agger, pass)*
Michael Brown og 34'
(A1 Kewell, A2 Fowler)
Fernando Morientes 71'
(A1 Cissé, A2 Gerrard)
Peter Crouch 89'
(A1 Gerrard, A2 Cissé)
Stephen Warnock 90'
(A1 Finnan, A2 Garcia)

Liverpool
25 Jose Reina, 5 Daniel Agger, 23 Jamie Carragher, 3 Steve Finnan, 21 Djimi Traoré, 8 Steven Gerrard, 16 Dietmar Hamann, 7 Harry Kewell, 10 Luis Garcia, 11 Robbie Fowler, 19 Fernando Morientes **Substitutions** D Cissé for R Fowler (68), P Crouch for F Morientes (81), S Warnock for H Kewell (88)
Fulham
30 Tony Warner, 31 Wayne Bridge, 6 Zat Knight, 35 Ian Pearce, 17 Liam Rosenior, 9 Michael Brown, 4 Steed Malbranque, 7 Mark Pembridge, 11 Luis Boa Morte, 15 Collins John, 13 Tomasz Radzinski **Substitutions** P Christanval for Z Knight (69), B McBride for T Radzinski (78)

March 19, 2006 – English Premiership

Newcastle   1 - 3   **Liverpool**
Shola Ameobi 41'   Peter Crouch 10'
(No mistake)   *(A1 Kromkamp, A2 Gerrard)*
       Steven Gerrard 35'
       (A1 Crouch, A2 Cissé)
       Djibril Cissé pen 52'
       (unassisted)

Newcastle
1 Shay Given, 33 Celestine Babayaro, 6 Jean Alain Boumsong, 3 Robbie Elliott, 26 Peter Ramage, 5 Belozoglu Emre, 14 Charles N'Zogbia, 17 Scott Parker, 4 Nolberto Solano, 23 Shola Ameobi, 9 Alan Shearer **Substitutions** L Bowyer for C N'Zogbia (28), K Dyer for S Ameobi (62), L Clark for B Emre (90)
Liverpool
25 Jose Reina, 5 Daniel Agger, 23 Jamie Carragher, 4 Sami Hyypia, 2 Jan Kromkamp, 8 Steven Gerrard, 16 Dietmar Hamann, 7 Harry Kewell, 28 Stephen Warnock, 9 Djibril Cissé, 15 Peter Crouch **Substitutions** Luis Garcia for P Crouch (63), X Alonso for S Gerrard (74), R Fowler for S Hyypia (90)

March 21, 2006 – English FA Cup

Birmingham   0 - 7   **Liverpool**
       Sami Hyypia 1'
       (A1 Sissoko, A2 Gerrard)
       Peter Crouch 5'
       (A1 Gerrard, A2 Sissoko)
       Peter Crouch 38'
       (A1 Garcia, A2 Gerrard)
       Fernando Morientes 59'
       (A1 Gerrard, A2 Finnan)
       John Arne Riise 70'
       (A1 Gerrard, A2 Finnan)
       Olivier Tebily og 77'
       (A1 Kewell, A2 Riise)
       Djibril Cissé 89' (A1 Garcia)

Birmingham
1 Maik Taylor, 3 Jamie Clapham, 4 Kenny Cunningham, 29 Mario Melchiot, 31 Marcos Painter, 2 Martin Taylor, 25 Stephen Clemence, 10 David Dunn, 22 Damien Johnson, 7 Jermaine Pennant, 9 Mikael Forssell **Substitutions** O Tebily for M Taylor (45), N Kilkenny for D Dunn (71), A Bruce for D Johnson (75)
Liverpool
25 Jose Reina, 23 Jamie Carragher, 3 Steve Finnan, 4 Sami Hyypia, 21 Djimi Traoré, 14 Xabi Alonso, 8 Steven Gerrard, 10 Luis Garcia, 6 John Arne Riise, 22 Mohamed Sissoko, 15 Peter Crouch **Substitutions** H Kewell for D Traoré (22), F Morientes for P Crouch (56), D Cissé for S Gerrard (71)

<u>March 25, 2006 – English Premiership</u>

Liverpool	**3 - 1**	**Everton**

Liverpool   **3 - 1**   **Everton**

Phil Neville og 45'
(A1 Alonso)
Luis Garcia 47'
(A1 Crouch, A2 Reina)
Harry Kewell 84'
(A1 Finnan, A2 Garcia)

Tim Cahill 61'
(M1 Crouch, marking/reaction)

Liverpool
25 Jose Reina, 23 Jamie Carragher, 3 Steve Finnan, 4 Sami Hyypia, 14 Xabi Alonso, 8 Steven Gerrard, 7 Harry Kewell, 10 Luis Garcia, 6 John Arne Riise, 22 Mohamed Sissoko, 15 Peter Crouch **Substitutions** S Warnock for H Kewell (87), F Morientes for P Crouch (90)
Everton
1 Richard Wright, 22 Tony Hibbert, 3 Gary Naysmith, 18 Phil Neville, 15 Alan Stubbs, 5 David Weir, 17 Tim Cahill, 14 Kevin Kilbane, 21 Leon Osman, 8 James Beattie, 11 James McFadden **Substitutions** D Ferguson for J McFadden (67), A Van der Meyde for K Kilbane (68)

Monthly Summary

Team Form

March	G	W	D	L	F	A	GD	GFA	GAA	PPG	Pts	Rank	League Position
Total	7	4	1	2	19	7	12	2.71	1.00	1.86	13	-	-
Premiership	5	3	1	1	12	5	7	2.40	1.00	2.00	10	2	3rd

A bad start to March, with a draw against Charlton, a defeat at Highbury, and being dumped out of Europe 0-2 (0-3 on agg) by Benfica. The Reds scored just once in those first three games. A miraculous transformation ensued, as Benítez's men racked up 18 goals in four straight victories to finish the month. Liverpool's 10 Premiership points ranked them 2nd in March, topped by the 15 points claimed by Manchester United, and thus keeping the Reds in the 3rd spot overall.

Player Form Summary

Player	Games	Goals	Assists	Points	Mistakes leading to goals
Steven Gerrard	7	1	2	3	-
Luis Garcia	5	1	1	2	-
Sami Hyypia	8	1	1	2	2
Steve Finnan	8	0	2	2	-
Peter Crouch	5	1	0	1	-
Harry Kewell	8	1	0	1	-

The floodgates well and truly opened in March, but not until three disappointing games had passed. The 19 Liverpool goals in the period came from 11 different players, plus three courtesy of the opposition's own-goals. An absolute monster of a month from Steven Gerrard with 10 points, with only one registered via a goal (against Newcastle). He picked up two assists in the 5-1 win against Fulham and a season-high five against Birmingham in the 7-0 rout. Luis Garcia had his most productive month of the season, scoring the only Liverpool goal at Arsenal and scoring just after half-time from a Crouch flick against Everton. The Spaniard also picked up five assists in the month, with two apiece against Fulham and Birmingham. A great month was also had by Peter Crouch scoring four goals in a three game period in the month, netting one against Fulham, one against Newcastle and two in the big win against Birmingham along with a couple of assists. Djibril Cissé continued to be effective even when being played out of position, netting a point per game with two goals and three assists during March. Steve Finnan was again effective going forward, collecting four assists to make up for his two mistakes leading to opposition goals (Arsenal, Benfica).

April 2006

April 1, 2006 – English Premiership

West Brom   0 - 2   **Liverpool**
Robbie Fowler 7'
(A1 Cissé, A2 Alonso)
Djibril Cissé 38'
(A1 Alonso, A2 Reina)

West Brom
29 Tomasz Kuszczak, 14 Martin Albrechtsen, 19 Curtis Davies, 3 Paul Robinson, 24 Ronnie Wallwork, 16 Steve Watson, 8 Jonathan Greening, 10 Andy Johnson, 22 Nathan Ellington, 15 Diomansy Kamara, 25 Nwankwo Kanu **Substitutions** Z Gera for D Kamara (45), K Campbell for N Kanu (62), N Clement for S Watson (62)
Liverpool
25 Jose Reina, 23 Jamie Carragher, 3 Steve Finnan, 4 Sami Hyypia, 14 Xabi Alonso, 7 Harry Kewell, 6 John Arne Riise, 22 Mohamed Sissoko, 9 Djibril Cissé, 15 Peter Crouch, 11 Robbie Fowler **Substitutions** Luis Garcia for R Fowler (65), F Morientes for P Crouch (71), J Kromkamp for D Cissé (78)

April 9, 2006 – English Premiership

Liverpool   1 - 0   **Bolton**
Robbie Fowler 45'
(A1 Crouch, A2 Carragher)

Liverpool
25 Jose Reina, 23 Jamie Carragher, 3 Steve Finnan, 4 Sami Hyypia, 14 Xabi Alonso, 8 Steven Gerrard, 7 Harry Kewell, 6 John Arne Riise, 9 Djibril Cissé, 15 Peter Crouch, 11 Robbie Fowler **Substitutions** Luis Garcia for D Cissé (45), D Hamann for R Fowler (75), D Traoré for H Kewell (88)
Bolton
22 Jussi Jaaskelainen, 26 Tal Ben Haim, 2 Nicky Hunt, 5 Bruno N'Gotty, 25 Abdoulaye Faye, 11 Ricardo Gardner, 7 Stelios Giannakopoulos, 4 Kevin Nolan, 10 Jay-Jay Okocha, 6 Gary Speed, 14 Kevin Davies **Substitutions** H Pedersen for S Giannakopoulos (53), M Jansen for J Okocha (61), I Campo for A Faye (74)

April 16, 2006 – English Premiership

Blackburn   0 - 1   **Liverpool**
Robbie Fowler 29'
(A1 Morientes, A2 Riise)

Blackburn
1 Brad Friedel, 33 Michael Gray, 3 Zurab Khizanishvili, 2 Lucas Neill, 6 Ryan Nelsen, 29 David Bentley, 12 Morten Gamst Pedersen, 14 Steven Reid, 8 Robbie Savage, 11 Craig Bellamy, 10 Paul Dickov **Substitutions** S Kuqi for P Dickov (67)
Liverpool
25 Jose Reina, 23 Jamie Carragher, 3 Steve Finnan, 4 Sami Hyypia, 14 Xabi Alonso, 6 John Arne Riise, 22 Mohamed Sissoko, 28 Stephen Warnock, 9 Djibril Cissé, 11 Robbie Fowler, 19 Fernando Morientes **Substitutions** Luis Garcia for R Fowler (63), H Kewell for S Warnock (69), J Kromkamp for F Morientes (81)

April 22, 2006 – English FA Cup

| **Chelsea** | 1 - 2 | **Liverpool** |

Chelsea 1 - 2 **Liverpool**
Didier Drogba 70'   John Arne Riise 21'
(M1 Riise, clearance/header   *(A1 Gerrard)*
M2 Reina, failed punch)   Luis Garcia 53'
                                        (A1 Finnan)

Chelsea
23 Carlo Cudicini, 3 Asier Del Horno, 13 William Gallas, 20 Renato Paulo Ferreira, 26 John Terry, 5 Michael Essien, 14 Njitap Geremi, 8 Frank Lampard, 4 Claude Makelele, 9 Hernan Crespo, 15 Didier Drogba **Substitutions** A Robben for A Del Horno (45), D Duff for N Geremi (62), J Cole for H Crespo (62)
Liverpool
25 Jose Reina, 23 Jamie Carragher, 3 Steve Finnan, 4 Sami Hyypia, 14 Xabi Alonso, 8 Steven Gerrard, 7 Harry Kewell, 10 Luis Garcia, 6 John Arne Riise, 22 Mohamed Sissoko, 15 Peter Crouch **Substitutions** D Cissé for P Crouch (69), D Traoré for H Kewell (78), F Morientes for S Luis Garcia (82)

April 26, 2006 – English Premiership

West Ham 1 - 2 **Liverpool**
Nigel Reo-Coker 46'   Djibril Cissé 19'
(M1 Traoré, positional/   *(A1 Sissoko, A2 Morientes)*
holdline/awareness)   Djibril Cissé 54'
                                        (A1 Fowler, A2 Morientes)

West Ham
23 James Walker, 19 James Collins, 5 Anton Ferdinand, 17 Hayden Mullins, 22 Elliot Ward, 15 Yossi Benayoun, 11 Matthew Etherington, 20 Nigel Reo-Coker, 2 Lionel Scaloni, 8 Teddy Sheringham, 25 Bobby Zamora **Substitutions** C Fletcher for J Collins (45), M Harewood for Y Benayoun (77)
Liverpool
1 Jerzy Dudek, 23 Jamie Carragher, 3 Steve Finnan, 2 Jan Kromkamp, 21 Djimi Traoré, 16 Dietmar Hamann, 22 Mohamed Sissoko, 28 Stephen Warnock, 9 Djibril Cissé, 11 Robbie Fowler, 19 Fernando Morientes **Substitutions** S Hyypia for S Finnan (63), Luis Garcia for R Fowler (80), J Riise for F Morientes (85)

April 29, 2006 – English Premiership

Liverpool 3 - 1 **Aston Villa**
Fernando Morientes 4'   Gareth Barry 58'
(A1 Alonso, A2 Cissé)   *(M1 Team, Marking)*
Steven Gerrard 61'
(A1 Alonso)
Steven Gerrard 66'
(A1 Morientes, A2 Alonso)

Liverpool
25 Jose Reina, 23 Jamie Carragher, 4 Sami Hyypia, 2 Jan Kromkamp, 21 Djimi Traoré, 14 Xabi Alonso, 8 Steven Gerrard, 6 John Arne Riise, 9 Djibril Cissé, 15 Peter Crouch, 19 Fernando Morientes **Substitutions** R Fowler for P Crouch (62), M Sissoko for D Cissé (65), S Warnock for J Riise (74)
Aston Villa
1 Thomas Sorensen, 6 Gareth Barry, 16 Wilfred Bouma, 21 Gary Cahill, 18 Aaron Hughes, 4 Olof Mellberg, 12 Steven Davis, 8 Gavin McCann, 11 James Milner, 30 Gabriel Agbonlahor, 10 Milan Baros **Substitutions** J Angel for M Baros (45), K Phillips for G Barry (82), C Gardner for S Davis (86)

Monthly Summary
Team Form

April	G	W	D	L	F	A	GD	GFA	GAA	PPG	Pts	Rank	League Position
Total	6	6	0	0	11	3	8	1.83	0.50	3.00	18	-	-
Premiership	5	5	0	0	9	2	7	1.80	0.40	3.00	15	2	3rd

Liverpool maintained the pace this month with a perfect six wins in six games, five in the Premiership. The Reds are finishing off the season better than any team in England. The 15 points in the Premiership were only second to Newcastle's 16, but that total came from six games. The Reds maintained their good scoring form this month, notching 11 goals, and picked up three clean sheets.

Player Form Summary

Player	Games	Goals	Assists	Points	Mistakes leading to goals
Djibril Cissé	6	3	2	5	-
Fernando Morientes	5	1	4	5	-
Xabi Alonso	5	0	5	5	-
Robbie Fowler	5	3	1	4	-
Steven Gerrard	3	2	1	3	-
John Arne Riise	6	1	1	2	1

The 11 goals scored in April came from six players, with both Cissé and Fowler scoring three each. Cissé added two assists to his points haul, one against Aston Villa and one with a cross for Fowler's goal against West Brom. Morientes had a good month, also gaining five points, courtesy of a goal and an assist against Aston Villa, a brace of assists against West Ham and the assist on Fowler's last goal of the month against Blackburn away. Xabi Alonso just pipped his fellow Spaniard in the assist department, finishing with five for the month, all in just two games: he had a major hand in both goals against West Brom and in all three goals the Reds scored against Aston Villa in the last game of the month.

May 2006

May 7, 2006 – English Premiership

Portsmouth	**1 - 3**	**Liverpool**
Ognjen Koroman 85'		Robbie Fowler 52'
(M1 Hyypia, positional/marking)		*(A1 Morientes, A2 Kewell)*
		Peter Crouch 84'
		(A1 Cissé, A2 Kewell)
		Djibril Cissé 89'
		(A1 Crouch, A2 Hyypia)

Portsmouth
33 Dean Kiely, 2 Linvoy Primus, 6 Brian Priske, 3 Dejan Stefanovic, 14 Matthew Taylor, 4 Andres D'Alessandro, 28 Sean Davis, 22 Richard Hughes, 26 Gary O'Neil, 25 Benjani Mwaruwari, 9 Svetoslav Todorov **Substitutions** O Koroman for R Hughes (62), W Routledge for A D'Alessandro (68), N Pamarot for L Primus (86)
Liverpool
1 Jerzy Dudek, 23 Jamie Carragher, 3 Steve Finnan, 4 Sami Hyypia, 14 Xabi Alonso, 8 Steven Gerrard, 7 Harry Kewell, 6 John Arne Riise, 22 Mohamed Sissoko, 11 Robbie Fowler, 19 Fernando Morientes **Substitutions** J Kromkamp for X Alonso (41), P Crouch for F Morientes (67), D Cissé for R Fowler (83)

May 13, 2006 - English FA Cup Final

Liverpool	**3 - 3**	**West Ham (aet)**
Djibril Cissé 32'		Jamie Carragher og 21'
(A1 Gerrard, A2 Finnan)		*(M1 Alonso, pass)*
Steven Gerrard 54'		*M2 Carragher, clearance)*
(A1 Crouch, A2 Alonso)		Dean Ashton 28'
Steven Gerrard 90'		*(M1 Reina, save)*
(A1 Riise)		Paul Konchesky 64'
Liverpool win 3-1 on penalties		*(M1 Gerrard, positional/pulled inside)*

Liverpool
25 Jose Reina, 23 Jamie Carragher, 3 Steve Finnan, 4 Sami Hyypia, 14 Xabi Alonso, 8 Steven Gerrard, 7 Harry Kewell, 6 John Arne Riise, 22 Mohamed Sissoko, 9 Djibril Cissé, 15 Peter Crouch **Substitutions** F Morientes for H Kewell (48), J Kromkamp for X Alonso (67), D Hamann for P Crouch (71)
West Ham
34 Shaka Hislop, 5 Anton Ferdinand, 4 Daniel Gabbidon, 3 Paul Konchesky, 15 Yossi Benayoun, 11 Matthew Etherington, 6 Carl Fletcher, 20 Nigel Reo-Coker, 2 Lionel Scaloni, 9 Dean Ashton, 10 Marlon Harewood **Substitutions** B Zamora for D Ashton (71), C Dailly for C Fletcher (77), T Sheringham for M Etherington (85)

Monthly Summary
Team Form

May	G	W	D	L	F	A	GD	GFA	GAA	PPG	Pts	Rank	League Position
Total	2	2	0	0	6	4	2	3.00	2.00	3.00	6	-	-
Premiership	1	1	0	0	3	1	2	3.00	1.00	3.00	3	6	3rd FINAL

The 3-1 win over Portsmouth saw the Reds finish the year in 3rd place in the Premiership, missing out on 2nd by only one point, and finishing nine points short of Chelsea. The slow start made by Liverpool proved costly. With only one win and four draws in August and September the Reds found themselves 14 points behind Chelsea, who had won all seven games. The Reds were also four points behind United who had won three, drawn two, and lost one. From October onwards Liverpool won 24 games and collected 75 points, five more than Chelsea and three more than United. The FA Cup victory in Cardiff offered plenty of consolation.

Player Form Summary

Player	Games	Goals	Assists	Points	Mistakes leading to goals
Djibril Cissé	6	3	2	5	-
Fernando Morientes	5	1	4	5	-
Xabi Alonso	5	0	5	5	-
Robbie Fowler	5	3	1	4	-
Steven Gerrard	3	2	1	3	-
John Arne Riise	6	1	1	2	1

Steven Gerrard finished off a prodigious season in style with a three-point game in the FA Cup Final in Cardiff. A fantastic assist for Cissé's goal was followed by two game-tying goals, the second of which went down as the club's goal of the season. Djibril Cissé added a goal and an assist from the Portsmouth game, to go along with his Cup final goal, while Peter Crouch also scored at Pompey and assisted in Gerrard's first goal in the final.

Final FA Barclaycard Premiership table - 2005/06

	P	W	D	L	F	A	W	D	L	F	A	GD	Pts
1. CHELSEA	38	18	1	0	47	9	11	3	5	25	13	50	91
2. Manchester United	38	13	5	1	37	8	12	3	4	35	26	38	83
3. Liverpool	**38**	**15**	**3**	**1**	**32**	**8**	**10**	**4**	**5**	**25**	**17**	**32**	**82**
4. Arsenal	38	14	3	2	48	13	6	4	9	20	18	37	67
5. Tottenham Hotspur	38	12	5	2	31	16	6	6	7	22	22	15	65
6. Blackburn Rovers	38	13	3	3	31	17	6	3	10	20	25	9	63
7. Newcastle United	38	11	5	3	28	15	6	2	11	19	27	5	58
8. Bolton Wanderers	38	11	5	3	29	13	4	6	9	20	28	8	56
9. West Ham United	38	9	3	7	30	25	7	4	8	22	30	-3	55
10. Wigan Athletic	38	7	3	9	24	26	8	3	8	21	26	-7	51
11. Everton	38	8	4	7	22	22	6	4	9	12	27	-15	50
12. Fulham	38	13	2	4	31	21	1	4	14	17	37	-10	48
13. Charlton Athletic	38	8	4	7	22	21	5	4	10	19	34	-14	47
14. Middlesbrough	38	7	5	7	28	30	5	4	10	20	28	-10	45
15. Manchester City	38	9	2	8	26	20	4	2	13	17	28	-5	43
16. Aston Villa	38	6	6	7	20	20	4	6	9	22	35	-13	42
17. Portsmouth	38	5	7	7	17	24	5	1	13	20	38	-25	38
18. BIRMINGHAM	38	6	5	8	19	20	2	5	12	9	30	-22	34
19. WEST BROM	38	6	2	11	21	24	1	7	11	10	34	-27	30
20. SUNDERLAND	38	1	4	14	12	37	2	2	15	14	32	-43	15

Exclusive Bonus Chapter
If...

> *"If you can keep your head when all about you*
> *Are losing theirs and blaming it on you,"*
>   Rudyard Kipling

If: the most desperately grabbed-at word in the history of football fandom. "If only we had won that game in August, we would be Champions by now." "If only we hadn't conceded those eleven goals and had three men sent off, we would have *definitely* won that game." And, of course, "If only Sean Dundee had been as good as Maradona we'd have won another six league titles, and sold him for enough money to buy a new team and build two new stadia."

Some of the "ifs" fans trot out might actually be true — if an unlucky bounce of the ball hadn't occurred at that crucial point, it might indeed have all been so different — but then again plenty are merely false hope. In this section we will not look back to determine what could have been done differently to win more games, but instead look forward, using everything we have learnt over the past two seasons to better predict what the future might hold for Liverpool Football Club and its players in 2006/07, providing they maintain much of the form of 05/06, and continue to improve in a few key areas.

> *If you can dream — and not make dreams your master;*
> *If you can think — and not make thoughts your aim;*

This is the crystal ball section of the book. Of course, some of the predictions herein may seem rather fanciful, but they are all based on facts from 2005/06. While plenty of the suggestions will inevitably prove false, given the unpredictability of the game of football, and the *force majeures* that occur in sport and, indeed, life in general, everything is rooted in reality, and what is *disctinctly possible*. Where possible we've tried to look at the more realistic patterns that have emerged, rather than working from brief and seriously skewed samples. (Example: after his first appearance in a Liverpool shirt at the start of the new season, Mark Gonzalez's goals-per-minute rate had him on course for 684 goals by mid-May. We can confidently predict that this is highly unlikely.)

Some of the statistics posted in Benítez's second season will be very difficult for the team to match in his third, let alone beat. And for every area that sees predictable improvements there will almost certainly be another that sees a surprising regression; if it's relatively easy for the strikers to improve on 2005/06's strike rates, it'll be nigh-on impossible for Pepe Reina to keep as many clean sheets. An improvement in the balance between the two, however, and it could be a season to remember. Fractionally fewer clean sheets in return for 15-25 more goals would just about do it.

Team "ifs"
In this section we will be looking at the team statistics from 2005/06, and extrapolating them ahead of 2006/07, factoring in the kind of improvements we could expect to see if (there's that word again) Rafa Benítez has successfully addressed the weaknesses of the preceding two campaigns.

To start with, if Liverpool improve their points-per-game average at the same rate as seen between 2004/05 to 2005/06, the Reds will win 2.79 points-per-game. This would result in 106 points — a distinctly unrealistic total, exaggerated by the low starting point of Benítez's disappointing first league campaign, and made difficult to match due to the fact that the better you do, the less scope it leaves to pick up extra points. However, improve at half of that rate in the new season, and that would take the Reds to 94 points, which would guarantee the title nine times out of ten.

If Liverpool carve out as many chances in 2006/07 as they did in 2005/06, but improve their collective finishing from five shots-on-goal-per-goal to four, the team would score 71 goals. This would be an improvement of 14 goals, and put the Reds near the top of the league in the category (Chelsea and Man United led the Premiership in 05/06, scoring 72 goals).

If Liverpool make it even more difficult for their opponents to score this year, lowering the opposition shots-on-goal-per-goal figure by only one shot for every goal scored, the Reds would concede only 21 goals, an improvement of four goals. If Liverpool did make the previous two improvements, the team would have a goal difference of +50, the same total Chelsea had in 2005/06 on their way to 91 points and the Premier League title.

If Liverpool could reduce their 'Failure to score' figure from nine games in 2005/06 (one in four) to somewhere in the region of five next season, whilst maintaining their total of 22 clean sheets, that should prove to be worth an extra eight points, and give a total approaching 90 points for the year.

If Liverpool win an away game in the Premiership against one of Arsenal, Chelsea or Manchester United, it will be their first since Rafael Benitez took control. In fact, if Liverpool draw an away game in the Premiership against one of Arsenal, Chelsea or Manchester United it will be their first since Benitez arrived. Any of these results, as well as boosting Liverpool's points tally, would also lower that of their rivals.

If Liverpool can improve the percentage of corners they concede from by just 0.5%, then they will only concede one solitary goal from a corner in 2006/07.

Similarly, if the Reds can halve the number of goals they concede from free-kick crosses in 2005/06 they will concede only one goal from this type of situation in 2006/07. If Benítez's men can halve the number of goals they concede from outside the 18-yard box in 2005/06 they will concede only one goal from that range in 2006/07.

> *If you can meet with Triumph and Disaster*
> *And treat those two imposters just the same;*

Formations and line-ups "Ifs"
In this section we will be looking at the statistics posted by different team selections and units during the 2005/06 season, and apply these to the '06/07 Premier League campaign, in an attempt to gauge the potential effect this would have on results. It is highly unlikely that we will ever see any of the units play all 38 league games, or even get close, especially in the current era of rotation — and with a manager who chops and changes on a weekly basis — but it is interesting to look at all the same.

If the best back five of Reina, Riise, Carragher, Hyypia and Finnan were to play the full 38 game Premiership fixture list in 2006/07, and exactly maintained their 2005/06 form throughout, the Reds would score 67 goals, concede only 14, keep 27 clean sheets and collect 91 points.

If Alonso and Gerrard were to play all 38 Premiership contests this season in the centre of midfield, and maintained their 2005/06 partnership rates in the process, the team would score 88 goals, concede only 19, keep 23 clean sheets and collect a total of 92 points. However, if Alonso and Sissoko were to take their '05/06 form into all 38 Premiership games in '06/07, Liverpool would score 63 goals, concede 28, keep 20 clean sheets and collect a total of 84 points.

If John Arne Riise played left midfield and Steven Gerrard right midfield for all 38 Premier League contests in 2006/07, then based on their 2005/06 form the team would score 95 goals, ship 24, keep 18 clean sheets and finish with 90 points. If Harry Kewell played left midfield and Steven Gerrard right midfield for all 38 Premier League games in 2006/07, then based on their 2005/06 form the team would score just 42 goals, concede 29, keep 19 clean sheets and finish with 86 points. If Luis Garcia was partnered up-front with Peter Crouch for all 38 Premier League games in 2006/07, then based on their 2005/06 form the team would score 78 goals, keep 22 clean sheets and finish with 87 points.

> *If you can make one heap of all your winnings*
> *And risk it on one turn of pitch-and-toss,*

Player "Ifs"
For many of the 'Ifs' in this section we will be using a weighted average of the rates posted by players over the last two Premiership seasons, and factor in an

improvement/decline quotient to predict their potential production in 2006/07. To do this we have come up with an estimate of the playing time (to the nearest 500 minutes) they can expect to play, barring serious injury.

If Pepe Reina escapes the antics of Arjen Robben, and plays all 38 Premiership games (3420 minutes) for Liverpool in 2006/07, he will save 165 shots, pick up four goal assists, make three costly mistakes, and keep 24 clean sheets; almost certainly seeing him win the Premier League's golden gloves award for the second year running.

If Jamie Carragher can avoid making a costly error in his first 225 minutes (2.5 games) of the 2006/07 Premiership season he will have totalled 5000 minutes (the equivalent of 55 full games) without being at fault for a goal. If he can further continue his streak and match last year's faultless Premiership form, his total errorless streak will reach somewhere in the region of 7500 minutes, or the equivalent of 83-84 games.

If Steve Finnan is able to improve his Premiership form in terms of attacking involvement to the level of his overall form from last season he will assist at a rate somewhere around 0.35 per 90 minutes. To put that into context, if he plays 3000 minutes (approx. 34 starts) this season in Premiership play he can be expected to pick up 12 goal assists that would almost certainly place him in the top five for assists from full-backs in the league during 2006/07.

If a number sequence starts two, five, three, three, four, two, one, what is the next number in the series? Well if you can answer that if you will know how many goals Sami Hyypia will score in 2006/07. If the big Finn can improve on the average of his last two seasons by 5% in the Premiership in 2006/07 he will score two goals, pick up four goal assists and have five mistakes leading to goals in 3000 minutes.

If John Arne Riise plays 2500 minutes (approx. 27 starts) this year in the Premiership he will get two goals, six assists and have one mistake leading to an opposition goal. If all 2500 minutes are from left-back, then Riise will score one goal and have six assists, whilst if all 2500 minutes are in left-midfield then the Liverpool No.6 will pick up five goals and ten assists. If Stephen Warnock were to be promoted to the first choice left-back for the 2006/07 season and play somewhere in the region of 3000 minutes (approx. 34 starts) he would potentially collect two goals, two assists and five mistakes leading to goals. Those figures could potentially be one goal better than those calculated for John Arne Riise but four assists and, more worryingly, four goal costing mistakes worse. If Fabio Aurelio plays 1500 minutes (approx. 16 starts) this year in the Premiership and matches his *La Liga* form he will collect two goals and four assists. If the left-back position in the league was shared between John Arne Riise, Fabio Aurelio and Stephen Warnock in the ratio of 22, eight and eight games respectively, then the left-back position will produce three goals and eight assists for 11 attacking points. These figures in 38 games would approximately match the figures posted by Liverpool's left-back's in all 62 games of 2005/06 (two goals and eight assists for ten attacking points).

If the centre-back position in Premiership play was shared between Sami Hyypia, Jamie Carragher and Daniel Agger in the ratio of 33, 33 and ten games respectively, then the centre-back position will produce four goals and 12 assists for 16 points. Last year the centre-back position produced 15 attacking points in 62 games.

If, in the league in 2006/07, the right-back position is shared between Steve Finnan and Jamie Carragher in the ratio 34 games to four, then the right-back position will produce no goals and nine assists. If the left-back, centre-back and right-back positions were shared as the above three paragraphs suggest, the Liverpool back-four would produce seven goals and 29 assists for 36 attacking points in 38 league games. In 2005/06 the Liverpool defence produced only one goal and 22 assists for 23 attacking points in 38 games.

If Xabi Alonso plays 2500 minutes (approx. 27 starts) in Premiership play this season the Spaniard will score three goals, assist on a further 12 and commit one mistake leading to an opponent's goal. If Alonso can reproduce the rates of his first Premiership campaign in 2004/05 during 2006/07 he will score three goals and pick up 14 assists in 2500 minutes. If Steven Gerrard plays 3000 minutes (approx. 34 starts) up to the form of his last two league rates during the 2006/07 Premiership season he will score ten goals, pick up 12 goal assists and commit one mistake leading to a goal. However, if Gerrard matches the form he has produced in all competitions over the last two seasons he will collect 14 goals, 18 assists and two goal mistakes in 3000 league minutes. If Mohamed Sissoko plays 2500 minutes (approx. 27 starts) this year in the Premiership he will collect three goal assists. If Liverpool played with a central midfield pair all season and shared it equally between Steven Gerrard (central midfield rates), Xabi Alonso and Momo Sissoko (2280 minutes each) the position would produce a total of 19 goals and 32 assists for 51 attacking points a 46% increase on the total produced in 2005/06 where the two positions combined for 57 attacking points in 62 games.

If Harry Kewell plays 2000 minutes (approx. 22 starts) in the league in 2006/07 he will score two goals and assist on a further seven for a total of nine attacking points. If Bolo Zenden plays 449 league minutes without Liverpool conceding a goal whilst he is on the pitch he will reach 900 minutes (or the equivalent of ten straight games) without being on the pitch when the Reds concede a goal. If Zenden plays 2500 minutes on the left flank in Premiership play this season he will score four goals and pick up nine assists for a combined 13 attacking points.

If Mark Gonzalez plays 2000 minutes (approx. 22 starts) in league play in 2006/07 he will pick up eight goals and five assists for a total of 13 attacking points. If the Liverpool left-midfield spot is shared between Mark Gonzalez, Harry Kewell, Bolo Zenden and Fabio Aurelio in the league in 2006/07, in the form of 18, 11, five and four games, respectively, the position will produce ten goals and 11 assists for 21 attacking points, the exact same production produced by the position in 2005/06.

If Luis Garcia plays 2000 minutes (approx. 22 starts) in the Premiership in

2006/07 he will collect eight goals — five of which could prove to be game-winners — and nine assists for a total of 17 attacking points. If Jermaine Pennant plays 2000 minutes (approx. 22 starts) in the Premier League in 2006/07, and his attacking play improves by 20% due to playing in a better team, he will score two goals and pick up 11 assists for 13 attacking points. If the right-midfield spot is divided into 17, 13 and eight games between Jermaine Pennant, Luis Garcia and Steven Gerrard (based on his right-midfield rates) respectively, the position will produce ten goals and 19 assists for 29 attacking points — an 8% increase on production from the position last season.

However, it's up front where the greatest changes can be expected, with new strikers and, beyond that, new wingers to supply the ammunition.

If Peter Crouch plays 2000 minutes (approx. 22 starts) in the league in 2006/07 he will fire in ten goals and assist on a further ten for 20 attacking points. However, if Crouch can match his England goal scoring form of 10 goals in 837 minutes — including his two goals against Andorra on 2nd September — he will score 24 goals in 2000 minutes of football. If Robbie Fowler plays 2000 minutes (approx. 22 starts) in league play this season he will score 12 goals, assist on five, totalling 17 attacking points based on the last two years. However, if Robbie can match his form since he came back to Anfield — including his one goal in 83 minutes versus Sheffield United — he will register 14 goals and five assists in 2000 minutes. If Craig Bellamy plays 2000 minutes (approx. 22 starts) in Premiership play this season he will collect 12 goals and six assists for 18 attacking points. If Dirk Kuyt plays 2000 minutes (approx. 22 starts) in the league campaign in 2006/07 and scores at the rate he posted in Holland he will net 18 goals. If you take into account his final two seasons, and factor in a drop-off (about 25%) in scoring rate from the Dutch *Eredivisie* to the English Premiership, he will score 12 goals.

If Benítez plays two strikers in all 38 Premiership games in 2006/07, with each of Fowler, Crouch, Bellamy and Kuyt playing equal minutes (1710 minutes, the equivalent of 19 starts) those players might be expected to score 10, eight, 11 and 10 goals respectively. That would combine for a total of 39 goals from the four main forwards, 18 goals greater than Fowler, Cisse, Morientes and Crouch combined to score when playing up front in 2005/06.

Whether or not these impressive rates are maintained, or indeed improved upon as anticipated, remains to be seen. But if sufficient levels from all areas of the team are kept constant from 2005/06, and the noted shortfalls addressed, then there's every chance of the Reds being crowned Champions in May 2007. To paraphrase the final line in Kipling's poem, Liverpool will own the Earth and everything that's in it.

"Tomkins examines the
reawakening of Liverpool
Football Club with a
keen eye, balancing raw
emotion with a rare sense
of perspective"

Oliver Kay, *The Times*
on *Golden Past, Red Future*

Red Revival

Rafa Benítez's Liverpool Revolution

Paul
Tomkins

Available now. ISBN 0-9549580-3-9